FAMILIAR STRANGERS

Brendan Kennelly was born in 1936 in Ballylongford, Co. Kerry; and was educated at St Ita's College, Tarbert, Co. Kerry, and at Trinity College, Dublin, where was Professor of Modern Literature from 1973 until his retirement in 2004. He has published more than twenty books of poems, including three earlier Bloodaxe selections, *A Time for Voices, Breathing Spaces* and *Begin. Familiar Strangers* replaces those and also includes the whole of *The Man Made of Rain* (1998), written after he survived major heart surgery.

He is best-known for two controversial poetry books, *Cromwell*, published in Ireland in 1983 and in Britain by Bloodaxe in 1987, and his epic poem *The Book of Judas* (1991), which topped the Irish bestsellers list: a shorter version was published by Bloodaxe in 2002 as *The Little Book of Judas*. His third epic, *Poetry My Arse* (1995), did much to outdo these in notoriety. All these remain available separately from Bloodaxe, along with his other recent titles, *Glimpses* (2001), a collection of short poems, and *Martial Art* (2003), versions of the Roman poet Martial.

His translations of Irish poetry are available in *Love of Ireland: Poems from the Irish* (Mercier Press, 1989). He has edited several anthologies, including *The Penguin Book of Irish Verse* (1970; 2nd edition 1981), *Between Innocence and Peace: Favourite Poems of Ireland* (Mercier Press, 1993), *Ireland's Women: Writings Past and Present,* with Katie Donovan and A. Norman Jeffares (Gill & Macmillan, 1994), and *Dublines*, with Katie Donovan (Bloodaxe Books, 1995). He has published two novels, *The Crooked Cross* (1963) and *The Florentines* (1967).

He is also a celebrated dramatist whose plays include versions of *Antigone* (Peacock Theatre, Dublin, 1986; Bloodaxe, 1996); *Medea*, premièred in the Dublin Theatre Festival in 1988, toured in England in 1989 by the Medea Theatre Company, and broadcast by BBC Radio 3 and published by Bloodaxe in 1991; *The Trojan Women* (Peacock Theatre & Bloodaxe, 1993); and Lorca's *Blood Wedding* (Northern Stage, Newcastle & Bloodaxe, 1996).

His *Journey into Joy: Selected Prose,* edited by Åke Persson, was published by Bloodaxe in 1994, along with *Dark Fathers into Light,* a critical anthology on his work edited by Richard Pine. John McDonagh's critical study *Brendan Kennelly: A Host of Ghosts* was published in The Liffey Press's Contemporary Irish Writers series in 2004.

His cassette recordings include *The Man Made of Rain* (Bloodaxe, 1998) and *The Poetry Quartets: 4,* shared with Paul Durcan, Michael Longley and Medbh McGuckian (The British Council / Bloodaxe Books, 1999).

Brendan Kennelly

FAMILIAR STRANGERS

NEW & SELECTED POEMS
1960-2004

BLOODAXE BOOKS

ISBN: 1 85224 662 6 hardback edition
       1 85224 663 4 paperback edition

First published 2004 by
Bloodaxe Books Ltd,
Highgreen,
Tarset,
Northumberland NE48 1RP.

www.bloodaxebooks.com
For further information about Bloodaxe titles
please visit our website or write to
the above address for a catalogue.

Bloodaxe Books Ltd acknowledges
the financial assistance of
Arts Council England, North East.

Cover printing by J. Thomson Colour Printers Ltd, Glasgow.

Printed in Great Britain by
Bell & Bain Limited, Glasgow, Scotland.

For Peter, Kristen, Meg, Hannah
and Grace Mary Murphy

ACKNOWLEDGEMENTS

Familiar Strangers: New & Selected Poems 1960-2004 replaces all previous selections of Brendan Kennelly's work, including three published by Bloodaxe Books: *A Time for Voices: Selected Poems 1960-1990* (1990), *Breathing Spaces: Early Poems* (1992) and *Begin* (1999). It also includes his book-length poem *The Man Made of Rain* (1998); Brendan Kennelly reads the whole work on a double-cassette which is still available from Bloodaxe Books. The arrangement of poems is thematic and also draws upon a few poems from *Cromwell* (1983/1987), *Poetry My Arse* (1995) and *The Little Book of Judas* (2002), but the selection from those three books is very small since they are available separately. The selection does not cover two other recent Bloodaxe titles, *Glimpses* (2001) and *Martial Art* (2003), nor does it overlap with *Moloney Up and At It* (1984), which is separately available from Mercier Press, the Moloney poems here being reprinted only from *Up and At It* (1965).

This book includes many poems published in earlier collections and selections, and the contents page shows each poem's publication (see initials after titles listed below). Poems listed without any title initials are previously uncollected. Thanks are due to the editors of numerous magazines and anthologies in which the new and previously uncollected poems first appeared.

The Rain, the Moon (with Rudi Holzapfel). Dublin: Dolmen Press, 1961 (TRTM).
The Dark about Our Loves (with Rudi Holzapfel). Dublin: John Augustine and Co, 1962 (TDAOL).
Green Townlands: Poems (with Rudi Holzapfel). Leeds: University Bibliography Press, 1963 (GT).
Let Fall No Burning Leaf. Dublin: New Square Publications, 1963 (LFNBL).
My Dark Fathers. Dublin: New Square Publications, 1964 (MDF).
Up and At It. Dublin: New Square Publications, 1965 (UAAI).
Collection One: Getting up Early. Dublin: Allen Figgis, 1966 (COGUE).
Good Souls to Survive. Dublin: Allen Figgis, 1967 (GSTS).
Dream of a Black Fox. Dublin: Allen Figgis, 1968 (DOABF).
Selected Poems. Dublin: Allen Figgis, 1969 (SP69).
Bread. Dublin: Tara Telephone Publications, 1971 (B).
Selected Poems, enlarged edition. New York: Dutton, 1971 (SP71).
Love Cry. Dublin: Allen Figgis, 1972 (LC).
Salvation, the Stranger. Dublin: Tara Telephone Publications, 1972 (STS).
The Voices. Dublin: Gallery Books, 1973 (TV).
Shelley in Dublin. Dublin: Anna Livia Books, 1974; Dublin: Egotist Press, 1977 (SID74); revised edition. Dublin: Beaver Row Press, 1982 (SID82).
A Kind of Trust. Dublin: Gallery Books, 1975 (AKOT).
New and Selected Poems, edited by Peter Fallon. Dublin: Gallery Books, 1976 (NASP).
Islandman. Dublin: Profile Press, 1977 (IM).
The Visitor. Dublin: St Bueno's Press, 1978 (TVR).

A Girl: 22 Songs, 1978. Song cycle sung by Bernadette Greevy. Music: Seoirse Bodley to poems by Brendan Kennelly. Fully published in *BS* (AG); recorded by Gael-Linn, Dublin, 1981.

A Small Light. Dublin: Gallery Books, 1979 (ASL).

In Spite of the Wise (also entitled *Evasions*). Dublin: Trinity Closet Press, 1979 (ISOTW).

The Boats Are Home. Dublin: Gallery Books, 1980 (TBAH).

Shelley in Dublin, revised edition. Dublin: Beaver Row Press, 1982 (SID82).

The House That Jack Didn't Build. Dublin: Beaver Row Press, 1982 (THTJDB).

Cromwell: A Poem. Dublin: Beaver Row Press, 1983; corrected edition, Newcastle upon Tyne: Bloodaxe Books, 1987 (C).

Selected Poems, edited by Kevin Byrne. Dublin: Kerrymount Publications, 1985 (SP85).

Love of Ireland: Poems from the Irish. Cork & Dublin: Mercier Press, 1989 (LOI).

A Time for Voices: Selected Poems 1960-1990. Newcastle upon Tyne: Bloodaxe Books, 1990 (ATFV).

The Book of Judas: A Poem. Newcastle upon Tyne: Bloodaxe Books, 1991 (BOJ); see also *The Little Book of Judas* below.

Breathing Spaces: Early Poems. Newcastle upon Tyne: Bloodaxe Books, 1992 (BS).

Poetry My Arse: A Poem. Newcastle upon Tyne: Bloodaxe Books, 1995 (PMA).

The Man Made of Rain. Newcastle upon Tyne: Bloodaxe Books, 1998 (MMR); published simultaneously as a complete reading on cassette.

The Singing Tree. Newry: Abbey Press, 1998 (TST).

Begin. Newcastle upon Tyne: Bloodaxe Books, 1999 (BG).

The Little Book of Judas. Tarset: Bloodaxe Books, 2002 (LBJ); shorter edition of *The Book of Judas* (with 30 additional poems).

CONTENTS

3 *Bodies of spirits*

PREFACE

I called this book *Familiar Strangers* because the more familiar one becomes with certain poems, the stranger they are. This is also true of certain people, streets, rooms, voices, cliffs, cats, dogs, roads, fields, hills, beaches. True, in fact, of almost everything to which one pays attention. Not to pay attention is to let familiarity become boredom, to stifle the innate strangeness of people and things. And especially, perhaps, of words.

In 1957, a young Englishman said to me over a drink, 'Did you know, Brendan, that the British Empire was spread by an accent?' Well, no, I didn't know. But since then I have come to think that the real British Empire became, not an Empire of territory, but an Empire of language. More specifically, an Empire of Englishes. An Empire of words and accents, emphasis and intonation, aggressive rhetoric and shrewd reticence, images and rhythms.

Looking back over poems which I've written during the past fifty years, I can see and hear different Englishes, ranging from the language of a North Kerry village and parish (where words and accents changed from townland to townland) to the many Englishes of Dublin where I've lived, for the most part, since 1953; to the Englishes of London and Leeds where I worked on and off during the 50s and early 60s; to the Englishes of many cities throughout the world. Englishes seem to fit in more or less everywhere; they are adventurous, flexible, daring and capable. They delight in the fluency of change and difference. I think one should surrender to them no matter where they come from, no matter what they say or how they say it.

Two days ago, Christmas Day, 2003, I walked the cold, deserted streets of Dublin. A solitary, staggering drunk accosted me in the icy emptiness of Leeson Street and said, 'D'yez know wha? Yez look bike a bleedin' snowman!' I couldn't think of a reply. Not smart enough. I moved on. A snowman. Bleedin? But not bleedin' smart enough. Still, my favourite encounter was with that most familiar of all strangers, Santa Claus, one darkish December day in Thomas Street. He fixed a long, hard stare on me and said, 'I think I know you. Tell me this, me ould flower. Were you an' me in Mountjoy Jail together?' I gave Santa the most political reply I knew: 'Not to the best of my recollection, sir.' It seemed to satisfy him. He jingled on.

Stories. Yarns. Ireland lacks a developed philosophical tradition. What it has instead is a tradition of ferocious, funny, poisonous, caricaturing, good-natured, self-delighting, endless gossip and yarns passed around like drinks among a group in a pub. Gossip is a kind of snoopy, self-sustaining interest in others. There's a fair amount of gossip in much poetry. And most poems have stories behind them. And stories are told by people, by men, women, boys, girls. Even history is turned into stories.

When I was writing *Cromwell* I listened to stories about history, about Cromwell himself, voted one of the top ten 'Great Britons' of the Millennium in Britain, considered an inhuman monster in many parts of Ireland. Such is the power of stories behind poems. History. His story. History deals in facts. The question is, do some facts become stories as quickly as some stories become facts? Stories float in the air, drifting like life-giving forces, drifting as if choosing a mind or imagination to alight on and animate. So a fair section of this book has to do with men, women and youngsters, and therefore with history, mythology, rumours, conversation, gossip.

Frequently, to a surprising degree, people *are* the words they use. Or do words use people? No single section of *Familiar Strangers* is rigidly structured because poems from different sections, written in different decades, overlap and echo each other. It's as if one's mind and imagination have a number of deep-rooted, obstinate obsessions that still assert their presence, no matter how frequently expressed. They, too, are familiar strangers. Perhaps their fascination lies in the fact that they can never be fully understood. They choose the moment or decade when they'll pay me a visit. Well, come in, you're welcome, where have you been? Well, I'm here now, is the reply. Say me, say me.

Englishes demand voices. Say me. Some forty years ago, I began to understand that poetry is a house of voices, that objects need voices as people, ideas and feelings need them. Furthermore, it is the damaged and outcast, the unforgivable and unspeakable who need voices most of all, perhaps, because these very voices – repulsive and horrific though they may be – help us to understand our own mysterious humanity, or lack of it. Cromwell and Judas educated me. So did Ace de Horner in *Poetry My Arse*. So did that visionary, pouring being in *The Man Made of Rain*. Voices. Total strangers. Coming closer. Growing familiar. Here, now. Even silence is a voice. Silence most of all, perhaps, at certain moments in the masterful darkness of a winter's night, sleep gone, three o'clock, the rain is starting, what's it saying?

Listening to a voice means making a space in yourself, deepening your capacity for surrender to such things as difference, diversity and memory, which are three strong sources of challenge and stimulation. I think there's a fair amount of difference, diversity and memory in this book.

History sometimes screams with difference. History is, among many things, the shaping of memory. From a personal viewpoint, memory is a lightning invader of one's mind, one's being. It can take possession of that mind, that being, at different times throughout the years. Memory is a stalker, a colonising power, a source of warmth and appalling chill, at once insistent and unpredictable. Memories range from the beautiful and sacred to the horrific and obscene, from the consoling and reassuring to the hurtful and accusing.

Ibsen said that poetry is a court of judgment on the soul. So is memory. Poetry must let all the different kinds of memory speak and sing, clarify, assert, and make known their judgments. Memory can alter the present and educate the future, give us roses in December, ice in July. But this will happen only if and when poetry surrenders unconditionally to memory.

The power of poetry is directly linked to, and measured by, its capacity for surrender. To memory, to difference, to dreams, to what is perplexing or frightening, to diversity, to voices, to history and mythology. To Englishes. Different Englishes make the same story different; the story becomes many stories, the poem many poems. This sense of echoing connection across decades, across cities, cultures and countries, this sense of multiple identity may help to account for the blend of familiarity and strangeness in many poems.

It's not unlike one's memory of a school friend going to another country for fifty years. He returns. You meet him, recognise him, perhaps not immediately, but you do. O it's yourself, Jimmy O'Grady. Now, he's like that poem you learned by heart together, you were both in the same class at school, some of the words of 'Elegy in a Country Churchyard' have lived in both your heads and hearts over the years. You look at your friend. He looks at you. Strange. Familiar... *and leaves the world to darkness and to me*. Good to see you again. Where have you been? What's the story? Tell me, Jimmy, tell me.

The familiar strangeness of renewed friendship possesses not only some of the haunting power of poetry but also of dreams. The sheer "madness" of many dreams is quite haunting. I had such dreams while writing *Cromwell*. I once made the mistake of trying to explain a dream but soon recognised the futility of this. The best one can hope to do when writing about dreams is to capture some of the thrilling reality of new feeling and images, that exciting lostness, that daft narrative which many people experience in dreams. It may well be that it is in dreams, even more than in poetry that we find the ultimate capacity for surrender.

The state of being haunted is what poetry and dreams have most in common. This is tantamount to a constant companionship, not always easy, sometimes troubling, always engaging, always, somehow or other, new. How does something one knows (or thinks one knows) nearly all one's life, seem new, each passing day? I don't know. Sometimes I think it has to do with how we experience time. There is the straightforward, necessary, chronological way, the way of the clock, the watch and the calendar. Then there is the sudden, surging way of memory and dream, of lightning mental relationship, of surprising, even shocking connection, of image begetting image, of 1950 leaping forward unstoppably to 2004.

In writing, I favour this second way, which is another reason why the different sections of this book should not be seen as fixed or rigid since they connect and echo forward and backward, jumping over the heads and shoulders of decades to relate to instinctive kin. I think this second way is truer to the way we are, the way we live, or refuse to live, in the depths of our being, while the first way is necessary for making a living from day to day. I respect both ways but prefer the way leading to the leap of light and kinship, the thrill of celebratory connection, the sense that it inevitably dictates, in the shaping of a *Selected Poems*, its own necessary architecture.

I hope there are moments in this book which have the kind of celebratory thrill I refer to. I've seen huge changes happening in Dublin over the past fifty years. One of the most disturbing changes is the increasing violence, the murders, the savage beatings, the barbarous, ever-deepening lack of respect for life. And then there is what appears to be the casual acceptance of such horror, which amounts to a dark, complex change of consciousness. All this has happened, and continues to happen, at a time marked by what many call 'unparalleled progress'. And, without any doubt, there has been remarkable 'progress' in several areas. But there has also been regress, by which I mean loss of respect for life, for people. And while poetry must always explore and reveal the realities of this barbarous darkness in a post-colonial land (or anywhere), confronting the violence, cynicism, corruption and "sophistication" that seem to accompany wealth, it must also, somehow, always, cling to a vision of plain human dignity, celebrate the gift of life, the very act of giving that is poetry itself.

Poetry is a gift that challenges and questions everything, including itself, as it also celebrates the inestimable value and beauty of the gift of living, and of the instinct to taste and share that gift with others, as long as possible. So this book begins with 'A Giving' and ends with 'Begin'.

Perhaps it's that word 'Begin' that prompts me to end this note with another Dublin streetbite. A woman in Dame Street asked me recently, 'How long have you been writing?' 'About fifty years,' I replied. 'Stick at it,' she said encouragingly. 'You never know. You might make a career of it yet.' You never know. I might. I bleedin' might.

BRENDAN KENNELLY

1

Lifting the moon

A Giving

Here in this room, this December day,
Listening to the year die on the warfields
And in the voices of children
Who laugh in the indecisive light
At the throes that but rehearse their own
I take the mystery of giving in my hands
And pass it on to you.

I give thanks
To the giver of images,
The reticent god who goes about his work
Determined to hold on to nothing.
Embarrassed at the prospect of possession
He distributes leaves to the wind
And lets them pitch and leap like boys
Capering out of their skin.
Pictures are thrown behind hedges,
Poems skitter backwards over cliffs,
There is a loaf of bread on Derek's threshold
And we will never know who put it there.

For such things
And bearing in mind
The midnight hurt, the shot bride,
The famine in the heart,
The demented soldier, the terrified cities
Rising out of their own rubble,

I give thanks.

I listen to the sound of doors
Opening and closing in the street.
They are like the heartbeats of this creator
Who gives everything away.
I do not understand
Such constant evacuation of the heart,
Such striving towards emptiness.

Thinking, however, of the intrepid skeleton,
The feared definition,
I grasp a little of the giving
And hold it close as my own flesh.

It is this little
That I give to you.
And now I want to walk out and witness
The shadow of some ungraspable sweetness
Passing over the measureless squalor of man
Like a child's hand over my own face
Or the exodus of swallows across the land

And I know it does not matter
That I do not understand.

Yes

I love the word
And hear its long struggle with no
Even in the bird's throat
And the budging crocus.
Some winter's night
I see it flood the faces
Of my friends, ripen their laughter
And plant early flowers in
Their conversation.

You will understand when I say
It is for me a morning word
Though it is older than the sea
And hisses in a way
That may have given
An example
To the serpent itself.
It is this ageless incipience
Whose influence is found
In the first and last pages of books,
In the grim skin of the affirmative battler
And in the voices of women
That constitutes the morning quality
Of yes.

       We have all
Thought what it must be like
Never to grow old,
The dreams of our elders have mythic endurance
Though their hearts are stilled
But the only agelessness
Is yes.

I am always beginning to appreciate
The agony from which it is born.
Clues from here and there
Suggest such agony is hard to bear
But is the shaping God
Of the word that we
Sometimes hear, and struggle to be.

The year

It was the year of first love,
          a burnt leg, two months
of glorious, car-stopping snow.

          But O my God
how can it be so near
          and yet
          so long ago?

The True Thing

I don't know anyone who knows what became of the true thing.
If poets think they sing, it is a parody they sing.
In the beginning men of common sense
Knew that for the damned dream to grow
Wholesale massacre of innocence
Was necessary, prophets' blood must flow,
Thieves of little apples be crucified, rebels be put down,
Conspiracies of messianic troglodytes be strangled
And saviours be given the bum's rush out of every pub in town.

Out of the smashed cities
Works of art adorn the Vatican walls
A comfortable living is right for the Archbishop and his wife
Lads and lassies study till their eyeballs burn and their souls know
One must never heed the bitter cries, forsaken calls
Of the man in the beginning burning fear
Like old papers, kissing his death, having given his life.
Yes, and we have double-glazed hearts and committees and promotions and
          pensions

And time off to enjoy and bless
The kids shining out to discos and parties
In the holy light of progress.
And we have learning, we could put Hell in a couplet, Eden in an epigram,
Dish out slices of epics like gifts of land in the Golden Vale
And sweat blood or what feels like blood
To get the right rhythm and thereby hangs a tale
Of an abortive experiment in love
That began in bestial company and ended in public shame
And started all over again in a sad parody
Of what cannot be understood

Only followed as a blind man follows his expensive dog
Through visionary streets of fluent slavish traffic
Calmly-crazily living the rhythms of my mechanical blood
Yearning occasionally, nevertheless, for dialogue with God.
I would ask, to begin with, what became of the true thing
And after that, well, anything might happen.
I can even imagine a poet starting to sing
In a way I haven't heard for a long time.
If the song comes right, the true thing may find a name
Singing to me of who, and why, I am.

Measures

It was just that like certain of my friends I, Buffún, could not endure the
emptiness. They took the measures open to them. I invited the butcher into
my room and began a dialogue with him, suspecting that he'd follow a strict
path of self-justification. Imagine my surprise when, with an honesty unknown
to myself (for which God be thanked officially here and now) he spoke of
gutted women and ashen cities, hangings and lootings, screaming soldiers and
the stratagems of corrupt politicians with a cool sadness, a fluent inevitable
pity. But I wasn't going to let that fool me. So, from a mountain of indignant
legends, bizarre history, demented rumours and obscene folklore, I accused
the butcher not merely of following the most atrocious of humanity's examples
(someone was sneezing and shouting 'Mary' outside my room) but also of
creating precedents of such immeasurable vileness that his name, when uttered
on the lips of the unborn a thousand years hence, would ignite a rage of hate
in the hearts of even the most tolerant and gentle. Imagine, I said, to create,
deliberately, a name like that for yourself, to toil with such devotion towards
your own immortal shame, to elect to be the very source of a tradition of
loathing, the butt of jibing, despising millions. (I was really riding the old
rhetoric now.)

The butcher calmly replied that the despising millions were simply millions; he was one. One. Yes, I agreed, one who makes Herod look like a benevolent Ballsbridge dad frolicking with his offspring in Herbert Park. I would remind you, returned the butcher, that you invited me here. I am the guest of your imagination, therefore have the grace to hear me out; I am not altogether responsible for the fact that you were reared to hate and fear my name which in modesty I would suggest is not without its own ebullient music. I say further that you too are blind in your way, and now you use me to try to justify that blindness. By your own admission you are empty also. So you invited me to people your emptiness. This I will do without remorse or reward. But kindly remember that you are blind and that I see.

The butcher walked out the door of my emptiness, straight into me.

Let It Go

Let it go
Out of reach, out of sight,
Out of the door and the window,

Through the city,
Over the mountains
And the sea.

I do not mean a mere escape,
A deliberate loosening
Of a brutal grip

Like that of church on soul,
Father on son
Or even love on the lover's beautiful

Surrender to the dear pain,
Or any sin or sickness that could
Swallow a man.

I mean a different thing
Beyond desire to acquire or captivate,
A felt relinquishing

Such as can be seen
When the air yields to the bird
Or the green

Trunk of a tree surrenders
To the tactful advance of moss
Or when the river stirs

Its surface
To accept a drifting stick.
I feel such courtesy

When I let it go
From me to countries
I will never know

And I stand, hoping to discern
Its breath in my heart
At its return.

Conference

It takes a while but then
yes, I believe my eyes.
Half-way up the quiet laneway
where drinkers and stray dogs make their beds
I stumble on a conference of dreams.
One whispers all the dreams are back
from nightjourneys through human heads
and are swapping stories
about what they've been up to
in all the sleeping blood and brains.
This gives them a laugh and helps them
face the coming night
when they must up and out again
into the sleeping beings
of children, women, men.
Unseen, for some unreason, I glide past,
listening to the talking dreams:

'I am a frog on a table, eating leftovers.'

'I am a pink light-bulb, flickering but not extinguished.
This has been going on for years.'

'Last night, I re-designed the map of Europe and, for the first time, got it
        right.'

'I was Napoleon's hat at an auction. I went for half-a-million Euro to a retired
     wrestler from Copenhagen.'

'I am Hitler's diary. Then I am eyes devouring it.'

'I am a bell no one can stop ringing'

'I am the photograph hidden in Beethoven's wallet.'

'I am the early sparrow fortune-teller in Pimlico.'

'I make children happy, I tell them stories about an old man who can turn
     stones into chocolates.'

'Every time the Minister for Health speaks, I make him burp and burp. This
     improves his English.'

'I drive mad cyclists through a nun's head.'

'I am back at school, crying.'

'Her perfect body prone, I make her scream.
Who can tell the dreamer from the dream?'

'First, I was an apple. Then, a rose. Tonight, who knows?'

The nightmares (I am told) are the cheekiest of all.
You never know what they'll get up to,
they're determined to get havoc raging
in the blood and brains and bones
of snoring innocents, tired creatures
who, next morning, will suffer
a special kind of hangover.
But in the laneway now, as if
to emphasise their different styles,
the nightmares sit and share
their nightmare smiles.
They contribute to the conference too:

'I am Chinese torture with an Irish passport.'

'Honeymoon night, I am her mind
owned by the man she left behind.'

'I am the conviction
her left breast is rotten.'

'I am the house shaking all round him
asking the question, Will I fall? Will I fall?'

'I concoct and arrange the lies
in the spin-doctor's head.
I laugh as the knackers swallow my lies,
soft succulent lies; sharp stabbing lies.'

'I am the bomb-maker inviting you to coffee.'

'I am the abuser, I am respectable.'

'I am the art of forgetting, the curse of remembering.'

'Time is a football. Head it home. I'm a striker
without a club. Will I be bought?'

'I ask her, have you met each other?
I like her eyes when she can't recognise herself.'

'I make him illiterate, then I beat him with the whip of knowledge.'

'You escape into sleep. I am inescapable.'

'I am the needle stitching her lips. I convince her she'll never know what's
         going on.'

'On and on and on, I whisper whisper whisper
as I make minds and bodies
heave and blunder.'

On and on and on. What is going on?
Reaching the far end of the laneway
I turn and look back.
Although my midnight eyes are reeling
I see the dreams are gone.
So are the nightmares.

         I have a feeling
this was a most successful conference,
revealing, vigorous and deep,
enabling every kind of dream
to shred, amuse, ravage and delight
strange human sleep.

Is it any wonder
I hardly know
whether to laugh or weep?

A Host of Ghosts

Night: the pits are everywhere.
I am slipping into the pit of my own voice,
Snares and traps in plenty there.
If I ponder on shadows in the grass
I will find Oliver, Mum, The Belly, Ed
Spenser down in Cork, the giant, He, a host of ghosts
Who see in the living the apprenticed dead
Merging with insidious mists
Lit here and there by a flashlamp sun
Slaving away like a human mind
To clarify the mist for anyone
Who thinks he'd like to understand
Through nightmare,
           laughter,
                a ridiculous wit,
The symmetry of his particular pit.
If I am nothing, what shall I become?
I here suggest the bobbing sea's debris
Throbbing like Oliver's stimulating drum
Before the export trade in slaves to the Barbados
Inflames my old teacher three hundred years
Later; he stands in the middle of the floor
Raging at rows of shivering youngsters,
Cursing their stupidity and his own anger.
Now he is a ghost as well
Gone to his spot in the symmetry
Of heaven or hell or where you will. You will.
Such happy, tortured ultimates have vanished now
Into the whittling ground
Where dances, for a moment, my nightmare mind.

Whatever

'What is poetry?' the girl in blue
    asked the man in black.
'I'm not sure,' Pat Tierney said. 'I think it's whatever
    lifts the moon off my back.'

A Language

I had a language once.
I was at home there.
Someone murdered it
Buried it somewhere.
I use different words now
Without skill, truly as I can.
A man without a language
Is half a man, if he's lucky.

Sometimes the lost words flare from their grave
Why do I think then of angels,
Seraphim, Cherubim, Thrones, Dominions, Powers?
I gaze amazed at them from far away.
They are starting to dance, they are
Shaping themselves into vengefully beautiful flowers

Someone, Somewhere

'I do not believe this language is dead.
Not a thousand years of hate could kill it,
Or worse, a thousand years of indifference.
So long as I live my language shall live
Because it is mine, do you hear me, mine,
No, of course you don't hear me, why should you,
You who believe what has always been said,
Let us bury our language, our language is dead.
I have a notion, I have a bike
And I'm going to ride it through the back roads
Of Ireland. Each road, in its turn,
Will twist me to people, my people, whose minds
Will dance to those words buried
In their hearts. Someone, somewhere, will learn.'

Proof

I would like all things to be free of me,
Never to murder the days with presupposition,
Never have to feel they suffer the imposition
Of having to be this or that. How easy
It is to maim the moment
With expectation, to force it to define
Itself. Beyond all that I am, the sun
Scatters its light as though by accident.

The fox eats its own leg in the trap
To go free. As it limps through the grass
The earth itself appears to bleed.
When the morning light comes up
Who knows what suffering midnight was?
Proof is what I do not need.

Leaving

Relihan stood at the door of the council house,
Muttered 'Now is no time for grieving';
Wife and children stared into his face
Refusing to believe he was leaving
Them for good. His hand circled the dull knob
Of the door between him and anonymity,
Heart hardening to each broken sob
Stabbing the air. Already he could see

Strangers in the eyes begging him to stay,
More strange to him than all that lay unknown
In the deep adventure of England.
He looked at his own for the last time, turned away
From the warm squalor of home.
Worlds died, were born in the turn of his hand.

The Prodigal Son

To go away is not to die
And to return is to begin again
But with a difference.

I had a lot to spend; I spent it;
Men's eyes opened in wonder
At my extravagance.

You know what it is to spend –
Ecstatic moments of release
That spring from, lead to boredom.

But in the spending was the joy
Those who hoarded never knew –
Know-alls, planners, calculators,

Safe adventurers who watched me as I
Flung my portion to the wind and women.
Some seemed to love me. They did not. They soon forgot.

Lose! Lose! – beat in my ears from dawn to dark,
The only lesson one should learn,
The exacting savage art.

Not forgetting anyone, but outstripping all,
I cross your threshold once again
With such a history of loss

It stirs what you believe is your forgiveness.
Forgive yourself, forgiving me.
You offer; I accept.

We'll go into a room, draw up two chairs,
Share a bottle till the early hours.
I have things to tell you before I begin.

2

Questioning answers

As the twig is bent the tree inclines.

VIRGIL

To Learn

There were nine fields between him and the school.
The first field was deep like his father's frown
The second was a nervous pony
The third a thistle with a purple crown
The fourth was a suspicious glance
The fifth rambled like a drinker's talk
The sixth was all wet treachery
The seventh was a man who did too much work
The eighth was downcast eyes, determined to be tame,
The ninth said hello, goodbye.
He thought of the nine fields in turn
As he beat the last ditch and came
In sight of the school on the gravelly rise.
He buckled down to learn.

The Stick

The man walked out of the classroom
And strode to the end of the yard
Where the ash tree was in bloom.
It was a calm day, the leaves barely stirred
As he searched the tree for the right strip.
He tried many pieces, threw them aside.
At last, he found the right size and shape
And with his knife sculpted
A thin hard stick, his work of art.
Back in the room, he looked at the boys' faces.
They'd be farmers, labourers, even singers, fiddlers, dancers.
He placed the stick on the mantlepiece above the fire.
His days were listening to boys' voices
Who'd know the stick if they didn't know the answers

words

what's words ozzie assed me
sounds dat kum outa peepul's mouths i said
where dey kum from first sez ozzie
dunno i replied

fukken fish have no words ozzie went on
but dey enjoy de fukken sea
and fukken tigers have no words
but dey enjoy eatin you and me

only peepul has words ozzie said
an luk at de shit dey talk
if i kud reed i'd say buks are shit as well

words are to kummyunikate sez i

like shit sez ozzie won good bomm
blow de whole fukken world ta hell

prades

ozzie is stonemad about prades
so he say kummon ta belfast
for de 12th an we see de orangemen
beatin de shit outa de drums
beltin em as if dey was katliks' heads

so we set out from dublin
an landed in belfast for de fun
it was brill
dere was colour an music an everyone
was havin a go at sumtin i dunno

what but i'll never forget ozzie in
de middul of all de excitement
pickin pockets right left and centre

on de train back to dublin he was laffin his head
off, dere shud be more fukken prades he said

flushed

ozzie kum to me all flushed sez he
i want a fukken ride
i was lukken at de telly lass nite
sumwun played here kums de bride

sum fukken bride i can tell ya boy
i very nearly hopped inta de box
kummon now sez ozzie we'll go ta
our pub down de keys an get our rocks

off so down we toddle like a pair
o' young bulls up from de cuntry

fifteen pints o' cider a man i never lied
about drink in me life we pick up two
fine tings an screw em crosseyed up in de park
ozzie said tis hard ta whack de fukken ride

skool

dis jesus fella sez ozzie who was he
how de fuck do i know sez i
you went ta skool forra bit sez ozzie
didn't learn much dayre sez i

but he died on de cross sez i
for you an for me de teetchur said
what de fuck you talkin about sez ozzie
de man is dead dat's all de man is dead

but everywun sez jesus dis an jesus dat
pay de jesus rent by us a jesus pint
till i get de jesus dole

but who de jesus hell was he sez ozzie
i dunno sez i yoor jesus iggerant sez he
shuv yoor iggerance up yoor bleedin hole

Small Black Stars

Then the brown horse wheeled and galloped across the field
Clean flanks glittering in the sun,
Terror that might impoverish a man
Gave it a savage dignity revealed
In hooves that beat as though in frenzy or pain,
Creating small black stars that flashed and fell
Like souls a moment poised between heaven and hell
Then plunging down to earth again.
The brown horse slowed, shivered, then was still;
I knew the dread that's always nameless, near,
And thought of small black stars that flashed and fell
To make a broken firmament of fear.

Catechism

Religion class. Mulcahy taught us God
While he heated his arse to a winter fire
Testing with his fingers the supple sallyrod.
'Explain the Immaculate Conception, Maguire,
And tell us then about the Mystical Blood.'
Maguire failed. Mulcahy covered the boy's head
With his satchel, shoved him stumbling among
The desks, lashed his bare legs until they bled.

'Who goes to hell, Dineen? Kane, what's a saint?
Doolin, what constitutes a mortal sin?
Flynn, what of the man who calls his brother a fool?'
Years killed raving questions. Kane stomped around Dublin
In policeman's boots. Flynn was afraid of himself.
Maguire did well out of whores in Liverpool.

My Mind of Questions

Did Jesus have brothers and sisters?
        Did they give him a rough time?
What was it like on a Saturday night
        In the Holy Family home?

Did they mock his God-like talents?
        Laugh at wise things he said?
Did he fight with them for an extra spud
        Or a cut o' brown bread?

Did he have a favourite sister
        Who understood him better than most
And agreed that he was the Father
        Son and Holy Ghost?

If challenged, would he fight back,
        Square up to a bully?
Was he a handy lad with the mitts
        Sidestepping beautifully

When a bigger lad charged at him,
        Expecting to knock him down?
Did Jesus trip him up
        Then go to town?

What was he like in the scrap
        When the dirt blinded his eyes?
Did he ever get a kick in the balls
        From some frigger twice his size?

When, in the streets of Nazareth,
        Did he first hear the name of God?
Did he know it was his own name
        When he first tasted blood?

Did he go in search of birds' nests
        In meadow, field and glen?
And if he found a thrush's nest
        Did he rob it then?

Did he ever fish for eels
        And watch them die at his feet
Wriggling like love in the dust?
        Gospels, you're incomplete.

What was he like at school?
        Was he fond of poetry?
Did he make the teacher feel like a fool
        Because he lacked divinity?

What did the teacher think of him
        Doing his father's business?
Did he wonder at times if Jesus
        Was out of his tree, or worse?

Did Jesus like to sing?
        Did he whistle and hum
As he walked the streets of Nazareth
        Going home to mum?

(I've heard it said he lacked
        A sense of humour,
That his mind was grim and grew grimmer
        And grimmer and grimmer).

What was his appetite like?
        What did he like to eat?
What did he see the first time he washed
        His hands and feet?

What were his fingers like? His mouth?
        His throat, toes, thighs, teeth, eyes?
Did he often cry? For what? And what
        Was the sound of his sighs

At night when he was alone
        And no one had ever been created
Except as shadowy strangers
        Who went their separate ways?

What did he think of his neighbours?
        His neighbours of him?
Was he a quiet little fella
        Fond of his home?

Or did he sometimes seem
        As if he were biding his time
Like a man with a job to do
        That took up all his mind?

At what moment did he know
        That home is not enough
And he must scour the darkness
        To give and find love

Among strangers waiting out there
        Full of need,
So full his heart inclined
        To bleed?

Did he break up his family?
        Did they resent him?
From the day he left did he ever
        Get in touch again?

Was he handsomely made
        Or humped, mis-shapen?
Was his life a preparation
        For what can never happen?

When he saw the sadness of sex
        Did he sit and think
Or slip down a Nazareth laneway
        For a happy wank?

Back in the Holy Family
        All hope and despair on the shelf
Did he look in the eyes of others
        Or smell himself?

Did he stand in a doorway of time
        Look at a street
Hear people bawl for his blood
        And then forget

He'd ever existed? Did he shudder
        To know the future now?
Did he know? How could he bear it?
        The sweat on the boy's brow

Turns to blood in my mind of questions,
        How foolish they are,
What do I know of anything,
        Even my own star?

My own star above all, perhaps?
        My own blood?
My own tracking, trackless, shapeless, restless,
        Sleepless head?

After School

The teacher sneered, 'Carmody, I know you're dull
But try to answer.' Carmody's wild eyes
Floundered. 'Ah Carmody, you fool, you fool!'
The anguish in his face
Speared his heart. After school
The children badgered him beneath a bridge.
'Open his trousers! Quick! Pull out his tool!'
He stood there shivering on the edge

Of madness; their taunting fouled his ears,
Sent horror screaming through his mind.
Then amid the soul-insulting jeers
He heard the river at his side
Saying he should close his eyes on all his kind.
The river cried and cried and cried.

A Return

The insolence of the dead! With the same black scarf
The worried shirt open at the throat
The forehead high as Shakespeare's
The eyes convinced that every child is a brat
Or parasite, he strides, after more than thirty years,
Into my dream, sits facing me as I sit
Transfixed by the wrestlers stuck in each other.
I feel again a wave of hate
Begin to drown my mind and there
In the struggling arena, I rise, I live,
Amazed at obscenities scalding my lips,
Untouched when his great head cowers
Then lifts – O God, that unforgettable shape –
Begging the pardon that I will not give.

The Brightest of All

The man who told me about the fall
Of the brightest of all the angels
Was Sean McCarthy
Who suffered badly from varicose veins
In the enormous cold classroom.
It wasn't always cold.
On certain days when the sun
Strode like All-Ireland victory into the room
Warming the windows the ceiling the floor
And the chipped desks where the boys
Sat in rows, devoted and docile
As slaves in a Roman galley
Arranged to cope with the sea
And no questions asked,
I thought of the brightest of all
Thrown out of home
Falling, falling
Down through the alien air.
People working the fields
Walking the streets of the cities
That were red circles and squares
On McCarthy's map of the world
Bluegreening a yellow wall
Gaped in wonder at brightness
That darkened the sun to a disc of shame
In the humbled sky.
In this piteous fabulous fall
The brightest of all
Crashed through the crust of the earth
Coming to rest
Deep in its secret heart.
When the scab fell away from the wound of the world
Healed in its own good time
The brightness was trapped in the secret heart
That sustains our birth
Accepts our death
And never complains or praises,
Patient and full of care
As my sister combing her rivery hair.
I was glad that the sun
Was no longer ashamed,
The people no longer dumb
At the sight of a shocking wonder.

And yet I was sad
That the brightest of all
Was trapped
And I thought
One gleam, one single gleam,
Not enough to shame the sun
But enough to brighten a man
May escape from the secret heart
Steal through the cold enormous classroom
Lessen the pain in McCarthy's legs
Where he stood
In the story of brightness expelled
From the painless kingdom
Of an angry God.
But the gleam never appeared.
Sean McCarthy's pain was no lie.
The secret heart is the deepest prison
Under the sky.

The Smell

The inside of the church absorbed the rain's thunder,
Lightning deceived and killed, the thunder never lied,
The thunder knelt and prayed at the high altar.
I was six years old. I knelt and prayed at her side.

She was a woman in black, she of the white head,
She whose lips rivalled the lips of the rain.
Someone closer to her than anyone had died far back.
That was the story. The story created her pain.

Out of her pain she prayed, always on her knees,
Her lips shaped secrets like rain in August grass.
Her white head, I knew, could not betray or deceive,
The thunder imitated the secrets of her heart.

I knelt at her side, my shoulder brushing her black,
Her lips surrendered visions of her private heaven and hell.
Drugged by her whispers, my head sank into her side,
My body and soul, in that instant, entered her smell,

Not merely the smell of her skin, but the smell
Of her prayers and pain, the smell of her long loss,
The smell of the years that had whitened her head,
That made her whisper to the pallid Christ on his cross,

The rent, dumb Christ, listener at the doors of the heart,
The pummelled Christ, the sea of human pain,
The sated Christ, the drinker of horrors,
The prisoner Christ, dungeoned in flesh and bone.

Her smell opened her locked world,
My closed eyes saw something of mine,
My small world swam in her infinite world
And did not drown but rose where the sun shone

On silence following the thunder's majestic prayer
For all the pain of all the living and dead,
I opened my eyes to the silence
Blessing her black clothes, her white head,

Blessing the smell that had told me something
Beyond lips' whispers and heart's prayer.
She took my hand in her hand, we moved together
Out of the church into the rain-cleaned air.

Thorn

When Fools' Day came the boy threw off his shoes
And galloped pellmell through the April air
That after winter tasted fabulous.
The road to Saleen Quay became a Milky Way
As he cavorted, trotted at his will
Until a vivid pain shot through his foot.
A thorn, spiky brown, lodged whole
And wicked near his heel. He probed, squeezed, got

It out, held it in the palm of his hand.
He forgot his foot's thinning trickle of blood
Watching the blood on the thorn, almost dried.
Winterbite he knew, how it gripped the land.
He thought of yellow spikes in the crown of God
And saw a long thorn stuck in the world's side.

Horsechestnuts

Everything in the room was too clean.
The boy watched the old priest nod over his crossword.
The pencil slipped from his grip, rolled on the floor.
Once or twice, the boy felt he was smothering.
All the words flew off into the darkness
Like frightened birds whose wings obscured the stars.
The boy said goodnight to the old man's silence,
Picked his way in blackness between two lines of trees,
Horsechestnuts rising beneath him, crowding about him.
They were coming alive, soon their loneliness would cry out.
He started to kick them though he couldn't see.
He picked them up and threw them at the night.
These were men's hearts he was flinging about
As if the flinging might set them free.
He threw hearts at the darkness till he came
To the gate and the first shocking timid light.

Lost

To crawl away then from the shame or hurt
Or whatever it was
And to hide below the depths in your heart
Was all you could think of
Because the world was not only
Empty of love
But was a vast rat gnawing through concrete
To find your flesh.
So you took to a street
And entered a house
Emptier than yourself,
A raw place
Bleeding with memories
Of dawning and dying days.
And you knew

They'd be out in the roads looking for you
In no time at all,
Looking, looking for you
As though they needed assurance

You'd once existed
Beyond the shadowed edges of their lives,
Their voices calling your name
Falling like light rain
On your hurt or your shame
There in the cold of the old empty house,
Calling your name
To the road and the street and the air,
Calling with echoing care
To come out come back come home
From your sanctuary of dark and cold.
Was it minutes or hours or days
Before you came out?
Child in the light

You were found
And were never the same again.

Moving through each known face
You are often lost in the darkest place
Tasting the loss that is yours
Alone,
Hearing the voices call and cry
Come back come out come home
And you wonder why
Being lost in yourself should stir
This cry in others
Who seem together
Behind the shadowed edges of their lives,
Their own cries slashing the air
As the day dawns, as the day dies.

The Horse's Head

'Hold the horse's head,' the farmer said
To the boy loitering outside the pub.
'If you're willing to hold the horse's head
You'll earn a shilling.'

The boy took the reins, the farmer went inside,
The boy stood near the horse's head.

The horse's head was above the boy's head.
The boy looked up.
The sun attended the horse's head, a crown of light
Blinded the boy's eyes for a moment.

His eyes cleared and he saw the horse's head,
Eyes, ears, mane, wet
Nostrils, brown forehead splashed white,
Nervous lips,
Teeth moving on the bit.

The sun fussed over it.
The boy stared at it.
He reached up and gave the horse's head
A pat.

The horse's head shuddered, pulled on the reins,
Rasping the boy's hands, almost burning the skin,
Drawing blood to attention.
The boy's grip tightened on the reins,
Jerked the horse's head to order.
The boy was not afraid.
He would be master of the horse's head
Made of the sun
In the street outside the pub
Where the farmer stood drinking at the bar.

Daylight said the boy was praying
His head bowed before an altar.
The air itself became the prayer
Unsaid
Shared between the boy
And the horse's head.

The horse's head guarded the boy
Looking down from its great height.
If the boy should stumble
The horse's head would bear him up,
Raise him, as before,
To his human stature.

If he should lay his head against the horse's head –
Peace.

The farmer came out of the pub.
He gave the boy a shilling.

He led the horse away.
The boy stared at the horse.
He felt the reins in his hands
Now easy, now rasping,
And over his head, forever,
The horse's head
Between the earth and the sun.
He put the shilling in his pocket
And walked on.

The Hill of Fire

I saw five counties of Munster
From the top of Scrolm hill,
And later the grey blankets of rain
Swaddling the far fields until

They seemed to disappear in greyness.
Minutes later, the rain was gone,
And the salmon-heavy Cashen
Like a river of silver shone.

The hob-nailed hours trudge slowly
Through that country; the brown
Mountain, bald-headed, lords it
Over the peaceful pastures down

Along the hillside. A name for every field –
Boland's meadow, marvellously green,
And the humped, crooked shoulder
Of grassy Garnagoyteen.

A touch of cold coming in the air,
I threw one last look around
At my mysterious province, and turned my back
On the cold purity of high ground.

From low ground, I saw the sun
Change the entire
World; that towering bulk became
A hill of fire.

The Fall

Three boys and a girl were standing there,
Hands linked in a circle. The circle broke
When Moynihan turned, darted like a hare
Through the grass, jumped, faced the others:
'I'm king o' the ditch! I'm king o' the ditch!
Who'll pull me down! Who'll pull me down!' The three
Advanced, stood at the base. Then one boy stretched,
Grabbed Moynihan's ankle fiercely

But a kick in the chest sent him reeling back.
'I'm king! I'm king!' roared Moynihan again,
Legs wide, a wild dominion in his eyes.
The second boy tried, failed to move that rock.
Then the girl reached as Moynihan reached down,
Fell from his throne, rolling between her thighs.

The Stones

Worried mothers bawled her name
To call wild children from their games.

'Nellie Mulcahy! Nellie Mulcahy!
If ye don't come home,
She'll carry ye off in her big black bag.'

Her name was fear and fear begat obedience,
But one day she made a real appearance –
A harmless hag with a bag on her back.
When the children heard, they gathered together
And in a trice were
Stalking the little weary traveller –
Ten, twenty, thirty, forty.
Numbers gave them courage
Though, had they known it,
Nellie was more timid by far
Than the timidest there.
Once or twice, she turned to look
At the bravado-swollen pack.
Slowly the chant began –

'Nellie Mulcahy! Nellie Mulcahy!
Wicked old woman! Wicked old woman!'

One child threw a stone.
Another did likewise.
Soon the little monsters
Were furiously stoning her
Whose name was fear.
When she fell bleeding to the ground,
Whimpering like a beaten pup,
Even then they didn't give up
But pelted her like mad.

Suddenly they stopped, looked at
Each other, then at Nellie, lying
On the ground, shivering.

Slowly they withdrew
One by one.

Silence. Silence.
All the stones were thrown.

Between the hedges of their guilt
Cain-children shambled home.

Alone,
She dragged herself up,
Crying in small half-uttered moans,
Limped away across the land,
Black bag on her back,
Agony racking her bones.

Between her and the children,
Like hideous forms of fear –
The stones.

Nails

The black van exploded
Fifty yards from the hotel entrance.
Two men, one black-haired, the other red,
Had parked it there as though for a few moments
While they walked around the corner
Not noticing, it seemed, the children
In single file behind their perky leader,
And certainly not seeing the van
Explode into the children's bodies.
Nails, nine inches long, lodged
In chest, ankle, thigh, buttock, shoulder, face.
The quickly-gathered crowd was outraged and shocked.
Some children were whole, others bits and pieces.
These blasted crucifixions are commonplace.

Innocent

Only the innocent can be total monster.
Myles Bartishel, bored at seven years old,
Scoured holes and crevices for hungry spiders
But found none. Thwarted and blackening, he held
His patience but didn't change when the sun
Emerged, kind as a father, to throw its light
On the spiderless world. Myles turned to a pane
Of glass, warm to the touch. On its face a fly

Moved as if it wanted to pierce the glass
And flit forever in that blue infinity
Of cool reflection and intangible things.
He let it flounder; then got it between his
Fingers. Two tugs. On the ground, the fly's body
Jerked. Myles held in his hand two silver wings.

The Visitor

He strutted into the house.

Laughing
He walked over to the woman
Stuck a kiss in her face.

He wore gloves.
He had fur on his coat.
He was the most confident man in the world.
He liked his own wit.

Turning his attention to the children
He patted each one on the head.
They are healthy but a bit shy, he said.
They'll make fine men and women, he said.

The children looked up at him.
He was still laughing.
He was so confident
They could not find the word for it.
He was so elegant
He was more terrifying than the giants of night.

The world
Could only go on its knees before him.
The kissed woman
Was expected to adore him.

It seemed she did.

I'll eat now, he said,
Nothing elaborate, just something simple and quick –
Rashers, eggs, sausages, tomatoes
And a few nice lightly-buttered slices
Of your very own
Home-made brown
Bread.
O you dear woman, can't you see
My tongue is hanging out
For a pot of your delicious tea.
No other woman in this world
Can cook so well for me.
I'm always touched by your modest mastery!

He sat at table like a king.
He ate between bursts of laughter.
He was a great philosopher,
Wise, able to advise,
Solving the world between mouthfuls.
The woman hovered about him.
The children stared at his vital head.
He had robbed them of every word they had.
Please have some more food, the woman said.
He ate, he laughed, he joked,
He knew the world, his plate was clean
As Jack Spratt's in the funny poem,
He was a handsome wolfman,
More gifted than anyone
The woman and children of that house
Had ever seen or known.

He was the storm they listened to at night
Huddled together in bed
He was what laid the woman low
With the killing pain in her head
He was the threat in the high tide
At the back of the house
He was a huge knock on the door
In a moment of peace
He was a hound's neck leaning
Into the kill
He was a hawk of heaven stooping
To fulfil its will
He was the sentence tired writers of gospel
Prayed God to write
He was a black explosion of starlings
Out of a November tree
He was a plan that worked
In a climate of self-delight
He was all the voices
Of the sea.

My time is up, he said,
I must go now.

Taking his coat, gloves, philosophy, laughter, wit,
He prepared to leave.
He kissed the woman again.
He smiled down on the children.
He walked out of the house.

The children looked at each other.
The woman looked at the chair.
The chair was a throne
Bereft of its king, its visitor.

Tasty

About two and a half miles up a muddy by-road
Past hedges where summer lovers were wont to rut,
Some ten feet from a sturdy five-bar gate
On a frosty November night,
Dark sparkles jewelling the countryside,
Close to a row of oak trees
Whose roots, trunks, boughs and leaves
Flourished in the folklore of that parish,

The giant met The Belly. The giant's eyes
Appraised this rural scene with epic relish.

'I'm going to eat you, Belly,' smiled the giant.
'Pray don't,' The Belly pleaded, 'At least not now;
Ponder somewhat, reflect, be merciful, not hasty.'

For answer, the giant stuffed The Belly in
His gob, chewed the screams, swallowed all
And mumbled, 'Not bad. In fact, unusually tasty.'

The Big Words

The first time I heard
Transubstantiation
My head fell off.

'Explain it,' the teacher said.
I looked around the classroom
Searching for my severed head
And found it near a mouse-hole
Where we used to drop
Crumbs of bread
Turning to turds

Twice as transcendental
As holy words.

'Explain it to me,' I said to my father.
From behind the great spread pages of *The Irish Independent*
'It's a miracle,' he said,
'I'm reading John D. Hickey on the semi-final
But come back later and we'll see
What's happening to Gussie Goose and Curly Wee.'

I found out what *Transubstantiation* meant.
I trotted out my answer
But the trot turned into a gallop
And I found myself witnessing a race
Between all the big words
Used by all the small men.
I use them myself, of course,
Especially when I have nothing to say,
When I cannot raise dust or hackles, go to town, or make hay
With the little bit of life in my head
Suggesting I should drink the best wine,
Eat the best bread
And thus, with a deft flick of my mind,
Transfigure the blackest hours
On this most holy ground
Where some would make their god
Hide behind big words,
Shields to stop him showing the colour of his blood
And be safe as the bland masters of jargon
Whose blindness is an appetite
For whacking great vocabularies
That cough resoundingly
In some bottomless pit
Of self-importance.

Some night soon, I'm going to have a party
For all the big words.
By the light of a semantic moon
I'll turn the race into a dance,
And with my little words
Both hosts and servants
Catering beyond their best
For even the teeniest need
Of every resonant guest,
Big and small will all be thrilled to see
Exactly what has happened
To Gussie Goose and Curly Wee.

Poem from a Three Year Old

And will the flowers die?

And will the people die?

And every day do you grow old, do I
grow old, no I'm not old, do
flowers grow old?

Old things – do you throw them out?

Do you throw old people out?

And how you know a flower that's old?

The petals fall, the petals fall from flowers,
and do the petals fall from people too,
every day more petals fall until the
floor where I would like to play I
want to play is covered with old
flowers and people all the same
together lying there with petals fallen
on the dirty floor I want to play
the floor you come and sweep
with the huge broom.

The dirt you sweep, what happens that,
what happens all the dirt you sweep
from flowers and people, what
happens all the dirt? Is all the
dirt what's left of flowers and
people, all the dirt there in a
heap under the huge broom that
sweeps everything away?

Why you work so hard, why brush
and sweep to make a heap of dirt?
And who will bring new flowers?
And who will bring new people? Who will
bring new flowers to put in water
where no petals fall on to the
floor where I would like to
play? Who will bring new flowers
that will not hang their heads

like tired old people wanting sleep?
Who will bring new flowers that
do not split and shrivel every
day? And if we have new flowers,
will we have new people too to
keep the flowers alive and give
them water?

And will the new young flowers die?

And will the new young people die?

And why?

Nineteen Forty-Two

A tangled briar, a bleeding hand,
a berry on a bed of ants,
a boy who sips at fear,
his torn pants.

Children's Hospital

Huge-headed, this petrified freak of clay
stares at the staring visitors bearing flowers,
fragrant tokens of a mute desire to see
the prone ones on the highway to recovery.
Recovery? This one, girl, five years stretched,
looks and looks and says
nothing. Behind her eyes,
bright mornings of her body's freedom.

Intruding rays of sunlight bring
the sky's immaculate benediction
on suffering
that happens in the dullest way
while innumerable children blunder towards
the dangerous light of day.

While things endure or break, while winter comes again
and prowls morosely through dark places,
I read the clammy script of pain
on children's faces.
In Ward 11, Unit 4, St Mary's Hospital,
neatly arranged, paralysed creation
lies limp between the lime-white sheets.

Intruding sunlight hovers on
the unfathomable fruit of God's imagination.

The Learning of Pity

There is hate in the child's eyes
For his father's father
Who prowls the house half-naked late at night
Looking for whiskey and a little water.
The whole house is changing
And the child's eyes are progressive.
The old man knows what's in the air
And seems hardly disposed to forgive.

What did Oliver's son think of him?
What does any son think of any old man
Withering away, shanks thinning, eyes rheumy,
Hands trembling, speech foolish? Yet this is the custom
And strangely there are those, even the occasional son,
Hurt and renewed in the learning of pity.

Girl on a Tightrope

They've set up the tent in the blacksmith's field
And the village children
Stare at the girl on the tightrope
As if they were astronauts
Staring at the world
Like men on the first morning of creation
Seeing mountains valleys rivers lakes
In colours never seen before

While down below
A clown grins
A greasy grin
And prepares to ride a horse
Around the ring
In the tent
In the blacksmith's field
Where the world begins

She is stepping a line
The children have never known
Somewhere between earth and sky
Somewhere they have never been

A line of danger and adventure
A line of longing and of love
A line of breathing and of breathlessness
A line of poised humanity and vigilant divinity

In the tent in the blacksmith's field
With the children watching

She is stepping there
Between girl and goddess
And her hair is black and tight
And bound with a ribbon of light
At the back of her head
Neat as a bird's

And the light of eyes is on her
Guiding her
Willing her
To move safely in her silence

Billy O'Sullivan is praying for her
And Tony Crow is begging God to bring her safe
And Martha Kane's lips freeze in terror
And Tommy Doran's mouth is an o of awe
And Mona Coleman's hands are locked together
And Danny Dalton shuts his eyes
More tightly than ever he shut them before
But he cannot shut her out
He cannot shut her out

For she is there
On a line in the air

With a ribbon of light in her hair
Looking neither up nor down
But straight ahead
As though there were a road in the air
With fields on either side
She will look at later
Or even enter
For a moment's rest
After a journey through her own silence
And the children's silence
And their riveted eyes
On legs hands body head
Neat as a bird's

O if only she could fly
There would be no danger then
That she might fall and die

But she steps her way
To where she must go
And she will reach that spot
And smile
And wave
At children happy in her moving
And arriving
Children clapping stamping shouting
Till they're hoarse

And the lumpy clown
Grins
A greasy grin
Tries
And fails
To ride a horse

Around the ring
In the tent
In the blacksmith's field

Where the world begins

Rebuke

A man will scold his own child in a trice.
So Ritchie scolded Mosh, a boy of four
Who blindly sought the river's sympathies
And stumbled, dropping tears, down to the shore.
He slipped and fell, went down, came up,
Went down again. MacDonagh pulled him in,
Took him, dripping, to Ritchie's crowded shop.
Ritchie screamed to see his chastised son

So changed, as though the quick rebuke
Had driven him to a world unknown.
But now he lay there, still, beyond all pain;
The village watched and wept while Ritchie shook,
Two women pressed eager lips upon
Blue lips, giving their kiss of life. In vain.

Play

Picture the old man of seventy years
Rehearsing his death several times a day.
Between rehearsals, he calls the youngsters
To his side. If, in old men, it is possible
To speak of some belief in innocence
This old man has it in his drowsy way.
When he resigns the world for a spell
He does so only when the children promise
On pain of cross their hearts and hope to die
That they will quietly play about the chair
Where he sits staring down at heaven
Somewhere in his mind adrift in sleep.
'Angels of the earth, angels of the air,
All angels love to play about a sleeping man
And when they play, holy is the watch they keep.'

The Kiss

'Go down to the room and kiss him,
There's not much left o' him in the bed.
He had a good run of it, over eighty years.
In a few days he'll be dead.'

My nine years shook at the words 'kiss him'.
I knew the old man was something to my father.
I knew I had to do what my father said.
I trembled to the bedroom door

And entered the room where the drawn curtains
Foiled the light.
Jack Boland was a white wreck on the pillows,
His body a slight

Hump under the eiderdown quilt, starred white and red,
Everything under the black crucifix
With gaping mouth and bleeding head.
He saw me, half-lifted a hand. 'Here, boy,' he said.

I walked across the bedroom floor
And felt the ice in his hands enter mine.
His eyes were screwed up with sickness, his hair was wet,
His tongue hung, slapped back. Every bone

In my body chilled as I bent my head
To the smell and feel of the sickspittle on his lips.
I kissed him, I find it hard to say what I kissed
But I drank him into me when I kissed him.

I recognised something of what in him was ending,
Of what in me had scarcely begun.
He seemed without fear, I think I gave him nothing,
He told me something of what it is to be alone.

There is no way to say goodbye to the dying.
Jack Boland said 'G'wan, boy! Go now.'
I shivered away from his hands, his smell,
The wet blobs of pain on hair and brow,

The weak, eager touch. My childfear
Went with me out into the corridor, stayed
Inside me till I stood again at my father's side,
Head down, thinking I was no longer afraid

Yet feeling still the deathlips rummaging at my lips,
The breath a sick warmth mingling with my breath.
It's thirty years since I bent my head to the kiss.
Ten thirties would not make me forget.

A Leather Apron

After he cut the lamb's throat
He held it out from him by the hind legs
And let it kick for a minute or so.
Then he laid it on the table
That was hacked and scarred like a few faces
I've glimpsed in streets. Slowly then he drew
The bleeding knife across the leather apron
Covering his belly.

      I saw the lamb's blood
Wiped from the knife into the leather,
From the leather through the clothes, through the skin
Until it lived again in every butchering vein.
Unless he absorbed what he killed, I'll never
Tell the gentling touch of the man.

Ten Bob

I stood with a catechismical God
In the gravelled yard of the National School
Listening to teacher shouting across the road
To a tinker leaning on a bicycle
Rusty, groaning rebelliously out of date,
'Any chance you'd borrow a farmer's shovel
And shift a few cart-loads of the boys' shit?'
'How much?' 'Ten bob.' 'Yer on.' That was all.

God and myself were idle watching the tinker
Hefting three cart-loads into Herlihy's field
To earn his few drinking pence.
God sang dumb, the tinker hummed through his black muffler,
Teacher questioned, at peace with his world,
Herlihy's field soaked the shit of innocence.

The Stammer

A river might start from his mouth
But rocks mock the flow over the gravelly bed
Breaking the water like paper tearing
Breaking the flow like a belt in the head
When the flood of a thought is strong.
The questions wound
But do not kill him.

Only, in the mind, blood's thundery sound
And, like a pain through the eyes, the sense of wrong.

The questions
Are stones from a sling
Made of forked alder,
Tongue of a shoe, twin
Strips of rubber from a discarded
Tube at the back of a garage
Where nettles thrive, wickedly fluent.
Men batter crashed metal back into shape.
A girl was maimed in that accident.
The questioner, tall, fair-minded,
Aims,
The stone round and smooth
Hits the inside of his throat
He has often seen in a mirror,
A scrawny blood-necked fledgling gawking from a nest,
A fish pulsing in dust
The hook stuck in the mouth
The rhythmical foolish lift and flop of the tail.

The fish has a dry mouth, not a note
Of the music of whales
Wave-making lovers humping for fun
Strumming the dumb leagues.
The sea played from pole to pole
Sings with their appetite.

With what delight they will plunder their grounds
And, for long months, eat.

Dust is dulling the scales.
Sunlight grins at the back
Belly

Mouth gulping silence
Unshuttable eyes.

Lips pumping silent cries
He drowns in the questioner's eyes
Sweat on his forehead
Sweat in his spine
Dribbling down to swim in the slit
Of the cheeks of his arse,
Flow like the river making the pool,
The Soldier's Hole
Under the alder trees,
Prim twigs
Laws
He cannot understand
But must observe

Going down, down,

Eyes open
For spawn and redbreast
Of the watery-delicate bones
Pulsing in stones
Shadows of stones
Eyes like old men
Who have said too much
Darting at his approach
To the deeper water
At the far end
Green with secrets
A poetry book
With its own smell
One of his friends
Might read aloud

Beyond all shame
Never a faltering
Rhythm or word
Spawns' and redbreasts' shadowy sounds
Focussed from rivers around
In the room with yellow walls
The nailed boarded floor unshaken
By the pains of learning
Fires cries communion festivals
Bluegreen map of the world
Deserts cities islands seas

The eyes of questions
Four broken
Desks
Names and dates so scarred
Each desk is a part
Of the sadness
Bagging the heart
Freezing the lips
Where nothing
Cannot be spoken.

The Learning

The learning goes on forever.
A pigeon dozing in the ivy
Is sending out bulletins
I am trying to decipher.

The streets survive, offering their thoughts
At no cost. Lost
Rivers plead under our feet,
Astray in themselves,
Sharing our anonymity.

With what devotion
The children of ignorance
Apply themselves to learn
The streets' wisdom, the rivers' rhythms
In the spell of the flesh
Failing through self-repeating evenings.

Listen!
Is it a bomb or a heart-beat?
A tired sigh of the past
Or the future's optimistic eye?
Touch of some habitual defeat?
The sound of a kiss
That cannot be returned
Though all our lives
We have yearned, we have yearned.

I will spend what I have to spend
And never accuse my pockets of time
Of hoarding or squandering, getting or shedding
Possessions.

It is as though I were straining to hear
Low, happy laughter
Vanishing in the grass of an occupied garden
One summer evening
That lays itself down

Like a cat in the corner of a shed
After taking its prey
That lost day.
It rests now, sweetly surfeited
While round the corner of the hour
Hunger waits like the bad news
We fear to hear.

The spending burns on.
I will always turn to this burning
As the days
To the repeated losing of themselves,
Throwing themselves away as though
They could not bear the burden of themselves
That must come again as they happened long ago,
Each one a child, a corpse, a proven fighter

In the learning that goes on forever.

John Keane's Field

John Keane's field is edengreen
After a shower of rain in August.

Here by the brown river
Mushrooms whiten the green
Like feelings of confidence
Or images out of a dream
Persisting in daylight,
And I know something again
Of the meaning of brotherhood.

It is an intent walking through wet grass
In a silence old as growth,
Eyes rejoicing at every discovery,
Words drifting out over the brown river
Like flickering birds without names,

Getting rarer now
Because some of the fields are poisoned with progress.
And I know our kind
Would kill river and field
If green and brown
Stood between them and money.

Our eyes look down into the green
And find the white surprises
That did not die with childhood.
We stumble on the eternal
When we walk crookedly.

Other moments,
Killers of sudden wonders,
Are where we live.
Our days endure the small murders.

The brown river drags through the long summer,
John Keane's field is ready for winter,
We are going our different ways
Powerless against what threatens
The land.

'We got the pick o' them,' you laugh,
Pinkwhite cups of August
In either hand.

God's Eye

Beneath the stare of God's gold burning eye,
Two crisp hands clap; a thousand plover rise
And wheel across the clean meadows of the sky.

Black wings flash and gleam; a perfect white
Makes beautiful each rising breast,
Sovereign in the far-off miracle of flight.

Their terror is a lovely thing,
A sudden inspiration, exploding
In the thunder of each beating wing;

A startling rout, as of an army driven
In broken regiments
Against the proud, fantastic face of heaven.

And yet, no mad disorder, no raucous accident
Deforms the miracle; high flocks
Fulfil an inbred, furious intent.

In screams of dread, perfection whirls
Along the headlands of the sky;
They circle, gabbing now like girls,

And wing to safety in Carrig Wood,
Dip through branches, disappear; across the sky,
The pale sun throws a quilt of solitude.

After terror, they are safety's prisoners,
Momentary victims of security
In labyrinths where surly winter stirs.

They breathe on branches, hidden and alone.
Fear will flare again, but now the abandoned sky
Is turning cold and grey as stone.

I think about that marvellous rout, the empty sky,
A flight of plover hidden from
The stare of God's gold burning eye.

3

Bodies of spirits

Ella Cantillon

The watcher saw her walk the empty street
The crinkled yellow scarf about her head.
Her face had the waxen polish of the dead
And her walk was crooked. She dragged her feet
As though in pain or shame,
Anguished parody of movement. Across
His mind slipped the sweet syllables of her name –
Ella Cantillon. Then he was
Standing about five yards from the stage
In an open field on an August day,
One with that summer crowd entranced
By the slight girl waiting, purely
Poised. The sunlight became homage
When her body married music and she danced.

Litter

Her mind snapped like a summer-dry twig
And fell in pieces at her feet
To be trampled on by people going to work,
Coming from work, till it seemed stamped into the concrete
Pavement. A man pushing a barrow
Brushed the pieces in with other bits of litter,
Cigarette-boxes, butt-ends, burnt matches
And a democratic sludge of dirty paper.
By a corporate process, all this was sent
To a dump ten miles outside the city.
Her mind lay buried under mountains of waste
While she sat staring at the base of a monument
Or crying and screaming in the streets
About something stolen from her, or she had lost.

A Mad Woman

Her hair blowing about her head
she careers before my eyes,
screaming about her beloved dead
and their deep mysteries.
How passionately she gabs aloud
her mostly incoherent words
at the imperturbable crowd,
at the full air and the wheeling birds,
at the great monuments of stone
and little children at their play,
she shouts, 'Remember you are all alone!
So pray, God damn you! Pray! Pray! Pray!'

Union

When salmon swarmed in the brown tides
And cocks raised their lusty din
And her heart beat like a wild bird's heart,
She left her kin.

A black ass brayed in the village,
Men ploughed and mowed,
There was talk of rising water
When he struck the road.

Words stranger than were scattered
Over the shuttered dead
Were faint as child-songs in their ears
When they stretched in bed.

A Kerry Christmas

The frost transfigures and the wind deceives,
A warring season bickers to its end,
The exiles gather and the land believes
It knows a birth, commemorates a friend
Who scatters crumbs of love to north and south,
Countering the scrounging winter light;
Goodwill dribbles from the swilling mouth,
The mad Atlantic thrashes in the night

Where Mollie Connor, shawled in total black,
The smell of clay telling where she has been,
A cross of generation on her back,
Nourished by the long, resurgent story
Explaining what ecstatic voices mean,
Stumbles to her private, certain glory.

A Cry for Art O'Leary
(from the Irish of Eibhlín Dubh Ní Chonaill)

My love
The first time I saw you
From the top of the market
My eyes covered you
My heart went out to you
I left my friends for you
Threw away my home for you

What else could I do?

You got the best rooms for me
All in order for me
Ovens burning for me
Fresh trout caught for me
Choice meat for me

In the best of beds I stretched
Till milking-time hummed for me

You made the whole world
Pleasing to me

White rider of love!

I love your silver-hilted sword
How your beaver hat became you
With its band of gold
Your friendly homespun suit
Revealed your body
Your pin of glinting silver
Glittered in your shirt

On your horse in style
You were sensitive pale-faced
Having journeyed overseas
The English respected you
Bowing to the ground
Not because they loved you
But true to their hearts' hate

They're the ones who killed you
Darling of my heart

My lover
My love's creature
Pride of Immokelly
To me you were not dead
Till your great mare came to me
Her bridle dragging ground
Her head with your startling blood
Your blood upon the saddle
You rode in your prime
I didn't wait to clean it
I leaped across my bed
I leaped then to the gate
I leaped upon your mare
I clapped my hands in frenzy
I followed every sign
With all the skill I knew
Until I found you lying
Dead near a furze bush
Without pope or bishop
Or cleric or priest
To say a prayer for you

Only a crooked wasted hag
Throwing her cloak across you

I could do nothing then
In the sight of God
But go on my knees
And kiss your face
And drink your free blood

My man!
Going out the gate
You turned back again
Kissed the two children
Threw a kiss at me
Saying 'Eileen, woman, try
To get this house in order,
Do your best for us
I must be going now
I'll not be home again.'
I thought that you were joking
You my laughing man

My man!
My Art O'Leary
Up on your horse now
Ride out to Macroom
And then to Inchigeela
Take a bottle of wine
Like your people before you
Rise up
My Art O'Leary
Of the sword of love

Put on your clothes
Your black beaver
Your black gloves
Take down your whip
Your mare is waiting
Go east by the thin road
Every bush will salute you
Every stream will speak to you
Men and women acknowledge you

They know a great man
When they set eyes on him

God's curse on you, Morris,
God's curse on your treachery
You swept my man from me
The man of my children
Two children play in the house
A third lives in me

He won't come alive from me

My heart's wound
Why was I not with you
When you were shot
That I might take the bullet
In my own body?
Then you'd have gone free
Rider of the grey eye
And followed them
Who'd murdered me

My man!
I look at you now
All I know of a hero
True man with true heart
Stuck in a coffin
You fished the clean streams
Drank nightlong in halls
Among frank-breasted women

I miss you

My man!
I am crying for you
In far Derrynane
In yellow-appled Carren
Where many a horseman
And vigilant woman
Would be quick to join
In crying for you
Art O'Leary
My laughing man

O crying women
Long live your crying
Till Art O'Leary
Goes back to school
On a fateful day

Not for books and music

But for stones and clay

My man!
The corn is stacked
The cows are milking
My heart is a lump of grief
I will never be healed
Till Art O'Leary
Comes back to me

I am a locked trunk
The key is lost
I must wait till rust
Devours the screw

O my best friend
Art O'Leary
Son of Conor
Son of Cadach
Son of Lewis
East from wooded glens
West from girlish hills
Where rowanberries grow
Yellow nuts budge from branches
Apples laugh like small suns
As once they laughed
Throughout my girlhood
It is no cause for wonder
If bonfires lit O'Leary country
Close to Ballingeary
Or holy Gougane Barra
After the clean-gripping rider
The robust hunter
Panting towards the kill
Your own hounds lagged behind you
O horseman of the summoning eyes
What happened you last night?
My only whole belief
Was that you could not die
For I was your protection

My heart! My grief!

My man! My darling!

In Cork
I had this vision
Lying in my bed:
A glen of withered trees
A home heart-broken
Strangled hunting-hounds
Choked birds
And you
Dying on a hillside
Art O'Leary
My one man
Your blood running crazily
Over earth and stone

Jesus Christ knows well
I'll wear no cap
No mourning dress
No solemn shoes
No bridle on my horse
No grief-signs in my house
But test instead
The wisdom of the law
I'll cross the sea
To speak to the King
If he ignores me
I'll come back home
To find the man
Who murdered my man

Morris, because of you
My man is dead

Is there a man in Ireland
To put a bullet through your head

Women, white women of the mill
I give my love to you
For the poetry you made
For Art O'Leary
Rider of the brown mare
Deep women-rhythms of blood
The fiercest and the sweetest
Since time began
Singing of this cry I womanmake
For my man

I Met a Woman

I met a woman in a street somewhere.
She was serious and beautiful. She said
Of the killings, 'Some people are devil-gripped
And many who are not might as well be dead.
If we could only see what is happening
We would never cease to pray.
We would surrender to God's love, knowing
His need for us. There is no other way.'

I said 'Do you pray?'

'I do,' she said, 'I let God into me.
I open my heart. He comes.
I pray for the killers, the killed, the ditched women.
I pray for you who are throwing yourselves away.
My heart is stamped with my people's names.'

Actaeon
(after Ovid)

Actaeon, conqueror of hunting-grounds,
Feeling the noonday sun was good
Because the morning dripped with blood,
Called off his hounds

And ambled in a lazy manner
Into a pine and cypress valley
Where in a pool of crystal water
Bathed the goddess Diana,

Tired from the hunt. Like the light of day
Her limbs, her knotted hair
Drifted on the water.
Naked to the world she lay.

Not the smallest sound was heard,
Only the heart of silence beat
In the guilty noonday heat
When Actaeon on Diana stared –

Hunter at the Goddess of the Hunt.
Happy with his morning he
Strolled into her privacy,
His life's worst error. She bent,

Scooped water in her fist and flung
It at his hair.
From his head there
Sprouted horns of the longlived stag.

All stag but for his human mind
Actaeon sought the solitude
Of highest hill and deepest wood
But always, just behind,

The hounds that he had trained to kill
Yelped and bayed while he
Tried to lose them but they
Howled and hungered still

Till Blackfoot, Grabber, Harpy sprang.
He screamed 'I am your master.'
They tore him deeper, faster.
His wet flesh shredded on their fangs.

Who can imagine Actaeon's terror?
Dare anyone define
(It might be yours or mine)
The nature of his error?

Far from his death, the sunlight blessed
Diana naked
While the waters of revenge
Cooled at her breast.

The Hope of Wings

The girl forces the gull's beak open with
A spoon and starts to scrape the oil away.
Rampant the sky's colours, legend and myth
Sustain the attention of those beset by
Traditional hungers, but now I foresee
A bird-emptied sky, the world's shores

Hilled with crippled things, the thick, black
Smothering oil murdering the hope of wings.
And this girl – she can't be into her teens –
Would, if her working now is a guide,
Spend all her years remaking these stunned birds
Littering the sea, dead flops among stones.
She'd give a white-winged creature to the sky
Before black tides drown mere human words.

Girl in a Rope

By the still canal
She enters a slack rope,
Moves, slowly at first, round and round;
Gathering speed,
(Faster, faster now)
She clips the air without a sound –
Swift swirling sight,
Creator of a high design,
Orbiting in new delight
The red and white NO PARKING sign.

At the Party

When the woman at the party said
That she was dying of some incurable disease,
I stared into my glass and saw the red
Wine's glittering infinities
Dancing alive between my fingers,
Making me again confront her eyes –
No traces there of any special hunger,
No painful guess, hysterical surmise.
She said, 'Christmas in this land is cold,
Maguire's idea to go abroad is good;
As for myself, I like to take a stroll
On winter afternoons. Always heats the blood.'
Barely hearing, I agreed. She smiled again.
Her world approached, touched, recoiled from mine.
The room was loud with noise of dying men.
Her parted lips accepted the good wine.

A Great Day

She was all in white.

Snow
Suggests itself as metaphor

But since this has been so often said
I may be justified in considering it dead.
Something about snow is not quite right.

Therefore, she was all in white.

He was most elegant too
All dickied up in dignified blue.

They came together, as is habitual
In that part of the world,
Through a grave ritual,

Listening
With at least a modicum of wonder –
What God has joined together
Let no man put asunder.

Man in woman, woman in man.
Soon afterwards, the fun began.

It was a great day –
Long hours of Dionysiac festivity.

Songs poured out like wine.
Praises flowed as they had never done.

The people there
Seemed to see each other in a new way.
This added to the distinction of the day.

And all the time she was all in white
Enjoying every song and speech
Enjoying every sip and every bite.

Such whiteness seems both beautiful and true
He thought, all dickied up in dignified blue.

He looks so good in blue
(This warmed her mind)
Blue suits him
Down to the ground.

At the table where they sat
Things seemed to fit.

And the loud crowd sang and danced
The whole day long, the whole night long.
There could never be anything but dance and song.

I must change, she whispered,
I must change my dress.

He never saw the white dress again.

In the train, the trees wore their rainy veils
With a reticent air.

It's good to get away, she whispered,
Touching her beautiful hair.

She closed her eyes, the trees were silent guests,
A tide of thoughts flowed in her head,
In his head.

'Darling, it was a great day,' she said.

Moloney Discovers the Winter

'I had the love of a woman once,' Moloney said,
''Twas years ago. A fine cut of a girl she was too,
With hair the black of a crow's wing and eyes blue
As the sea; but what really marked that girl apart
Was that she knew my vagabond heart;
She saw the good in every man
Because she tried to understand,
And from all I knew of her, I could
Swear to Christ that she was good.
Manalive, you don't know what
It is to be loved by a woman like that;
And love me she did with her body and soul
In the height of love that cannot be told.

But women are the quarest creatures on the face
Of God's creation, and to my shame and disgrace,
Didn't she marry an ould man with a farm o' land,
Two miles south o' Banna Strand,
(The place where the Kerrymen let Casement down,
He was hanged like a dog in London town.)
Whatever got into her I can't tell;
Some schemin' devil from the floor o' hell
Promised her things that went to her head
And coaxed her into the farmer's bed;
Clothes and finery and pretty things,
Rubies and bracelets and diamond rings.
By money, sweet Jesus, my love was taken,
And I was left – alone and forsaken.
If a man has money, his heart may be rotten,
The black sins on his soul will be forgotten.
No consolation could I find,
Madness threatened my peace o' mind,
And I walked all roads in a terrible plight
Hardly able to tell the day from the night,
But could only think, as I walked on,
That my love was gone, was gone, was gone...

The madness took me soon after she wed,
And I knew I must see her in the farmer's bed,
So one winter's night I set out on my own
Till I came to my loved one's new-found home;
On the icy roads I nearly fell,
But I hardly noticed the ice at all
Or the wind that blew and howled at my head
As if ravin' at me not to near her bed;
But not hell and heaven's fury and might
Could have kept me from seein' her that winter night,
And I scorned all natural threats and harms
Till I saw her at last in the farmer's arms.
Outside their window I crouched while the black
Icy midnight cut into my back,
The bitter rain drenched me through to the skin
And I on the outside lookin' in
At my love denied by an old man's lust
And he stretched like a ram across her breast.

The very next minute, she caught sight
O' my face and started up in a fright,
Desire and terror in her eyes,
But a horny old man between her thighs,

Doin' his besht, to tell the truth,
To give my girl a belt o' the brute.
Then he turned his head and saw me plain
And he screamed like a pig in frightful pain
And rose from the bed and rushed to the door,
Shoutin' and callin' on dogs before
I knew what had happened, and I heard
The cries of hungry hounds as the farmer urged
Them on with his 'Kill! Kill! Kill!'
I looked at her face, so pale and still,
My only love, another man's wife –
And then I was runnin' for my life!

    I tore like a madman through the night
My heart hell-hammering with the fright,
Flyin' from hounds that came on and on,
I knew if they caught me all alone
How fiercely they'd strip the flesh from the bone;
Mad for the kill, as if loosed from a cage –
The hungry hounds of an ould man's rage.
I ran like the wind, their cries in my head,
Fear in my heart that gave me speed.
I ran with the terror in my blood
Till I staggered through a darkened wood;
I cut hither and thither through the trees
Till I lost the sound of the hungry cries,
And then, exhausted, I fell down,
Spent and weary on the ground.

    After a time, I opened my eyes,
Under the moonlit winter skies,
And I looked around. Suddenly I saw
That I'd been in that place before –
A little private moonlit grove
Where once, in the summer, I'd come with my love
And lain with her in the summer grass
And never believed that time could pass
And loved her with my body and soul
In the height of love that cannot be told,
Because words of mine could never express
The miracle of her tenderness.
The height of summer, the height of love,
The sacredness of the little grove!
And then – I shivered; the cold
Began to cut to my marrowbone
And all about me the winter's breath

Touched everything with the touch o' death;
Thorny bushes, branches o' trees, the wet
Grass growin' under my feet,
Animals stretched in their secret lair,
Beasts of the world, birds of the air.
God's creation became my cross,
All things crying out my loss.
Then, as if I were suddenly old,
I knew the meaning of the winter's cold;
I thought of her eyes and face and hair
And of the love that I'd known there
That now to me was as good as dead –
The plaything of an ould man's bed!
My Christ, I thought, that lovers must part,
And the cold of winter possessed my heart.

The Dose

'Strip her.
Whip her through the town.
Fling her into the river
From the bridge in Portadown.
Take her sister then
To a big important Protestant house.
Strip her, strip the owner, strip his working men and women.
Turn them all to ashes.

Retire to a nearby hillside,
Have a drink, relax, enjoy the screams, the flames.
The purged night,
Repeat the dose all through the province.
It is, you'll agree, satisfying work.
Don't delay, brothers. Get on with it.'

Fragments

What had he to say to her now?
Where was the woman he believed he had known
In a street, out walking, by the sea,
In bed, working, dancing, loving the sun

And saying so, always for the first time?
Who was this stranger with the graven face?
What led to the dreaming-up of a home?
And what was he, at sixty? Who was

That man lifting the blackthorn stick
With the knobbed top from its place
At the side of the fire, quietly dying?

He listened to his own steps in the walk
Past the reedy mud where plover rose
And scattered, black fragments, crying.

Steps

Steps on the street outside
Bring you to mind
High on a mountainside,
Your face stung by the wind,
Saying what it meant
To have to go away,
The happiness and disappointment
Of the irreplaceable day,
Of the summer night
When love lived until dawn
And in the breaking light
Put a brave face on
To counter later injury
By which it would be tried –
The sharp stab of memory,
Steps on the street outside.

It Was Indeed Love

I saw nothing making love to nothing
In that quiet place near the estuary.
It was a late October evening
And the autumn river turned to the autumn sea.
The sky was brash with crows, maybe they were
Noisy facing another winter,
A bleak enough scene, yet I could swear
A lover was waiting for another lover
Where trees and fields suggested love decayed.
Something that had begun a long time ago
Suffered in a moment its own ending,
The sky became a sky-devouring crow
Wings smothering sea and river in their shade
And though nothing made love to nothing
It was indeed love that was being made.

Santorini
(for Michael, Edna and Sarah Longley)

In this volcanic, dreaming place
Six Greek poets
Resurrect my mother's face
And set my father dancing again
As if death had never happened.

    Nikos, Yannis, Stella,
    Liana, Demosthenes, John

Smile as the Blasket Islanders
Make love to the sandwomen.
They grapple with my daughter's questions –
What happens all the flowers? What happens all the people?
And when a memory shivers
With images of love and loss
And Yannis asks 'What is this pain?'
I live it all again
And learn once more to let it go
As the people of this island
Living with their volcano

Muttering rumbling threatening
Take their daily lives in their hands
And go on making wine
And baking bread.
I'll take two volcanic stones
And put Atlantis in my pocket.
When will this earth explode again?

Liana, Demosthenes, John,
Stella, Yannis, Nikos,

Your precise fire will sing for me
In my explosive country
And when I look into your book
A small boat making a huge V
In that blue sea will astonish me
With gratitude.

I touch the stones.
My mother smiles, my father dances,
My daughter peppers me with questions,
A swimmer finds his music, an ambulance screams
In mercy, I build a bridge of love,
The willow speaks, the lightning dreams,
The blackbird sings, I make a wish, the gift appears
To bless this art
    that deepens friendship
        through the years.

The Exhibition

A girl hesitates under elm branches
Their shadows linking arms in the grass,
A few cobwebs depend on the logs of winter,
This tranquil cat suggests murderous ways,

A red setter shines across a road
To a child's muddy wellingtons thrown outside a door,
In a room of subdued music a woman
Fingers the gold in her hair

As if wondering whether to go on a spree
And spend every emotional coin
Or stay in that comfortable house
With himself and the children

Oh and a thousand other pictures
Are catalogued in my eyes.
I wanted to congratulate the artist
But he'd taken himself off down the sky

And was nowhere to be found.
Very soon, the show was over for the night.
I was grateful and decided to keep as a souvenir
My invitation printed in letters of light

Glowing more brightly in my head
The deeper my sleep.
My private collection is growing.
The more I give away the more I keep.

Love Cry

He mounted her, growing between her thighs.
A mile away, the Shannon swelled and thrust
Into the sea, ignoring the gaunt curlew-cries.
Near where the children played in gathering dusk
John Martin Connor cocked his polished gun
And fired at plover over Nolan's hill;
A second late, he shot the dying sun
And swore at such an unrewarding kill.

A quick voice called, one child turned and ran,
Somewhere in Brandon's river a trout leaped,
Infinite circles made nightspirits stare;
The hunter tensed, the birds approached again
As though they had a binding tryst to keep.
Her love-cry thrilled and perished on the air.

Lightness

The doctor and the sergeant, side by side,
Watched her as she walked the summer street
A girl light-stepping in her lissom pride
The ground a sudden Eden at her feet.
They watched, and each thought how he'd like to greet
Her smiling like the summer's chosen bride,
Legs the colour of the ripened wheat
Eyes making all other eyes grow wide

With wonder. But her lightness was the thing,
A gift that made you pity the poor blind,
A grace that told you why the best have cried
Because they know they are no longer young,
A miracle that made her leave behind
The doctor and the sergeant, side by side.

Love-child

Because the love-child in her belly stirred
She understood the stirring of the sea
And scorned in silence every hollow word
They thought consoled her wordless misery.
She knew the agony of the shot bird,
The threat to lovers' ecstasy;
Her cousins prattled on, she scarcely heard
But stared straight at the fire, then suddenly

Got up and quit the house of platitude
Where a small ring of astonished people sat
Looking at each other first, then at the flame
While she, tasting the air of solitude,
Felt them recede into the night
And in the private darkness, breathed his name.

Sister

Whenever Dillon ran the hundred yards
He won; and when he pitched the heavy shot,
Those who witnessed it could find no words
To tell their admiration. With what
Horror then they found that he
Was dead – rat-poisoned cleaning a spring-pit;
Two cut fingers in a nest of rats and they
Despatched him to the judgment when they bit.

The crowd he thrilled forgot him soon enough
But he'd a sister who remembered him forever
In the disciplined cold way that is love:
A link that neither time nor space would sever;
On rats she trapped at all times in a cage,
Slow, boiling water poured. She kept her rage.

Miss Anne

Seventy-five. White hair. Her feet at the fire.
Thus, for years. Sometimes she spoke of menace
Filling the air. She gave her few pennies
To the African Missions. God's desire,
It seemed, was the whitening of the black.
Miss Anne prayed. She prayed. Her feet touched warm ashes.
Fever burned in distant swamps and marshes.
For her prayers and pennies what she got back

No one could say. But often she lay awake
At four o'clock on a summer morning
And a far sound came nearer, on and on;
Above the driving men, the barking dogs, the crack
Of whip or stick, the sound of young bulls moving,
Hooves slipping, clipping the silence of the dawn.

Smell

She still got the smell of the bullcalf's blood
As she walked through Weir's field down to the sea,
Crossed among rocks, reached a high sand-drift, stood
Watching the rising tide. A fine bull, she
Thought, long in the back with the birthslime
Still on him, warm and wet. She watched the tide
Wash the stained shore, knew that in little time
It would surround her quietly on every side

If she but stayed where she was. The moist red beast
She'd seen totter into the light would grow strong
In time too. This tide would be high and full.
She bent to the fresh foam, took the salt taste
On her tongue, went back quickly along
The shore. The sea rose. She stroked the red bull.

Eyes

I want to speak of Moya Dyver's eyes –
Wrecked red lines on white,
Charts of pain's intricacies,
Maps of a strange country where the light
Dwindled among rivers of blood
Gone to God in a blink,
There again in a tick. Here was a wood
Where Moya Dyver sat down to think

Of all the other woods her shrunk eyes met,
Rivers where black and brown waters flowed
By roads crisscrossing oddly here and there.
She looked and saw, pulling a cigarette,
The smoke-ring her old lips blew
Perfect, breaking already on the air.

A Girl

It's amazing what we remember of people. You'd think we'd recall something "important" or "significant". Not at all, usually. We tend to be left with memories of little foibles, small gestures, odd phrases or words, snatches of songs, fragments of verses, bits of quotations from somebody, somewhere.

What I remember about the girl in this poem is the way she replied, simply, 'Yes, sir' and 'Yes, ma'am' to adults who were going to considerable lengths to advise her, praise her or chastise her over some matter. She refused to be drawn in to what they said; she remained deferentially apart. I also recall the quick, dark way she had of throwing a glance over her shoulder at you as she moved away from you. A quick, shy glance, at once searching and fugitive. She always seemed to be moving away into herself and always quickly scrutinising whoever she was leaving behind.

This girl worked for different people in the village where I was born and grew up. One day when she was sixteen or so she walked out of the village and into the river that we all knew so well. I was eight or nine then. I remember the men bringing her body through the streets. A couple of days passed before anyone recognised her.

Almost forty years later her phrases and her (to my child's eye) fascinating way of looking back over her shoulder returned to me. I began to write poems about her, through her. Or she wrote them through me. Who knows? Real memory is an irresistibly vivid and articulate moment in the present quickened by an image from the past. A swift glance over the mind's shoulder at time's legacy of fragments. The important thing is to be open to the inexplicable incursion of strange little features or aspects of people we thought we'd forgotten. If we allow these little aspects to return and speak, something essential manages to be born. Maybe the essential depends for its living expression on the apparently trivial and unrelated. Maybe the tiniest things have the ability to guide us towards the heart of the matter, if we let them.

1 *November Cloud*

November cloud is the colour of my mind.
My body is music.
I listen lovingly whenever I can.
I have wondered long at how blind

And ignorant I am.
I am beautiful too.
From the bits and pieces composing my body and mind
I choose what I think is true.

2 *The Room*

My room is surrounded by other rooms.
It is small and dark.
On one of the walls is a picture
Of the Sacred Heart.

If my own heart is sacred
How can I tell?
Sometimes I think it is poised
Between heaven and hell,

Poised like a gull on the wind
Down by the shore
Where all the cries of my life
Mingle together
As though the world itself were a room
Where humans lie
Listening to their sacred and unsacred hearts
Beat till they die.

3 *Familiar Things*

Strange how the most familiar things
– On my head the cold loved rain –
Say for me
What I cannot say of my pain.

I must not speak for myself.
Things speak for me.
Raindrops on a twig in February light
Are fragile and free.

There is no freedom that is not fragile.
O world beyond my skin
Shall I choose how to grow out of myself,
Shall I choose how to let you in?

Speak for me, then, familiar things
– On my head the cold loved rain –
Your voices constitute my voice,
Your freedom measures my pain.

4 *Lies*

I will not lie to myself
By saying that I betrayed another.
One can only betray oneself.
Do you hear me, sister? Do you hear me, brother?

It is this that is hard to bear –
I scarcely live, I rather
Endure the days like the dreams they are.
Do you hear me, mother? Do you hear me, father?

When I cut the lies out of my life
I still must live as best I can.
I was a brief lover, I'll not be a wife,
Do you hear me, boy? Do you hear me, man?

5 *Polka*

There is a road between great oak trees
I have walked since I was a child,
I danced when I heard the oakleaves singing
'That girl is wild.'

I followed the hoof-tracks of the working horses
Through winter into spring,
Whenever I stopped in my own silence
I heard the oakleaves sing.

Nightly, now, the huge-hooved horses
Pound where my body sleeps,
Along the road between the oak trees
A deepening silence creeps.

6 *Evil*

If I have no evil in myself
How shall I any evil understand?
Innocence, you are my enemy,
You split my heart and my mind.

Evil taught me whatever I know
And if it asks a price
Why should I not pay in full?
What if it asks my life?

Is my life worth more or less
Than the seaweed on the shore,
Than the midnight bark of a fettered dog
Or the wind's knock on the door?

Is my life worth more or less
Than the blackbird's body on the grass,
Than the old newspaper pitched in a drain
Or the despair of the half-heard rain?

7 *Birds' Wings*

There are times when I think my body
Is made of birds' wings –
Thrushes and larks and blood-breasted robins
And packed starlings.

I think I could fly
Out of myself into the air
Over the thin reeds to the swamp
Across the river

Into another country more peaceful than this
To find
The sort of peace that can exist
Only in my mind

When my body is made of birds' wings
That somehow refuse to fly;
Blackbirds, swallows, yellowhammers
Clamouring to die.

8 *Are women the only beings who feel?*

Are women the only beings who feel?
Is feeling stupid, vain?
I turn to the sound of rain falling
From a hedge into a drain.
If I walk here in three months' time
I shall find this hedge in bloom
Fresh blackberries will stain my fingers,
I'll pluck them, take them home

To my own family.
What do the blackberries feel
When I rip them off with my fingers?
I pluck the fruit that enters my soul.

I want to sing of how I feel
In my private cage of time,
How I am a groping creature,
How love is still a crime.

9 *The moment I found I was nothing*

The moment I found
I was nothing
Was the moment
I started to sing.

The moment I started to sing
I was something.
I was created
By a song

That came out of nothing
As, when a child,
I was told of this world
Called from a void.

I am nothing, I am a world
In my own sphere,
All the nothings move about me
Whirling together.

10 *The Puzzle*

My mind is a ray of sunlight
Making an angle on a kitchen wall.
The clarity of that moment
Stresses the puzzle.

Human filth is everywhere
And cannot be undone
By a vain human mind
Likening itself to the sun.

11 *The Dogs of Darkness*

The dogs of darkness howl
Across the fields.
Their smells lacerate my room,
Their fangs flash over half-sleep.

At the first light they quieten
But their fury has entered my blood.
Today's work will not appease
This angry god.

12 *Summer*

When summer came I threw off my shoes
As though to trust
Some promised goodness in the weather.
I grew to love the dust.

I felt each summer slowly yield
To autumn's sensual rust
And thrilled to find my heart at one
With summer dust.

13 *Darkness*

O the darkness of that room
Like the darkness of my womb,
Darkness here, darkness there,

What will the darkness bear?

Deeper darkness of the water,
Child-darkness moulding son and daughter,
Darkness of God's living air,

What will the darkness bear?

Darkness of my father's house,
Love so sweet and perilous,
Suffering no one dares to share,

What will the darkness bear?

Darkness of the world I know,
Darkness into which I go,
Darkness at whose face I stare,
What will the darkness bear?

14 *Sweetest postures of the heart*

In my life's ignored places
Noiseless, apart,
I have sensed
How I might stumble
On the sweetest postures of the heart.

I understand
But little.
I am usually mistaken
About what I try to grasp
But I would hope to be unshaken

By this sense of being wrong
And suffering wrong.
If I should stumble
On the sweetest postures,
Suffering would become a human song.

15 *All things move towards peace*

All things move towards peace,
The way is pain,
A trouble between two secrets
Of which nothing is known.

I live in nothing, I die towards nothing,
I am nothing. Then why
Do I read in the book
Of the earth and the sky

That all this nothing is a joy,
A miracle that grows
In its immensity
The less one knows?

This ignorance is the holiest thing.
Its influence lingers
In my heart when I let water flow
Between my fingers.

16 *Solitude*

The morning star is a solitary order.
The river at the back of my father's house
Makes its solitary journey
To the sea.

I love the solitariness of things.
I listen there
And hear the heartbeat of creation.
I see a God happy to bless

All that He has made.
Here, now, I thank Him for that blessing.
I love the cold centre of His fire.
He loves my gratitude.

17 *Possession*

Obscenities fall like rain –
My father, my daughter, my son;
The ultimate obscenity
Is possession.

Cut free, O my love that is not my love
Walk where your shadow
Follows you in a street
Or across a fresh-cut meadow

Saying
'You do not possess even me.
Embrace the blessing.
Exult in having nothing.'

18 *The Slaughterer*

My mind tonight is the squealing of pigs
Waiting for slaughter
All the days and nights of my life
Are a dream of water.

The slaughterer smiles through his knife
In the next room.
My hands encounter the seasons,
Hover about my womb,

Climb to my head to find
Screams nailed to my skull
And a child's bones before they grow
Pliable

As innocence itself.
Each pig squeals for its life.
The slaughterer turns to my room
Lifting his knife.

The water laps in my head
Deeper than ever.
Moonlight glints like a million blades
In my favourite river.

19 *Killers*

So many killers of women
Are loveable men.

Men do their daily good,
Work, consider, help, save
Money for further good,
Dig many a grave

Including their own
As did many a father and mother.

We know so little of what we kill
Though we kill each other.

20 *Strength*

They gather together to pool their weaknesses,
Persuade themselves that they are strong.
There is no strength like the strength of one
Who will not belong.

21 *Emptiness*

Let me be emptied of everything
Like a cup
Once brimming with milk or water.
Now there's not a drop.

The cup contains nothing.
Place it in the sun
It fills with sunlight
And is empty as a graveyard bone.

This emptiness is the presence I seek.
The sun wants to enter me,
Fill me with itself.
All this is accomplished lovingly.

22 *'I am going out...'*

I am going out, not down.
Out of my flesh
I pour like water.
Do I kick and thrash?

I am water
The colour of November cloud,
Mother, let me return
To the meaning of one word you said.

I am water
Cold above mud,

Cold, cold, cold
As man and God.

Smell of cruelty to the end
Hitting my heart,
Is the water sneering like men
Impressed with their own tricks,
Their callous clowning?
Surely to God
This moment is my friend
Mild air
Greenest grass
Twist in the river
November
Brother
Sister
Cloud
Water
Father
Mother

Working
Loving
Losing
Hoping
Drowning
The water a long shroud
My livingness drifting forever
Into a November cloud.

Eily Kilbride

On the North side of Cork city
Where I sported and played
On the banks of my own lovely Lee
Having seen the goat break loose in Grand Parade

I met a child, Eily Kilbride
Who'd never heard of marmalade,
Whose experience of breakfast
Was coldly limited,

Whose entire school day
Was a bag of crisps,
Whose parents had no work to do,

Who went, once, into the countryside,
Saw a horse with a feeding bag over its head
And thought it was sniffing glue.

Rebecca Hill

Half-hanging is the rage in Kildare
It is the rebels' will
So died Jonas Wheeler William Dandy James Benn
Rebecca Hill

Rebecca Hill was fifteen years
Half-hanged then taken down
As comely a girl as ever walked
Through Kildare Town

Taken half-hanged from an oak tree
She seemed to recover her wits
The rebels saw her flutter alive
Then buried her quick

Leaves of the oak tree still
Mutter like Rebecca Hill.

Feed the Children

Let my story feed the children
Who need a monster to hate and fear.
Arrange them in a classroom
Pour me into each innocent ear.
Be sure they know exactly what I've done
How I inflicted my own punishment
On myself, in a ropey place, alone.
Describe my face, my hands, my hair. Say I was sent
By darkness to commit the ultimate crime
Against the light and am the only man
Other men have not forgiven.
Tell the children all this, and more, so that their time
On earth will prove to all how no one
Of my kind can get within an ass's roar of heaven.

Citizens of the Night

The toothless old girl sang *A Dublin Saunter*,
ignored the sad look of being ignored
in her daughter's eyes.
The old man chirped 'I think I'll join in',
and began to sing
as though the joy of the citizens of the night
depended on his quavering fling.
The new boy worked at his first job,
conscience beaming from his forehead
like a miner's lamp in a pretty black pit.
He would be good, really good,
he was ready to sweat blood
in the crowd, getting the hang of it.

Helen Jones from Tullamore
pushed back her chair from the table,
walked to the door. Half-turning her head,
'Not a bad night for love,' she said.

Baby

I find it interesting to be dead.
I drift out here, released, looking down
At men and women passing judgement
In the streets of that moneymad little town.
I enjoy the jokes about me, scribbled in the Gents,
I like the lads in suits, their smart legal faces,
I follow them through every argument,
I note their gas antics at the Listowel Races.
There was a hope of love at the back of it all
And in spite of clever men making money
That small hope still survives.
Will I name the clever men for you? Yerra, no.
I smile to watch them prospering to their ends
But thanks be to Jesus I won't have to live their lives.

They're trying to find out who killed me,
A fascinating exercise.
If I were water I'd let them spill me
And I'd run out of their eyes.
If I were fire I'd burn books of law
And half-burn the men who study them.
If I were air I'd slip into their lungs
And out of pity revive them.
If I were earth – O now that I think of it
That's what I am or am becoming
A little more quickly than you, and painlessly.
Tell me what you think it means to be alive,
I'd love you on that topic, expounding.
Being dead, I must find out, you see.

And yet, being dead, I may grow
To be a small, cheeky flower
Peeping through a veil of snow
On the scarred face of the earth
That never grows ashamed;
Or I may be
A blade of grass to nourish you;

Or a book
Wherein the nosey world may read
Of lovers' luck
And what it means to bleed.

When I was being formed in her body
I could tell she was kind.
My toes my fingers my eyes
My hands my bum my tiny mind
Knew that.
She carried me everywhere.
I couldn't see where I was going.
She did.

Streets, roads, fields, kitchens,
Bedrooms, chapels, small hotels, fish and chip places,
Glances of men in cars, glances
Of women both barren and fulfilled –
I'm buried now under the strong feet
Of money. I'm dead. I hope my mother
Sings and dances.

A Drowned Girl

Waves' delicate fingers twined a tight noose of death around
Her beautiful body, destined, until then, to thrive;
When they scrambled her on to the rocks, she looked so young
You'd swear she was still alive.

She didn't look dead, but looked like any other girl
At whom you'd throw an admiring glance;
Quick brightness in a street, disturbing surprise at evening,
Frail truth in the impulse of the dance.

Heroisms happened swiftly; an old man, with bleeding toes,
Attempted things impossible alike to old and young;
Blew his stale breath between her frigid lips,
Too feeble to help stopped heart and water-stifled lung.

Doctor, priest, civilian prayed and probed and tried
To find one reassuring remnant of breath,
As if they couldn't see why a girl in a green swimsuit
Should be so irretrievably stretched in death.

There was no flood-tide of grief then, no cold consciousness
Of the essential tragedy, yet;
But the curious gaped, mumbled and stumbled
In a way impossible to forget.

Awareness wrapped itself like wet ropes of weed around the minds of all,
Rocks and beach became a mesmerised room,
And she, turning cold, looked somehow unwanted,
A blue child thrust from an impatient womb.

Various doctors pronounced her dead and everyone stood aside
While stretcher-bearers carried her from the rocks to a house on dry land;
Shortly afterwards, waves' delicate fingers twined white ribbons of foam
Around her footprints, perfect in the gentle sand…

Clean

'You know what these Irish bitches are like.
When they're not holy, they're cannibals
Out to munch a man's prick and balls
As an afternoon snack.
There was this mountainous cow of a creature
Who liked to kill and devour others
In a manner not uncommon among Irish mothers.
I decided to hang her.
She was so graceless that not once
Did she cry or call upon God to forgive her
But dangled in silence, gross and obscene.
Afterwards, I went to her house
And found the bones of three of my troopers
Picked clean.'

The Gift Returned

He was at the front on the right.
He could hear his brothers' breathing.
He could feel Jack's tight
Grip on his right shoulder. She'd said
'My death will teach you brotherhood.
There will be nobody younger, nobody older,
There will be brothers giving my death back

To the living grass.
The earth is crying out for us
And cares nothing for our grief.
When you bear me from this house
Where, on a fine day, from this hill I could see
Five counties and three rivers,
You will be farther from me
And nearer to each other
Than ever before.
All I know of dying
Tells me it is a tearing
Leading to new binding.
Wash my body
Before you give it back.'

Now, returning her to herself, they bore
Her washed corpse across the stony yard
Where she'd worked for seventy years
And he knew, feeling his brother's fingers
Cut for support into his shoulder
As though he were a drowning man,
Her deadweight was the lightest thing imaginable
To bear for a lifetime in his mind,
Making him adore the distance
That was the love between him and his kind.

Two five-bar gates between them and the road,
The people a black muttering sea,
The brothers four moving pillars
Bearing something familiar and incomprehensible
Over the stones
To the place of skulls and bones,
Small crooked roads ahead
Puzzling the hedges,
Supporting the living and dead
With earth's unkillable courtesy.
They shuffled through silent light
Becoming one under the weight
Of what had lived to be returned
To a deeper love
Than any moving man could ever imagine.

Yet it was there in the patient grass,
In her final silence,
In his brothers' breathing,
In the place authentic beyond words
Where the sense of returning
Swallowed the sense of leaving.

There Are Women
(after Osip Mandelstam)

There are women damp with their native earth.
Each of their steps is a hollow, sobbing sound.
To accompany the dead
To greet the risen dead
Is their calling.
To want a caress from them is criminal,
To part from them intolerable.
Today an angel
Tomorrow a worm in the grave
After tomorrow an outline.
What was a step becomes unreachable.
Flowers are immortal.
Heaven is whole.
What will be
Is a mere promise.

We Are Living

What is this room
But the moments we have lived in it?
When all due has been paid
To gods of wood and stone
And recognition has been made
Of those who'll breathe here when we are gone
Does it not take its worth from us
Who made it because we were here?

Your words are the only furniture I can remember
Your body the book that told me most.
If this room has a ghost
It will be your laughter in the frank dark
Revealing the world as a room
Loved only for those moments when
We touched the purely human.

I could give water now to thirsty plants,
Dig up the floorboards, the foundation,
Study the worm's confidence,

Challenge his omnipotence
Because my blind eyes have seen through walls
That make safe prisons of the days.

We are living
In ceiling, floor and windows,
We are given to where we have been.
This white door will always open
On what our hands have touched,
Our eyes have seen.

Muses

'Today I am a poet,' Big Island said
'And let me repeat you do not exist.
Behind me thrive the exemplary dead,
Behind you, scarecrows in a mist
Haggle over halfpennies in the dreepy streets
Of a scuttery town.
My Muse is clean.
Yours is a squat slut in
A cottage at the edge of a village,
Charging sixpence for a fuck.
If times were better, she'd cost more.
She sits there, waiting. Old men trudge
Through the muck towards their sixpenny knock
And a shagged gasp on a kitchen floor.
All lovers
Come and gone, she has a drop of whiskey
Then lies down on her own.
In the morning she goes to a grocer's house,
Scrubs the place from top to bottom.
The grocer emits a randy stink.
The grocer's wife wears a black dress
Suggesting she's a widow before her time.
Your Muse goes down on her knees
To scrub the floors of respectable people.
She's a slave, the way she applies
Herself, but she knows the important gods,
She's fit and willing, a trojan, a genuine girl,
She shifts the filth from decent houses
Then sighs homewards to wait for the lads.'

May the Silence Break

Because you do not speak
I know the shock
Of water encountering a rock.

Supremacy of silence is what I hate.
Only gods and graves have a right to that
Or one who knows what this is all about.

Perhaps you do.
If so, let something break through
The walls of silence surrounding you.

Out here among words
Your silence is like a magnet I am drawn towards.
Men's mouths, animals' eyes and the throats of birds

Fear this impenetrable thing.
So do I, all day long
And when the night drops like a confirmation

Of what you are,
Controller of every star,
Possessor

Of what the daylight struggled to reveal.
This possession kills
Whatever it wills.

Nothing I say matters tonight.
Nor should it.
This silence is right

Because it knows it is.
I shiver in the cocksure ice
And long for the warmth of bewildered eyes.

May the silence break
And melt into words that speak
Of pain and heartache

And the hurt that is hard to bear
In the world out here
Where love continues to fight with fear

And the war on silence will end in defeat
For every heart permitted to beat
In the air that hearts make sweet.

A Kind of Trust

I am happy now.
You rose from your sick bed
After three weeks. Your heart was low

When the world grew small,
A white ceiling
And four yellow walls.

Let me say again what this means
To me. As far as I know
Love always begins

Like a white morning
Of seagulls near the window,
Messengers bringing

Word that we must up and out
Into a small garden
Where there are late

Apples we shall find
So ripe that the slightest touch
Will pitch them to the ground.

Best things seem content to fall and fail.
I am not good enough for that.
I fight the drag and pull

Of any kind of dying
And bitterly insist
On that white morning

When you weakly climb the stairs,
Letting new life reach you like a gift
There at the brown banister.

I do not insist
Out of panic or vague dread
But out of a kind of trust

In this beginning
With late apples and early seagulls
And a young sun shining

When you let cold water flow into a cup,
Steady yourself between two chairs
And stand straight up.

A Passionate and Gentle Voice

Whatever contact I have with hope
Is clear to me on certain mornings
When a voice slips

Into my mind like a shy
Suggestion of love
That nothing will deny.

It is a passionate and gentle voice
Authentic as a patch of sunlight
On a floor inside a window

And it has always spoken the same words:
'I live in the stripped branch,
Dying flowers on the kitchen table,

Pools of water after a storm
Uncomprehending as children
Strayed from their parents in a crowded town.

You understand I do not exhort.
My state is one of waiting
For you, for the most part,

And I am helpless till you observe me
With your electric blood
And your eyes

Redeemed from tedium by the desire
To know
Why something begins to stir

In utter stillness like a memory
That will not let you sleep at night
But takes possession of you

And absorbs you into itself
So I await that morning
When you emerge

From the tired night as from a mist
Into a decision of sunlight
Where I exist.'

Separation

It breathes through the cherries,
Corn, virgin branches,
Hurts the eyes

Riveted on a dirtroad
Where stones snarl
At the car's backside

And a black squirrel electrifies an oak.
It walks in the wake of a forest fire,
Shells of trees hang like

A haggard army,
Roads without signs lead nowhere,
There are always some local gods wishing to

Lead us astray
Though we may be lost already.
With what gloomy defiance

It resists analysis
Though willing enough to reveal
Something in images –

Slow-motion pitch
And skid down the black face
Of a cliff,

Rainbow filth of oil
In a rut of water,
Dull

Seepage of self through grass
Seeking the ravenous kings
That set up their abode

In the dead and edible.
Oh yes
Many times it has come to this

But this, even this
(Heaven itself is but a glimpse)
Leads to the kiss

In the unknown village in the mountains,
Brings me the whitest knowledge
From the blood of shame

And asks salvation, the stranger, the reticent man
To open the door of his house
That I go in.

Willow

To understand
A little of how a shaken love
May be sustained

Consider
The giant stillness
Of a willow

After a storm.
This morning it is more than peaceful
But last night that great form

Was tossed and hit
By what seemed to me
A kind of cosmic hate,

An infernal desire
To harass and confuse,
Mangle and bewilder

Each leaf and limb
With every vicious
Stratagem

So that now I cannot grasp
The death of nightmare,
How it has passed away

Or changed to this
Stillness,
This clean peace

That seems unshakeable.
A branch beyond my reach says
'It is well

For me to feel
The transfiguring breath
Of evil

Because yesterday
The roots by which I live
Lodged in apathetic clay.

But for that fury
How should I be rid of the slow death?
How should I know

That what a storm can do
Is to terrify my roots
And make me new?'

Too Near

Do not come too near.
It is the space between
enables something to grow

and saves us from stifling.
I love to sweep the leaves
from the grass in the garden

and rejoice in the surgeon's skill
when he lops the branch
that keeps the tree from its full

stature.
No, I do not want to hear
everything about you

or possess the secrets
you do not wish to share.
Between us there are secrets in the air

too dear for knowledge,
too true to be fouled by the mind.
This morning I heard sounds of summer

resonant through the door
yet summer keeps itself
to itself

while acknowledging its debt
to winter and spring.
I cherish such reticence,

such private self-definition.
It permits me to see and hear
the best and worst of the current season
and nothing is too near.

A Viable Odyssey

I sit by the fire
Watching flameworlds leap and vanish.
It happens again – the desire

For another world and so,
Encouraged by a modest winter sun,
I go

To look at the sea.
The sea does not seek the wind
Nor the wind the sea

Yet the wind
Makes the sea shiver and blush
Like a boy whose mind

Is touched by images that come
From somewhere outside
And will not leave him alone

Till he goes in search
Of what takes him
Past bank and brothel, theatre, church,

Where disappointment lies.
When I stand where the sea is crisp
I think the wind tries

To upset it, or find
The sea bristles and frowns
To accommodate the wind.

Suddenly the sky is ice.
I feel on my head
The grey threat burst

Till it hurts my bones.
Whatever I looked for
I forget at once

And run from the thing I found
As little spiteful hailstones
Hammer the helpless ground,

I draw few lessons from ice
Except the conviction
That in winter fire is

Better company. Kind flames greet
My searching body
Warming to defeat.

bridge

and in the dark to lean across
like a bridge over a river on whose bed
stones are untroubled by what passes
overhead
and kiss the sleep in your body
with I love you I love you
like currents through my head
that is closer to deep water now
than at any time of the day

To You

I pass under the lamplight.
In that yellow world
I realise the night

Speaks its own language,
A dark idiom swelling
Perhaps with rage

Or love. I try to listen
But the words scurry
To the backs of stars. When

I tell myself I should settle for silence
Since better men have said
It is the purest eloquence

Leaves whisper at my feet
Or raise their rhetoric
About my head. What

Are my foolish words when
Set against the last gasp
Of a wave over a stone

Or the intense disclosures
Of shadows
Dancing together?

Nothing. Yet it is this
Nothing that compels me
To wake in the nightsilence

And feel the need to speak
To you. This is a universe
Of voices. They make

Me want to be a voice
Telling my fragments in words
That bid your heart rejoice

At the spider lunging to the kill,
Every sharp unshareable pain,
Dust that gathers on the window-sill.

Tonight You Cry

Tonight you cry
because you have no friend
and I

am not enough
though I would fill this cold house
with love.

I would lie at your side and bless
every icy spike
of loneliness

in your heart
but it would not suffice
because you suffer a hurt

beyond my reach.
I do not know where friends go.
I can say we lose touch

or forget
or grow beyond
or simply neglect

as I do those flowers whose
names I can never remember
but none of this

explains or consoles your tears
in the room
where shadows gather

about your head
like vague shapes of the lost
stalking through a cloud

in your mind.
Those you have loved
are all buried tonight

at the centre of that cloud.
It is a grey place,
a long stretch of beach in winter

waiting for waves
to run their cold hands
over its face

in a chill ritual of oblivion
advancing
to cover and drown.

The Furies

When the furies come
Their eyes stupid and bright
Hoofing into the room

How in God's name
May we hope
To cope with them

As they sit here,
Humped and dumb
Around the fire?

They do not respond to words
But take the shapes
Of starved carrion birds

Ready to feed
On reputation, love, kindness
Or hot bread.

Which they do
Until their own boredom moves them
To try something new

So they go together
Like a dull herd
In stupefying weather

And I realise
The mind's release in your words,
The heart's release in your eyes.

Warning

Her voice
when she spoke –
salmon muscle the waters;
driven from the deep
they drift dead,
bellies whiter than the blank sun overhead

whose light is yet denied
to algae growing on the seafloor
because the waste of countries
pouring, hour by hour,
builds a roof of slime
to strangle the seaflower.

Rain of cancer
corrodes the wheat,
soaks into the grass.
North, east, west and south,
berries steeped in the wind's poison
burst inside the mouth.

Death is pollen
drifting in the atmosphere.
A strontium snow
falls
on Washington, Madrid,
London, Moscow,

on fields where nothing
seems to live,
on villages that sleep inland
or hug wide estuaries
waiting
for what the tides may bring.

Her voice
follows me this morning.
On the tree that reaches to my window
a silent thrush upon a branch
sways
in warning.

The Moment of Letlive

When you look at me askance
In a moment I become
All I know of tolerance,

Altruism born of pain.
Gouged out of life for the most part
It questions what I am of man

And hurts me into love.
I hold your agony in my hands
And feel it enter me as if

Self cannot be contained
Within the body.
I am stunned

By this pained flowing
Out of your blood
But I have known

The moment of letlive
When it seemed possible
To subdue the beast

That turned your days to fear
And crouched in the corner of the room
Sneering.

Beyond Knowledge

On this quiet afternoon
When the shadows of branches
Make trembling sculpture
On a cracked wall
And a gull's cries
Recall the eyes
Of dying children,
I know enough to know
Most things worth knowing
Are beyond knowledge.

And I have now
The most chilling sense
Of the ignorance
That keeps us all from
Leaping into the abyss.

Down there is revelation
Or oblivion. Perhaps
They are one and the same.
Up here, some live as though
They were kings of knowledge.
The most ridiculous figure of all is your
Expert.
The only expert is death,
A most ubiquitous fellow,
There's nobody he doesn't know
And to this end, is not above
Crashing the party
Like some barging junior executive
Randy for brandy.
As he seeks introductions all round, I see
There are worse things than walking
Knowing one's limited
Capacity for love,
Half-glimpsing the most
Terrifying images in the March grass
Or on the pavement of a cul-de-sac
Or in a small
Apparently uncared-for garden,

Feathers ripped from the body
Of a robin killed when
We were sleeping,
His eyes closed in final
Terror or disbelief,
Or in this room the sound
Of your voice in sleep, torn words, half-crying,
And towards morning the sense
Of a world withdrawing
From you, from me, from all
We seem to half-know.
I lie here and watch it go
Through the wise light.
It has been so patient with us
I wish to thank it
As I witness its retreat
But reach instead
Towards you, limp in sleep,
And touch your head.

Mary Magdalene

(after Pasternak)

1

Night. The demons come,
Dragging my past.
Memories of lust
Savage my heart.
I'm an obvious fool, under a spell,
Slave to preying men.
The street is my home, my hell.

A few moments yet,
Then the silence of the tomb.
As these moments pass
I stand at the edge of the grim dream
And smithereen my life for you
Like a vase of alabaster cream.

O my teacher and Saviour
Where would I be now
If eternity weren't waiting
By my bed at night
Like a fresh client enticed
Into my alluring net?

Tell me what sin means,
And death and hell and hell's fire
When I, grafted on your tree,
Men's eyes rutting into me,
Am one with you in grief
Beyond human belief.

Jesus, I embrace the cross,
The four-square beam of the cross,
Your feet fastened to my knees.
How long since the demons came?
I weaken at your body
And make you ready for the tomb.

2

Make ready for the Feast.
Away from the crowd's thick smell
I wash your feet
With myrrh from a small pail.

I look for sandals. None.
My tears are blinding me.
My hair tumbles long and loose
Over my face like a veil.

Your feet rest on my dress,
Your feet wet with my tears.
Beads from my neck adorn your feet,
Your feet deep in my hair.

I see the future clearly
As if you held it whole
Before my eyes. Near you
I'm nothing at all.

Tomorrow the veil of the temple will split.
Our few people will meet,
Huddle apart. The earth, out of pity perhaps,
Will shudder under our feet.

The guards will break, re-form.
The horsemen will ride away.
The cross, like a waterspout in a storm,
Will penetrate the sky.

Stunned, biting my lips
I shall throw myself flat on my face
While your arms stretch out on the cross
In an unimaginable embrace.

Who on earth deserves this embrace?
What men? Women? Legends of old gods?
Are there so many hearts, lives, souls in the world?
So many rivers, villages, fields, hills, woods?

Three days will pass
Leaving me so empty and alone
I'll grow through ice, an impossible flower,
Resurrection, young, bearing my age, young, again.
And the sun of heaven will bless
Me with your caress.

She

She hears a landlord speak of the advantages of death
She goes through flames to save herself
She has a son murdered
She eats rawhides drinks puddles
She tries two churches
She cocks her piece and shoots a lord
She becomes a widow
She witnesses the burning of Lurgan
She sees Ruth Lynn hanged by the hair of the head
Anne Butler's brains scattered on stones
Toole McCann cut in pieces
Jane Hazleton die
Giles Whitehead burn
She does not ask why.

Wish

Out of the matted tangle of lies
Out of my betrayal of you
Your betrayal of me
Out of the crossed sea and the Star of David
Out of the jokes in the dreary streets
Of the cities where we never knew each other
Out of every accursed boring moment
When hatred furnaced our faces
And we knew that love can happen only
Between strangers for a moment in a cold place
Then gutter and cease

Out of the floors the walls the ceilings
Of houses where we fumbled through each other
Like branches swaying touching parting touching
I wish you peace.

Knives

Love is a knife in the daylight.
I shift, shiver, stabbed by an old thought
Of her shining like a blade
At my side.

Loneliness is a knife. As I sit
And cut my heart into interesting pieces
I see you walking down a street,
A stranger's face defining strangers' faces.

Assassin

In its own time and more decisive
than nightfall in December it surges
through you like the sea, love,

love.
When I say everything I mean it
and give

examples. A watch stops at night,
dead skin dissolves in water,
dustmotes dance in sunlight

and settle on the backs of books,
quiet monuments of passionate
men and women who had no truck

with stupid gods but chose the spider's art
becoming rivals of the sun.
Now they play another part

and fructify the dying earth or mingle
with the drowned or lie as much
at one as the chime and the bell

with the heartbeat of their struggle
silent but for voices between covers.
Nothing lives but the riddle

they left like a glove on a chair
or a split horsenut hanging
from its roots in mid-air

feeling the undermining force
of the wind that chills the blood
with ultimate divorce,

cocksure assassin whose aim is perfect,
whose music tilts the axis
when the ocean swells with shipwreck

or hands grow filthy with money
ignoring the infant's fascination
with its own shadow,

a woman feeling in her shrinking wrist
the pulse of terror,
a door closing in November mist.

Phone Call

A woman rings me at three in the morning to say
Fuck. Nothing else. Just fuck. Again fuck.
At that hour I'm not at my social
Best and don't know what to say back

To the voice. Yet I will not hang up.
I know the language of love and prayer,
I like that woman's voice and drowsily
Wonder what is the colour of her hair.

I hear
Womansadness pouring into my ear,
Sadness rivering heart and brain.

From Asia and Africa and India she speaks
On the phone at three in the morning to me.
Fuck. Sadness is never obscene. Fuck again.

Her Spirit

Once, when both of us were trying to solve the trouble,
I saw her spirit in her face.
It happened at a camping-site
in a dry, humpy country-place.
She'd gone to look for water and had found it
in a generous brown fountain.
Pumping the water into a red plastic bucket
she strolled towards me in the evening light.

That's when I saw the spirit of the woman.

Like the evening, she's easy, deep and bright.
The evening, everything living in the evening
focusses in her strolling figure and shines
through her skin. For a moment, no pain
exists, lost in the focus, the shining.
The water glitters as she sets the bucket down.
She turns her head. The trouble stirs again.

Keep in Touch

Like the birdthroats
Of a winter's morning
Anticipating spring

Flinging into our ears
Notes
We had almost forgotten

Or the ice we had begun
To accept as unbreakable
Melting in the sun

To resurrect the grass;
Like the neighbour
Who took ship one morning

Eleven years ago
To see a country
Where the snow

Lasts for nearly half the year
And then returned
As though from the next street

Where he had bought milk and bread,
Bringing stories that seemed like glad
Reports from the land of the dead –

Keep in touch, keep in touch,
My friend, my love.
When the old boredom begins to approach

With its ice in the blood,
Its manic wish
To shrivel and impoverish,

Keep in touch because I will be
Waiting for a word from you.
It means more to me

Than I can say
Or you imagine
That on any indistinguishable day

I touch through my hands, see through my eyes
Your face on the far side of the abyss
Bringing surprise.

Birth

I don't know if I shall be
Speaking or silent, laughing or crying,
When it comes to me

Out of this distant place
To shine at the window, rustle the curtains,
Brush my face

More lightly than gossamer,
So inspiring and fragile
I shall not dare to stir

Or hardly breathe until I sense
In my heart and mind
Its delicate omnipotence.

I may know then
The price and value of stillness
Commonly ignored by men

And be content to feel
It possess me,
Steal

Through my remotest countries
And establish its rule
Where, my bravest days,

I would not dare to venture.
Then, if I find courage enough,
I may speak in a manner

Befitting this thing.
God help me the moment
My heart starts opening

To comprehend and give.
I will be born in that hour of grace.
I will begin to live.

The Burning of Her Hair

(after Ovid)

I burst out in anger:
'For God's sake, don't silver-bleach your hair!'
No need for bleaching now. Your hair is gone.
Bald woman!
Imagine! You had incomparable hair
So silky-thrilling to the touch even girls' expert fingers
Baulked at braiding it, finer than the best
Silk of Asian girls at a feast,
Delicate as a spider's thread,
Its colours playing in a never-before-seen light.
Every time I looked, I saw it had
Changed, it was never the same sight

Twice, rippling, waving a hundred ways,
The comb's teeth never marked it, it was
Shy, bright, wild, it had never heard
The bruising anger of a human word,
Girls who dressed it had no fear, they knew
A love their blood confirmed was true,
No hairpin scratched their skin.

I have seen
You so at morning, naked, drowsily at rest
When young sunlight kissed your breasts,
Your hair a lazy, scattered magic on your shoulders,
Yourself a happy refugee from over beauty's border
Imprisoned in my stare
Your hair
All unaware
Innocent as first feathers
Surviving inquisitions, tribunals, terror, dread
Of heated irons pressing at your head.

'Don't burn it, don't torture it to death,' I said,
'Have mercy on your hair, gentle it, treat it well,
Don't force it into rings and waves of hell,
Let the wind tend it, the attentive wind, let the wind
Dress it so it claims all my heart and mind.
The wind is privileged to be
Responsible for this beauty.'

                    And now it's gone,
Charred, dirty, wronged, its light
The poisoned eyes of a broken-backed rat.
I saw a painting once, a goddess whose seawashed hair
Was almost yours.
You're stricken now, stupefied, appalled or
Simply not believing the mirror.
No jealous girl would run the risk
Of making you grotesque,
No scented queen of a beauty parlour
Reduce you to this horror.
Yourself! You only have yourself to blame!
Never mind! From conquered Germany will come
Hair to give you a new name.
When a man fixes on your false hair
You'll think 'This idiot loves a German stranger,
He doesn't even see me. A few days ago, I
Could have shown him hair to make him dizzy!'

I hear your small, burned cries.
I see the charred dribs and drabs stuck to your knees.
Your ruined head
Knows justice is dead.
But don't cry, my dear, stop, stop crying!
In no time at all your hair will be growing.
No burning could keep such glory down,
No torture guarantee its final destruction.
One day soon, every man in this hurrying town
Will stop and gape and stare
And say 'My God! What hair! What fantastically beautiful hair!'

A Holy War

'We suffered the little children to be cut out of women
"Their bellys were rippitt upp"
This was a holy war, a just rebellion
And little lords in the womb must not escape
Their due. Certain women not great with child
Were stripped and made to dig a hole
Big enough to contain them all.
We buried these women alive
And covered them with rubbish, earth and stones.
Some who were not properly smothered
Yet could not rise
(They tried hard) got for their pains
Our pykes in their breasts. People heard
(Or said they heard) the ground make women's cries.'

Sacrifice

How it was lived through her –
This giving of herself
That she never understood,

A sacrifice
A customary selflessness
A decimation and scattering of herself

To the four winds of the insatiate future.
Whatever men and women waited there
Were unknown to her

As the rain's lisping or belting secrets
At her windows
In the sleepless time.

And to what end?
To let some perfection steal through
Barely distinguishable days and nights of her life?

A device that helped her
Never to see herself?
A wish to imprint some version of herself

On the self of the unknown?
She listened to the rain,
To the rowdy wind,

To the gabble of unseen birds,
To the words of those under
What she took to be her care,

And felt something like love
Bleeding from her,
Wounding, renewing, confusing,

Like the touch of her fingers on another's skin,
The contact and vacancy
Of the aftermath of pain.

The Fire Is Crying

There are nine sods of turf in the fire,
Three at the centre flawlessly stacked,
Humpy brown ones on either side,
Black towers at the back,
It is a desert, a forest, a city,
Architecture of my own
Emptiness blazing under an exiled sky.

For the first time in my life as a man
I see a woman's face in the fire,
A long face, serious. Her hair is black,
Her skin grief-lined. She has the look
That knows the flesh is falling from her.

The hair tumbles to one side, the lips shake,
The fire is crying for her breaking neck.

A Half-finished Garden

Because her days were making a garden
She haunted that particular beach
Drawing rocks, sticks, shells and stones,
Random-pitched sea-gifts, over the years,
Bog-oak, sculpted and twisted,
She lugged from the beach up to the garden
That was half-finished when she had to leave it
To go to a place of which I know nothing.

Here is the picture (I have nothing but pictures),
The sea helpless to govern its giving
Through rumble and slither, bang, roar and hiss,
A house on a cliff-top with staring blue windows
And, work of the dead to pleasure the living,
A half-finished garden, epitaph, promise.

Her Face

The scrupulous and piercing hand of love
Wrote a few true lines into her face
Along the forehead, cheeks, about the eyes.
Her face was kind, or kind enough
To those who looked in it for hope or help
As if it were a holy well where men
And women came to stare into themselves,
To find the loving stranger buried deep within.

Her face drank pain, still offered its slow smile
As though the days were hungry and cried for bread,

As though itself, being lost, itself could save.
Her face sickened, either temple was a hole
Deep enough to contain the world's dead.
Her face broke in the grave, and is the grave.
O she is rich if she receives
The barest shred of what she gave.

The Hag of Beare
(from the Irish)

The sea crawls from the shore
leaving there
the despicable weed,
a corpse's hair.
In me,
the desolate withdrawing sea.

The Hag of Beare am I
who once was beautiful.
Now all I know is how to die.
I'll do it well.

Look at my skin
stretched tight on the bone.
Where kings have pressed their lips,
the pain, the pain.

I don't hate the men
who swore the truth was in their lies.
One thing alone I hate –
women's eyes.

The young sun
gives its youth to everyone,
touching everything with gold.
In me, the cold.

The cold. Yet still a seed
burns there.
Women love only money now.
But when
I loved, I loved
young men.

Young men whose horses galloped
on many an open plain
beating lightning from the ground.
I loved such men.

And still the sea
rears and plunges into me,
shoving, rolling through my head
images of the drifting dead.

A soldier cries
pitifully about his plight;
a king fades
into the shivering night.

Does not every season prove
that the acorn hits the ground?
Have I not known enough of love
to know it's lost as soon as found?

I drank my fill of wine with kings,
their eyes fixed on my hair.
Now among the stinking hags
I chew the cud of prayer.

Time was the sea
brought kings as slaves to me.
Now I near the face of God
and the crab crawls through my blood.

I loved the wine
that thrilled me to my fingertips;
now the spinster wind
stitches salt into my lips.

The coward sea
slouches away from me.
Fear brings back the tide
that made me stretch at the side
of him who'd take me briefly for his bride.

The sea grows smaller, smaller now.
Farther, farther it goes
leaving me here where the foam dries
on the deserted land,
dry as my shrunken thighs,
as the tongue that presses my lips,
as the veins that break through my hands.

She Sees Her Own Distance

Let no black disasters stop her course
When she, in the exploding countryside
Where boys like burning tyres are flung
High into fields and meadows to bleed

Into the all-receiving earth, decides
To let her daughter live in the world
Grinning on cynical axis. She knows this well
And yet she gives the child over to herself

To become what she is capable of becoming
Despite hurt speech, distressed hands, hungering eyes,
Despite do-gooders and civilised neglect.

She wishes the child well, waking, sleeping and dreaming.
Then, because she is suffering and wise,
She sees her own distance, and is not shocked.

A Restoration

Was it the lazy haze of the summer afternoon
Drifting into her, or the warm
Indolence of the sea caressing every bone
That made her stretch out on the sandy grass
And give herself into the arms
Of this prolonged, seductive moment?
Was she free a while of children's cries
Boring through her, shrill and insistent?
Whatever it was, she suddenly knew she was naked
And glancing at her left hand
Saw her marriage ring was missing.
She was panic as she searched and searched
Until she found it in the thieving ground
And restored it to its mark, dark and shining.

More Dust

Love is nothing but the wish to love.
When I pitched the eel back over my head
And saw its wet wriggling in the dust
I ran from the river up to the road
Where a man was sweeping more dust
Into a barrow old as himself.
He was muttering about work and no rest
For the wicked, smiling. A small sweat
Chilled my back as I came to the door
And ran into the room.
                              She stood
In front of the fire though it was summer.
I said nothing but ran up to her,
Laid my head against her belly.
I tried to listen to my brother.

Wings

The words have been said.
He towers above her, she pretends he's not there,
She concentrates on washing a heart of lettuce,
Wet leaves glitter in her fingers,
He folds his hands like wings about her black hair
And kisses her head.

The Habit of Redemption

I have felt the world shrivel to days
Beckoning me
Into a hell of indifference

Until I found
The habit of redemption
Living in my mind.

It breathed in the morning
As I wrote a letter
To a woman in mourning

For her dead brother.
He was sixty-six
And rare,

His days touched by imagination.
He died in October
Tending his garden.

It reached the deepest part of me
When the middle-aged man
Raking leaves turned quickly

And said 'how are you?'
Autumn died at his feet
But the day was new.

I would say nothing about all this,
Never bother to mention
The moment's metamorphosis

Were it not that hell gapes
At every step.
What I am given is not a means of escape

But of confrontation,
The truest education
That I know.

Moment that is all moments
Be with me when I grasp
A little of the meaning of transience,

A hint of the infernal night.
Come in the shape of a blade of grass
Stuck to the side of my boot

Or a kind word from stranger or friend
Or a yellow shedding from an old tree
That will not bend.

Gestures

She passed me on the street
Her hand a quick white arc
Motioning brown hair –
Sweet Narcissus vanished in the crowd.

A girl that I knew better
Her mouth twisted in rage
Closed her eyes of a sudden
And stared at her own darkness.

One I love
Walked on a summer strand,
Bent and picked a shell,
Remarked on its intricacy,
Its scrupulous profundity,
Then tossed it into the sea.

Myself when young
Crouched near a rough mud wall
Seeking a sheltering shade
And covered my face with my hands.
Afraid.

Only gestures remain
To tell me the truth of things,
To grasp the flashing essences
That leap, scatter and die;
Only simple gestures
Confound the usual lie.

Westland Row

Brown bag bulging with fading nothings;
A ticket for three pounds one and six
To Euston, London via Holyhead:

Young faces limp, misunderstanding
What the first gay promptings meant –
A pass into a brilliant wilderness,
A Capital of hopeless promise.

Well, mount the steps: lug the bag:
Take your place. And out of all the crowd,
Watch the girl in the wrinkled coat,
        Her face half-grey.
        Her first time.

The Celtic Twilight

Now in the Celtic twilight, decrepit whores
Prowl warily along the Grand Canal
In whose rank waters bloated corpses float,
A dog and cat that came to a bad end.
The whores don't notice; perfumed bargainers
Prepare to prey on men prepared to prey
On them and others. Hot scavengers
Are victims, though they confidently strut
And wait for Dublin's Casanovas to appear –
Poor furtive bastards with the goods in hand.

And in the twilight now, a shrill whore shrieks
At one stiff client who's cheated her,
'Misther! If you come back again,
You'll get a shaggin' steel comb through the chest.'
Then gathering what's left of dignity,
Preparing once again to cast an eye
On passing prospects, she strolls beside
The dark infested waters where
Inflated carcases
Go floating by into the night
Of lurid women and predatory men
Who must inflict but cannot share
Each other's pain.

The Girl Next Door

Alarmed to life, she encounters the cold floor,
Washes, dresses, gulps a quick cup of tea;
A vain glance for letters there at the front door,
Legs it through morning rain, hops the 15B.

The trivial hours pass by as pass they must,
One hour for lunch, the thick anonymous crowd;
Despite the evidence, who'd think they're dust?
Not she; a vague world flounders in her head.

Home at evening, the small ritual begins,
Knife, fork, spoon, meat, butter, tea and bread,
Soon, the dark, a drawing-down of blinds,
She stares into the fire; is tired; the bed.

Maggie Hannifin's way for women

Tend cheeky flowers of hope
from Stoneybatter to Japan.
Grow your own dope:
plant a man.

Irish proverb

Until the duck forgets to swim
and black is the colour of the swan's down
and mad dogs refuse to fight
a woman's mind will flabbergast a man.

Woman in a Doorway

Two men went in and out by that door.
The first was a gambler, even his laughter
gambled from one end of the year
to the other, scoffing at before and after,

attentive only to what was happening
now. Now he's gone. The second man
was easy, bit of a loner, took to drinking
till the flesh cartooned itself on his bones.

She never complained. She let them come and go,
live and die in their chosen, enslaved ways,
she lives now as she lived before

they entered and quit her life.
She lays no blame on anyone
but stands, strong and watchful, at her door.

Padraig Ó Conaire's Daughter
Visits Galway on Her Honeymoon

After the long journey, my husband is asleep.
Tense words of the interview stirring
like restless children in my brain, I lie beside him,
inches from his dream. For better and worse now, I am
part of it. Is that why, a child again, I rise and creep
over to the window, part the curtains, see the city
in the rain? There, in Eyre Square, rain blurring
his head, my father, a statue, sits and broods
as once he did beside the fire, the wet light
of Galway attending his neardistant form.
The rain is getting colder. A vindictive wind cuts
into his back. Wait a moment, father,
I'll come down with a blanket to keep you warm.

The Scarf

It strayed about her head and neck like a
Rumour of something she had never done
Because, the moment ripe, she had no mind to
Yet might have done often, had she chosen.
Where in God's name, I wondered, does it begin
And where on earth may I imagine its end?
Indolent headlands smiled at me, labyrinthine
Rivers flowing into each other wound
And wound about her like desires to praise
Every movement that her body made.
As she moved, so did headlands, rivers too,
Shifting with her as the winter sun laid
Emphasis on colours rumoured in its rays,
Grey-flecked lines of white, delirium of blue.

Speculations

After she passed the headland
why did she turn the car and drive back?
Did she sit for a while looking
at the grey rain caressing grey rock?

When she replied 'Money isn't everything'
what was drifting through her?
Did she turn the pages of the river
to find her peace written in water?

Portrait

She walks through the grass
(how it glitters in November sun)
searching for something.
Suddenly she drops on her haunches,
picks tiny flowers.
I can see nothing from here
but a girl in a white coat,
a yellow ribbon in her black hair.

She casts a long shadow in the grass.
It tucks itself under her
when she bends to pick the flowers.
It lengthens when she straightens
and follows her
as though to give encouragement.

She is leaving now,
walking off across the fields,
the flowers safe in a small cellophane bag.

Behind her the grass is still
though four yellowy leaves
frisk like children that have no care.

Ghost sculptures of her breath
drift backwards towards the leaves

then vanish in the air.

Nora O'Donnell

(for John Healy)

Nora O'Donnell knows how not to die.
This is the steel achievement of blood.
I see her coming out of hospital
pausing a moment at the side of the road
where the first house stood.
                              The first house.
The first garden. The first woman, Nora O'Donnell.
There's work to do, death must be put in its place.
This is acceptable and not without honour.
She is a small town, a fire, Botuney Bridge, a bed
where love is made in the silence it deserves
and you are born to say whatever is in you to say,
angered by the living, enlightened by the dead,
knowing the half-hearted thing is what is killing us.
Let the robin sing its heart out in the bush today.

The Work Was Coming Out Right

Anne Mulvihill lifted the box
Containing the shroud
Down from the top of the wardrobe,
Laid the shroud out on the table,
Ironed it with love
Or a care that looked like love.
She'd ironed clothes
For husband and children
All the long years
And would again
But this was different work.
She pressed every inch of the brown shroud
As though her life depended on it,
Not once did she lift her eyes
But pressed the cloth with her mind
As if she would get her death in order
Or consecrate her ignorance
Of past and future dying,
She pressed
With her heart's patience in her face

Her working days
Love-making nights
Beasts' and children's cries
The seasons' rhythms in her fingers
Fields changing colours
Like tired beliefs
Impassioned from within,
She pressed with her knowledge of sin
Her taste of grace
Her bargaining power with heaven
Her struggle with one who struggled with earth.

She hummed a tune as she pressed
Knowing the work was coming out right.
Then she lifted the shroud
A chalice of work
Up to the light
Admiring the shape in silence.
Folding it back in the box
She placed the box on top
Of the wardrobe again.

It was done,

Perfect as her smile
When she stood the hot iron on its end
To cool.

Last Kicks

'The power of the world is in the hands
of tired old men,' she said,
'and that's a cosmic sadness. In every land
I've met them, well-dressed, half-dead,
Bored, boring.

Why is this fulfilment a paralysis?
If a corpse could speak he'd be more exciting
than these figures at table, lifting a glass,
or in bed, last kicks of a landed fish
gasping in the dust for its lost element
before it swallows its death and peters out.

Power castrates them long before the finish.
Important, they squat in wealth, blunt
Buddhas of money's ruck and rout.
They trust no one. Themselves they never doubt.

I often laughed in their faces.
They thought they were funny. Dear Jesus!'

Her Laugh

It might have been something Hawley said
as they chatted together at the counter
where the grades weights and the white scales stood
monument to the notion of just measure
for decent people born suspicious
of everything that cannot be proved

but she laughed out of weariness into tears
and continued to laugh after Hawley left.

She was one of those folk who don't laugh much,
whose reasons for silence remain their own
locked property of heart and mind.
Her laugh when it tumbled free was such
a soaring out of work and children
there was nobody she mightn't leave behind.

The Good

The good are vulnerable
As any bird in flight,
They do not think of safety,
Are blind to possible extinction
And when most vulnerable
Are most themselves.
The good are real as the sun,
Are best perceived through clouds
Of casual corruption
That cannot kill the luminous sufficiency
That shines on city, sea and wilderness,

155

Fastidiously revealing
One man to another,
Who yet will not accept
Responsibilities of light.
The good incline to praise,
To have the knack of seeing that
The best is not destroyed
Although forever threatened.
The good go naked in all weathers,
And by their nakedness rebuke
The small protective sanities
That hide men from themselves.
The good are difficult to see
Though open, rare, destructible;
Always, they retain a kind of youth,
The vulnerable grace
Of any bird in flight,
Content to be itself,
Accomplished master and potential victim,
Accepting what the earth or sky intends.
I think that I know one or two
Among my friends.

Thérèse

She's out on the beach with the children having fun.
Atlantic breakers rear and scatter
foam like blessings in the sun.
Sea-breezes play in her tidal hair,
her eyes enjoy the sea, she looks and listens
to the inexhaustible Atlantic prayer
flung like rose-petals over sand and stones
to reach a man in a dark room where

his gangrenous tongue is healed. And then
her mind is arid-empty, her heart a dark
pit riddled with demons' mocking cries.
    Sick now, she persists, life nearly gone.
Eternity is time to do more work.
All tired, she writes a letter to love. Love replies.

Dying she grows a rose that never dies.

Saint Brigid's Prayer
(from the Irish)

I'd like to give a lake of beer to God.
  I'd love the Heavenly
Host to be tippling there
  for all eternity.

I'd love the men of Heaven to live with me,
  to dance and sing.
If they wanted, I'd put at their disposal
  vats of suffering.

White cups of love I'd give them
  with a heart and a half;
sweet pitchers of mercy I'd offer
  to every man.

I'd make Heaven a cheerful spot
  because the happy heart is true.
I'd make the men contented for their own sake.
  I'd like Jesus to love me too.

I'd like the people of Heaven to gather
  from all the parishes around.
I'd give a special welcome to the women,
  the three Marys of great renown.

I'd sit with the men, the women and God
  there by the lake of beer.
We'd be drinking good health forever
  and every drop would be a prayer.

To Marina Tsetaeva
(after Osip Mandelstam)

On a straw-packed sledge, barely covered
By our own matting, from Sparrow
Hill to a well-known church, we ploughed
Through the city of Moscow.

In Uglich, children play knucklebones,
Smell bread left in the ovens. I feel
Revealed through streets, bareheaded.
Three candles stand in the chapel,

Not three lit candles, but three meetings.
God Himself has blessed one, in His own name.
There will be no fourth. Rome is far.
He never loved Rome.

Is It Possible I Shall See You?
(after Osip Mandelstam)

Is it possible I shall see you,
Heart flowing with praise,
Bankers of mountain ranges,
Holders of mighty shares of gneiss?

With that eagle eye of professors,
Egyptologists and numismatists,
Of those birds, sombre-crested,
With hard flesh and wide breasts.

There Zeus, with the golden
Fingers of a carpenter,
Turns these amazing onion-lenses,
The psalmist's gift to the seer.

He sees in the glasses the splendid Zeiss,
King David's gift,
Sees everywhere wrinkles in the gneiss,
The pine, the little village nit.

4

The Man Made of Rain

For Maurice & Pat Neligan
and for David Thomas & Ian Graham

NOTE

There are many Englishes within English. These Englishes approach, collide and veer away from each other in startling, perplexing and revealing ways. They enjoy a mind-dazzling variety. There's Dayenglish, for example, and Night-english. There's the English of explanation and the calmly ecstatic, dream-energised English of pure being which has little or nothing to do with the English of good behaviour. Is there a different language for every different emotional planet? In this brief statement, I am applying the language of day to that of night, the language of explanation to the dreamenergised language of being. It is a process we all engage in. We must, in the interests of "communication". It is a civilised process, honest, heartwarmingly ludicrous, and necessary. Reason must worry itself, chew its nails back into its flesh, to explain the dream beyond its reach. If it explains the dream to its own satisfaction, it can tell itself it has the dream in its pocket, snug as a wallet.

I had major heart surgery, a quadruple bypass, in October 1996. The day after the operation I had a number of visions (they probably lasted a few seconds, in daylanguage terms). I saw a man made of rain. He was actually raining, all his parts were raining slantwise and firmly in a decisive, contained way. His raineyes were candid and kind, glowing down, into, and through themselves. He spoke to me and took me on journeys. His talk was genial, light and author-itative, a language of irresistible invitation to follow him wherever he decided to go, or was compelled by his own inner forces to go. Yet he gave no sense of being compelled to do anything, he seemed relaxed in his own freedom, he moved calmly and unstoppably. He led me to different places (I call them 'places') such as my father's grave, inside my father's bones, the land of no-language, the place where scars are roads through difficult territories, provinces of history and memory, the place of cold, true cold, and what is that? He took me into brilliant confusions to experience thrilling definitions, or moments of definition. He taught me the meaning of presence, what it means to be truly and fully in somebody's presence, a process of complete dreamsurrender to another's emo-tional and intellectual reality at its most articulate and vital. He was seeing, hearing and touching phenomena in a way he wished me to imitate so that I might be as real as he. He seemed to want to transfer, frequently with grace and humour, something of his essential being into mine. The interesting thing, now, is that, at this moment, I realise I was stricken in a bed, well, my body was, but I was also involved in a number of odysseys and conversations such as I'd rarely enjoyed or endured in the whole of my health, in the joy of my Dayenglish, in the world of explanation without which education would not exist, the explanation which is meant to make us establish, experience, and propagate the reassuring phenomenon of coherence that guarantees us the right answer to the question: Is it sane to be mad, or mad to be sane?

What is vision? It is completely normal when you're going through it, odd or tricky when you try to speak of it afterwards. The challenge of 'afterwards' is connected with 'afterwords', how to preserve the normality of the visionary moment without being distorted or even drowned in the familiar sea of Dayenglish. If that normality is not kept and sustained, what is sane and true at the moment of experience will come across as bizarre at the moment of telling. And vision is not bizarre though it may witness phenomena that are hair-raising in the telling. Vision, when experienced, is normal as rain falling on trees, grass, gravel, flowers, weeds, streets, people. Vision waits for us, ready to give itself; we use countless techniques to cut ourselves off from it. If I have failed to capture that normality in this poem, then this poem is a flop. If I have been able to suggest that beautiful and intense normality, then this poem may hold some kind of special interest for readers. This depends on how effectively I've persuaded Dayenglish to confront and express nighthappenings. The man made of rain would probably say that if I could surrender to the magical potential of Dayenglish to do the job, then I needn't worry. Nothing seemed to worry the man made of rain. There was a concentrated joy in him.

Well, I enjoyed writing this poem in the cold blue winter of 1996-97, just three months after my operation, in Dame Street in Dublin with crowds of young people happily drinking and carousing in the streets all night into early morning, and the man made of rain graciously and deftly flowing through 'afterwards' and 'afterwords' in my mind and imagination. Cold, blue light. Walks along the canal. Cries of lovers or would-be lovers drunk at night, threats and curses flung at the moon. Violence in the streets (you'll see the blood tomorrow), screams of homeless men beating each other up as they headed for favourite doorways or a place in the Saint Vincent de Paul shelter. They sought shelter in the shade of the Saint as I sought to re-create the sheltering, inviting, guiding presence of the man made of rain. In 'afterwards' and 'afterwords', I let these screams invade my being and the paper I wrote on. I wanted to see the dream absorb and transfigure its own violation by the "real". Time is a fierce river and language must do its poor best to keep up with the flow. Let it flow. The man made of rain would not leave me (not that I wanted him to leave me) until I let his presence flow in the best and only poem I could write for him. Though I appear in the poem, or what I recognise as my "own" voice sounds through it, the poem is essentially a homage to his presence, a map of his wandering discoveries, and an evidence of my inadequate witnessing of those discoveries and that presence. He is a real presence in the poem; I am more an absence longing to be a presence. How, equipped only with 'afterwords', could I possibly do justice to those thrilling voyages, excursions, expeditions, flings, conversations, moments of pure light, and pain that makes vision possible? What I feel now, afterwards, is gratitude to the man made of rain: to his raining light, shining gentleness, flowing sympathy, cheeky piss-taking of my hacked body, his smile inviting me to explore, explore, his pity, compassion, love. Dear man made of rain, dear guide, friend, genial pisstaker, (and whoever else you are), I hope you enjoy this ould poem.

December 1997

What?

'What is my body?' I asked the man made of rain.
'A temple,' he said, 'and the shadow thrown
by the temple, dreamfield, painbag, lovescene,
hatestage, miracle jungle under the skin.

Cut it open. Pardon the apparition.'

'What is my blood?' I dared then.
'Her pain birthing you and me,
the slow transfiguration of pain
into knowing what it means to be

climbing the hill of blood, trawling the poisoned sea.'

'Where have I been when they say I've returned?'
'Where beginning and end
combine to make a picture, compose a sound
reminding you that love is a singing wound

and I could be your friend.'

1

Between living and dying
is the calmest place I've ever been.
He stood opposite me and smiled.
I smiled too, I think, because this was the first time
I'd seen a man made of rain
though once or twice
my heart was chilled by men of ice.
The rain poured through him,
through his eyes, face, neck, shoulders, chest, all his body
but no rain reached the ground,
it ended at his skin.
          He looked at me with eyes of rain
and said, 'I'll be coming to see you
now and then from this moment on.
Today, I'm colours, all colours.
Look at me, I'll be colours again
but different next time, maybe.
See my colours today.'

I looked. I saw the flesh of rain,
I looked into and through the rain
and saw colours I'd never seen before.
As I looked, the colours began to dance
with each other, some were laughing,
some were crying, some said they were lost
and were looking for their brothers and sisters,
one said he was the colour of work
and it saddened him to see
how easily he made slaves of men.
I looked for the colour of slavery
but couldn't find it. I saw
the colours of poverty instead
like children in O'Connell Street.
'Pick one of us,' they sang in a chorus
'You'll have a friend for life.'
I was indecisive because I was
between living and dying
and anyway the colours
were vanishing into each other
like thoughts that cannot stand alone
but must seek out other thoughts
to stop going mad, why are thoughts
afraid to go mad?

The rain
is laughing at that fear,
I followed the rain of the eyes
and saw the terror
that makes reason necessary
and gives it authority,
an educated terror
that didn't trust the rain.
He never asked me to trust him but I
would trust the man made of rain
to the lip and into the mouth and belly
of eternity, it isn't even a question of trust
more of the kind of interest you find
when you put aside the fear of dying
and look at the light
or listen to the sound of water
or pay attention to pigeons
or her hair when she's unaware
or find yourself swallowing a nightsound
or like the way a scientist talks of ten dimensions.
It is calm in the place beyond trust
and especially calm if you walk there
in the company of your own hurt,
in the company of the man made of rain
pouring beside you
but more contained
than anything in the world
except the pain
waiting at the white door
one cold October evening, leaves falling,
traffic ranting, seagulls hovering,
swooping like dreams
that seek you out
for, it seems,
the fun of it.

O scars of living, the fun those dreams must have!

I won't have to open the door.

He steps forward, opens it, smiles.
I walk in, he vanishes,
nowhere to be seen,
the silver rain is everywhere,
the shadows creep
into the secret corners of the October evening

where live and die
secret and open
dark and light
chaos and wonderplan

are wideawake in the heart of sleep.

2

'There are those who'd say you're not normal,'
said the man made of rain.
'Follow me. Better still, walk with me.'

He lifted the pain from me
like you'd lift a cap from your head.
I walked with him.

Always the colours.
Now, the pictures.

A hill.
We climbed it.
I fell.
He picked me up.
There was such strength in the rain
unsuspected strength, the strength of drab,
neglected women and men.

A lime-kiln.
I went down into it.
I tasted the lime.
It changed to fountain-water
that cooled punishment
and made a pact with brutality.

'We'll go to the trees,' he said,
'Now that you know your chest is made of wood.'

The trees talked of folly and cruelty,
they told me of my blindness.
'If you write this down
you'll write it on the death of one
or all of us,' they said.

The man made of rain talked to the trees,
he touched them as he talked,
the trees flourished at his touch,
they were strong as he was gentle.

He cried a little, I think it was
the only time I saw him cry, I'm
wrong, the war between fear and music
draws his tears as well.

That's when he talks of hell.

Look at the children in the field, he said.

Tony O'Grady	Teddy O'Sullivan	Séan Creedon
Michael Mulvihill	Eddie Joe Dee	Scruffy Grace
Billy O'Shea	Noel O'Connell	Paddy Spring
Mick Flavin	Jer Enright	Tucker Heaphy
Patsy McKibben	Willie Cox	Dropsy Bawn

changed

to yellow flowers in the green field,
suddenly there was moonlight
and the flowers walked the streets of cities,
flowers out looking for work,
flowers walking streets in moonlight
and the man made of rain called for music,
the flowers danced at his bidding,
yellow flowers dancing in the streets
of New York and London
Liverpool and Boston,
flowers dancing because they'd found work
away far away
from sticks and stones will break my bones
but names will never hurt me
and don't you know
when poverty comes in the door
love flies out the window.

Do not distort me, twist me, misrepresent me,
let me be truthful as the dance,
do not pitch lies at me, or wrap them
like bandages around my mind,

I am with

the man made of rain, walking with him
through streets of yellow flowers
in the dancing light of exile
where happiness is possible and the edges
of the world are touched by what is gentle.

I hear you say flowers were born for human eyes.
Look into the eyes of the man made of rain.
It is time to go into exile,
pay attention to flowers in exile.
They could turn on each other now,
betray or kill each other

                    but not yet.

How hideous that would be, flowers killing each other
like men, like brother killing brother,
like de Valera in Listowel, 'I swear to God,
brothers will wade knee-deep through brothers' blood.'

They did. They do. They will.

Were flowers born for human eyes?

'Look at Callaghan making love to Julie Anne,'
said the man made of rain.

Julie Anne laughs at love, at men,
at Callaghan as she opens her legs
on the floor of Sunday, she laughs
at what he does and thinks, we know
she knows what he thinks
as we stand,
the man made of rain and I,
at the door of the place where coffins are made
for rich and poor and young and old
and love is made
in the light of mockery.

Keep the Sabbath holy but mix love with mockery.

'Here's the fountain,' he said.
'Callaghan is a flower in New York,
Julie Anne is a flower begetting flowers

in a small house down a side-road in Limerick
and you're a flower with thoughts making noise
in your head. I can hear them rattling.

When humans look at flowers,
flowers bear the burden of the eyes
that they enrich.'

The fountain leaped like a young goat,
the man made of rain mingled with it,
the fountain knelt in homage,
it told him its troubles, it asked him
to pray for the water of the world, the water
is threatened,

           I see the rain
in the man's heart, no poison there,
I see the rain composing his hair
relaxed and pure, I see
the rain pouring down his body
into his legs, pouring like grace
from head to toe, out to the edge
of his fingers, through his teeth
when he smiles.

He smiles. 'Wherever I am
is peace. Peace does not belong
to the dead alone.'

The fountain rejoices, back on its feet.
The water pours through his head
like questions through an eager child.

Why is peace so threatening to some?
Why do they try to strangle it?
Break its back and legs with clubs and hammers?
Why are they afraid to see it grow?

'You're slow,' he said, 'So slow, painfully,
pitifully slow.'

I know.

And yet I thought I moved.
I believed I moved.
Lord, that I may walk.

My pillow feathers whisper I'm made of lead.

That I may walk.

'There are those who'd say you're not normal,' he said.

3

'When you walk through my tongue
you're in a land of no language,' he said.

He opens his mouth, I walk in,
I wander through the tongue of rain.
I don't expect to meet such innocence again,
innocence that is, as I understood it then.

Are there words for innocence?
Let witnesses come forward.

Half-way through the tongue I see Dan Conners
push Mrs Morrisey's bread from her windowsill
                    into her backyard muck,
then hide behind a bush to hear her cry.
She has ten children to feed and what will feed them this night?

I did nothing about it.
I said nothing.

The tongue of rain is licking my mind.

I'm under it now, looking up.

He says it's a land of no language but I see
shadows of words running off his tongue,
word-shadows flicker and sway,
stop as if startled, then flow

in a river of silence through the tongue of rain.
I think I know what he means now,
this is before the first word is born,
anxious and puzzled, alone, pleadingly simple,
tense on the threshold of saying

or singing.

All that I say and am and can be
comes after,
but is born then.

At the back of his tongue, I see rooms
where they whimper and cry, men and women unheard.
Who is their word?
Where may it be found?
I taste his silver spittle, the blood of words
in the veins of the rain in his mind.

In the land of no language
I beg understanding of shadows,
I look, listen, wait to be born
in a word on the tip of the tongue
where I wander forever,
a guest at the feast of silence
soon to return to the room where I lie
conscious (they say), scarred and still,
pigignorant of words I kill.

4

I said,   'There's no way
          I could ever say
          you.'

          'Say I'm the air's notebook.
          Birds jot their thoughts on my pages.'

          'Have I the neck?'

          'Say I'm the heart-attack
                  Jupiter survived. Say
          Elvis reached Jupiter
                  in less than an hour.'

          'Can I believe that, even
                  in the light of my end?'

          'Say I'm the lost spirit-currency
                  you found
                  and are learning to spend.

          'Say I could be your friend.'

5

'You're dying tonight,' said the man made of rain.

'What can I do?' said my blood.

He understood.

'There are two mushrooms growing
under the tree outside your window.'

'Should I turn mushroom?'

'You might give it a shot.'

        Anxious leaves, plastic bags,
      envelopes, newspapers, birthday cards,
      rubber tyres and a clothes hanger
      rustled I was dying.

But he whispered, 'Dear mushroom,
        for the moment, you're not.'

Moment. For the moment. I'm not.

I see a house with a red roof
close to the hill of blood
that I must climb
wearing my favourite boots.
Will the man of rain accompany me?
Loneliness is a special kind of company,
it'll go anywhere with me, I don't have to ask it,
I can feel it close to my heart,
snuggling in there,
feathery, not rough, but with a kind
of cold tenderness I find
nowhere else.

I'll never forget these mushrooms
in late October.

The things that keep you alive
on the brink of November,
month of the dead where I come from.

I turn away from the hill of blood
and talk to the mushrooms.
They've had their own growing problems
but are enjoying maturity.
So would I if I ever reached it.
What is it?
Don't give me a cautious answer.

It is my stricken guess
that more men die of caution
than excess.

'Keep on talking,' he says. He's here.
'Keep on talking. You're among your own.'

The mushrooms don't object.

I'm drifting in a sea of warm blue oil,
I've been drifting for years, mushrooms
at my side, whispering, I'm listening,
I've never heard of dying here in this
oily sea of blue, suddenly there are
heads everywhere, bobbing, asking me
questions, voraciously bidding me welcome,
home at last, home, warm blue home,
no fear of drowning, that's over, where am
I from, am I alone, where did I learn
how to drift like this without a care,
in or out of the world, same thing, drifting,
the heads are singing to me and a woman
with a basket of flowers tells me to sleep
in the sea, I'm the sea's child, so sleep,
sleep in the sea, the clothes hanger rustles
says nothing, the anxious leaves are starting
to relax where they drift, broken and free.

If this is drowning, drowning's for me.

6

'So what if blood runs down the hillside,
it'll come home in time,' he said.

'It's mine,' I said. 'That blood is mine
and it's running all over the bloody place.'

'Right you are,' he said. 'And it's no harm
if you stain the green green grass now and then.
Mix the colours like women and men.
Some men never see their blood, is it
any wonder they're so keen to shed the blood
of others, some of the worst evil is spread
by men who've never seen their own blood
spilled.'

The rain poured through his forehead, shining,
I could see his brain, it was bigger
than America, dark as Ireland and necessary
as the old enemy so loved in ways. The rain
falling through the brain was itself the brain
and was light as praise
                touching
                        a child's head.

'Let me show you your blood,' he said.

'Some other time,' I answered. 'I'm too busy
dying right now.'

'You're full of excuses,' he said.
'But all right, I'll wait.'

He started to climb the hillside
the blood coming against him parted
and he walked the green path
not bothering to look back.

Blood on either side
he conquered the hillside.
The sun shone through the blood
the blood shone through him
but was no part of him,
it was a spectator, fifty thousand spectators
waiting

to pummel heaven with excited cries.
He let the blood be,
he let the blood flow
whichever way it chose or dared to flow
or was compelled to flow.

He reached the hilltop, stood alone
in the climbing light.

Shining, he was shining, maker and mover,
he laughed like rain in May, big drops
that land chuckling on your shoulders,
big generous drops, he sparkled, his brain
a storm of light in my darkness,
he stood at the top of the hill, shining,
free and easy, top of the hill.

In my vilest ignorance, in my cage of blood,
I see him still.

7

'Freedom is wings,' he said.

We passed Ballyseedy Cross, eight out of nine
blown to pieces.

'The German loves his mother,' he said.
'The cottage was lost and found in Cavan
of the jokes, not forgetting Kerry, mind you,
you will mind yourself, won't you, promise
me that, an' bless yourself goin' out the door,
never know what you're lettin' yourself in for.'

The man made of rain began to flow,
this flowing was for the pain that must
be forgotten, mustn't it?

> This flowing meant changes
>   in the old castles
>   the new estates
>   the bag on the thief's back
>   the old woman planning
>   a walk before Wednesday

                    the seven flowers
                  transfiguring the room
                in the house on the road
                  to nowhere.

It happened we were passing another house.

'That's a safe house,' he said. 'Killers rest there.
Murder must find a place to lay its head.'

'Jesus,' he said, 'the sadness of traffic.
The plight of people going places.'

There were nine flowers now.
There was a grey wall, had once been white,
love and sweetness through the night.

'Only when he sings is he real,' he said,
pointing to the young man advising
children how to go to hell pleasantly,
for a while, anyway.

'There are no brief visits to hell,' he said.
'I have a letter here, it's from a young man
drowned in America, he loved the sea, it
invited him, betrayed him, he knew he was free,
he writes of diving into childhood, it felt
like flying.'

I see the young man diving in his brain.
I hear the sea, the whispers, sighs.
I see the young man diving through his eyes.
You'd think he was flying.
Freedom is wings.

I can only repeat what I see.
I cannot say why
what I see
flows through me.
Eyes see what they see, that's history.

He sits in a chair in a corner of the room now.

'You might live,' he says.

I love the hint of laughter in the light about his head.

Put a head in the light, it displaces the light,
how does the light feel?
Does the light know the meaning of revenge?
The wild justice of striking back?
Has the light a history of dispossession?
I want to read the history of light
but that's a history no one made of flesh can write.

The laughter of the man made of rain
is the envy of people and books.
It's a sound like all the promises
chance or man or God makes it possible to fulfil.

It's a light striding sound,
a childrunner in the blood,
loving every moment of being,
its own being, mine, yours too.

Mary Ann Callaghan puts her hands on her hips,
laughs till her false teeth dangle
and her pension book threatens
to fall in the mud and the dust
where Keonach sells the Dingle mackerel
on the grounds that if you eat this fish
you'll find wisdom and a job in Dublin.

'Sure the Salmon of Knowledge is only
trottin' after it,' Keonach laughs,
cool silvery shillings in his hand.

'Eat fish from Dingle, fish from Dingle,
you'll be the brightest in the land.'

'Don't worry if you lose sight of me,' says
                        the man of rain,
'Something of me lingers
where I am not.'

He raises his hand, I am transfixed
by rain that composes his fingers.

It stretches away to the end of the world,
the edge of things, is there an edge?
It is closer to me than my own heartbeat.
He has perfect fingers,

fingers of silver rain, all light and shining,
don't blame me if I think of paradise,
yes, the fingers contain a garden
where love walks and meditates on all
that is not itself but may yet be part
of itself, I see a man
beautiful and blameless walking through
I papaveri, they are a revolution
against the grey conspiracies of swamps
oozing into the minds of men.

The hill of blood rebels against the swamps.

The garden vanishes.

There are flowers in his fingers.

I count them with all I know of love.

Ten.

One for bones and flesh
two for school
three for a bright lad
four for a fool
five for glad giving
six for peace
seven for loving

in a ruin made of stories

eight for children laughing in the eyes
of strangers to each other
till the moment flashes

nine for silence
the bequest of pain

ten for the music

of the man of rain.

8

Amor.
A man of rain.
Nobody intended that.
Yet he had to happen.
When he happened my world outgrew itself.

He is not born of intention.
He is what must happen.
He never heard of reason.
If he did, he pities it.

How do I know that?
Is the rain longing to be human?
Is there a human somewhere
longing to be rain?

A human being
longing
to flow forever,
to pour forever, yet be contained,
to fall on houses anywhere,
on first love, last words,
plans hatched in darkness,
bloody murder, fields of wheat
ripening through summer days

       longing to fall
          like blessings

           like praise.

9

'Let's go for a walk through your scars,' invited
                         the man of rain.

Away we went.

Half-way down my chest, he headed for an old castle,
climbed to the top and said 'You played love here
when you were seventeen. Nobody heard your words
but herself and the Shannon
and maybe a few seagulls on their way to Clare.'

Seventeen. What have I done? Where have I been?

He pointed to blood on a street.
'That's where Moriarty and yourself were beaten up,'
he said. 'That was the first and only time you saw
a mystic with a black eye and a broken jaw.'

A long stretch of road then. Calm. Small birds in hedges.
'I love it when the small birds sing,' he said.

I saw my scars becoming roads in his rainy head,
I saw small birds in cages, singing with such ecstasy
you'd swear to heaven they were wild and free.

'You filled two pints of Guinness for Jackie Carroll the night
he was killed,' he said. 'There's the small cross
to his memory.' I looked. A small cross.
All around, the soft implacable grass.

The next stretch festered. 'You were lost here,' he said.
'You were lonely and mean, your heart black as tar.'
Four o'clock in the morning, a woman is crying,
I don't know where I'm going but I go that road
because that's what roads are for, I bear
witness to this festering scar.

Travelling a hacked body is a healthy adventure.

Roads. Walked on. Driven on. Trampled. Used
like some of the women in the village I grew up in.
I want to listen to the voices of the roads,
voices of my scars, now more than ever I know
few voices are heard on this babbling stage.

Let go. Listen. Let go.

In the freedom of being lost, I hear choked voices flow.

'This road leads to a yellow house on a hill.
A woman taught you here. Try not to lie, she said.
She loved you. She's gone. So is the house. You see them still.'

I do.

He sees I'm tiring. 'Rest,' he says. 'Rest here.'
I fall asleep near a deep scar,
a thin, healing road of blood.

He walks away.

When I wake, I'll go back the roads I came.
I'll meet the hearts. A heart is laughing, a heart
is calculating, a heart grieves, a heart wonders,
a heart rages.

Jackie Carroll. Two pints the night he died.

What did the seagulls hear
on their way to Clare?

What is love in a yellow house on a hill?

Try not to lie.

Small birds sing in cages,
sing with such ecstasy
you'd swear that they were wild and free.

10

He pleaded   'Let me happen to you.
              Let me happen to you.'

It was a time when I'd no words.

            I watched him

            climbing a house
              opening a window
                rescuing a man
                  from himself.

The man of rain brought the man of flesh
              down to earth
                where he belonged
                  and laid him in the arms
                    of his brother

            who thought he was lost.

The man of rain walked off down the road
              that became a scar
              that became a river
              that became a line
                of poetry

burning

in his brain.

I saw the line of poetry burning in his brain,
            burning in the water of his brain.
      The water was on fire
            and the line turned cool
      in the middle of the fiery water
            still burning like revenge.

Amid burning revenge, one cool line of poetry.

On he walked, water and fire and poetry
            ready to rescue anyone
            trapped in himself
            and return him
                  to his brother.

It was a time when I'd no words
            but I let him happen
            to me as he
            had pleaded

and he poured through me
      with a look
            with a smile
            with a line

not mine, although I witness it, not mine.

The words are returning like workers from exile,
some of them want to tell me their stories,
            I want to listen,
the words of workers in exile will be mine
            and I will let them sink
                  into the darkness
                        where blood begins to think
                        of all that blood is not
                              but

                  thanks to pain

                  may be

                  yet.

11

A Dublin gangster,
now retired,
living with a hammer,
a mother, her daughter,
is hammering nails into my chest
which has of late become a block of wood.
As he hammers, he prays
my soul will find eternal rest
in the light of the mercy of God.
'You'll travel many a road,' he says
'Before you meet a gangster like me.'

I agree

yet wonder
how a brilliant Sunday paper
might decipher
how this gangster
relates
to a hammer
a mother
her daughter

and how the mercy of God
might make its sweet forgiving way

through a block of wood.

12

The man who said he was terrified
by the silence of the infinite spaces
must have looked through the eyes
of the man of rain.

Yet it is necessary to go beyond terror
and if you persist in looking through those eyes
you find a state of such clarity
peace is happy to live in you.

All words spoken and written
are drops of rain falling from a seagull's wings.
All the books are the forgotten famine dead
and no one knows the words of their song.

This in itself could be a source of the terror
but this too vanishes in that clear state
where the bones of all your dead foregather
to greet and welcome you, set you at your ease.

The creation of terror is a coward's art
and when I terrify myself by looking
at what I cannot begin to understand
I pray to be rain on a seagull's wings

falling on my cowardice creating terror
as a way out, a solution, to the eyes
of the man of rain looking through me
being looked through, seen, known, so what?

Think, say the eyes, of the beauty of nothing ;
call it the cheetah's speed or the Nine o'clock News,
the Weekend Supplement or Shakespeare in a nutshell,
a one-legged pigeon or a bubbly Millennium.

The beauty of nothing celebrates all the lost books,
the empty libraries of the infinite spaces,
words wandering, comets, lost starving children
whose eyes possess your eyes,
their silence saying, look into the eyes of the man
made of rain, cries of the victims of terror,
light on wet slates, the pain of admitting nothing
is the passion and the logic of beginning.

Meg Murphy is five. Eyes wide. 'I *lo-o-ve* reading!'

13

When I see a word
vanishing
into the rain of his head
I see a hand
shaping the word
'beginning'.
My eyes of a man
of flesh
explore the eyes of a man
of rain
and I see
there is no beginning,
no end.

There is a now
that cannot be grasped
so let me invent
my past
my future
to stop me knowing
the radiant nothingness
of now,
the drugged pain
of now,
the terrifying speed
of now
all through my slow carcass,
my slow soul.
This little now
is so beyond me
I'd better make haste
to invent
eternity.
Stranger at my door,
help me.

14

It was nice of death to stand aside a while
and make a little space, not much
but enough for me to see

a man beating a woman to death
with a red brick,
the kind of brick

lauded for the part it plays
in certain forms of architecture.
I'd read about such bricks

in smashing books, their epic
elegance filling my mind for days.
The red brick bashed the woman

till her spirit rebelled through her battered head
and passed through the veins
of the man made of rain

standing nearby.
Her clear spirit began its adventure
in the knowledge it would never die

but wander forever through veins and eyes
deeper than Homer's sea.
Feathers of gossip have a similar agility

and power of endurance
but nothing in her spirit was sick.
I saw it journeying. I saw the man with the brick

standing over her body in the shadow
of a gorgeous Cathedral renowned
in this city for the crowning of an English King

who approved of the music that evening.
The man with the brick was blind
to the man made of rain,
blind to almost everything, in fact.
He stood where death had created a space
for me, grim guilt on his face,

the Cathedral bells starting to toll,
the future plotting its revenge
in a small corner of the murderer's soul.

Otherwise, he was free to go, more or less.
The man of rain watched him hurry down Waterloo Road.
He watched her body too, the brick dumped near her head.

He carried her within him, gently as he could.

15

'Who's to say if you're sane or insane?'

'A normal man.'

'Who can say what it means to be a normal man?'

'I can.'

'Do, then.'

'I can't.
If I did
you might think I was mad.'

16

I look at rain pouring through him,
never breaking the skin,
just pouring in that world of light
visible behind skin, transparent man,
nothing to hide, I think of all our
hidden sicknesses, poems made of lies, skilful
things, fodder for prizes, consolatory,
ethical, I see him lucid, a man
of quiet clarity, pouring, contained,
who is the patron saint of rain?

Mary Ann Callaghan would be the woman
to answer that
and dare I disbelieve her?

''Tis all them clouds you have to thank for rain,'
        says Mary Ann,
''Specially the black wans with the snarly faces.
Them bastards is your patron saint.'

I saw him once stuff clouds into his pocket.
He reached up, gathered a crop of clouds,
white, grey, some black as anger,
put them in an inside pocket, I could
see through them, even the black ones,
they had fragments of the world in them,
oppressing them, I thought, weighing them down
but after a while he took the clouds
out of his pocket, threw them back in the sky
where they stretched themselves
like waking greyhounds,
and went for a race
delighted to be free.

To see delighted clouds enjoying themselves
shot fun through me.

I could have died with the thrill
of that shooting fun.
I thought for a moment I'd love to be
a cloudy man

but I was tied to a bed,
pumps sticking out of me.
You look a bit ridiculous, the pillowfeathers said.

He gets on well with clouds
but doesn't like to see them get too gloomy.
The gloomy ones slump in the sky
like bags under people's eyes,
sad and heavy and full
of poison waiting
to ooze into the eyes
and blind the people.
He doesn't like to see that happen.
He likes the clouds that move
and frisk a little in their freedom
like terrier pups
or lion cubs
or little leopards learning how.
The sky is a place of learning
and clouds should make the most of light,
kicking up their heels in their blue playground,
frolicking with heaven
never letting it get too serious
'cos all the gods are longing to smile
but men of flesh won't let them.

How may the gods escape
important, gloomy men?

I think if I had made the world
I'd smile, now and then.

My blood is happy when I stand
and look at clouds.

And is there anything more sweet and sane
than to lie
between living and dying

and listen to the rain?

17

It was a long time afterwards
(after what? please don't switch on the light)
I heard one of my father's bones say
'An epic is one word explored
like the inside of a bone,
explored until it's glad to surrender
secrets of highabove deepwithin downunder.
One word alone. Take
the word of an old man's bone.'

I take your word for it, fatherbone.
Who knows the loneliness of words,
thin, drifting flames in the infinite cold?
I am the child of a lost language
though I've run into it all over the world
and it runs through me now and then.
...agus ni baoghal duit an ragairne...
The ragairne stonecrushes my head tonight
(it must be night, please let it be night),
the ragairne
lashes the island until all I can do is leave it,
curse it
in words that never have enough of the lash,
let me live in an icy corner of Asia,
swim through the darkness of the epic Asian night.
Ragairne. Asia. I listen to him.
One word. Enough to eat my life. Darkness.
Switch on the light.

18

Birds of pain hover about my bed this darkness
singing their dark song to my rubbled flesh.
I taste the masterful blackbird, the gritty yellowhammer,
the passionate thrush

celebrating
my wish,

my trapped yet flying wish.

19

Everyone on this island knows everything that may be known
about rain.
There'd be a noticeable decline in life-giving talk if heaven
sent us less rain.
Many muttered blessings and curses are the children
of rain
and I know one sparkling woman who loves
to make love in the rain.

(Jesus, says Mary Ann Callaghan, is it any wonder
she'll be crippled with arthritis
when she's only forty-wan!)

20

What's the weight of flesh in the world just now?
The question bobbed in my mind like a red
ball in water at the foot of a monument

I know or remember or made up
in order to keep my grip on things.
First, you have these five continents

huge yet small enough when you place them
in atlaswater ; they contain much flesh
with millions of tons more on the way

because we love each other, that's what we say,
or slip into bed or get a good ride
or enjoy feast and speeches with bridegroom and bride.

Even as it burns to ashes or merges with clay
flesh is replaced by promising cries
and new names chosen most lovingly.

What's the weight of it? Weight of it all?
Heavy heavy heavy despite
testosterone, epitestosterone, what you will

and the earth bears it all with a grin
of winter or spring, bears millions of tons
of flesh sleeping and waking, flesh of men,

women, children, flesh everywhere, all the time,
flesh making flesh, killing flesh, loving flesh,
punishmentbeating flesh, being born is the crime

and the sentence is living, the mad Dean said.
I lay beyond living, still trying
to calculate the weight of the dead

before I'd advance on the problem of now,
the living, bless them all days, all ways.
I'd like mathematics to learn how to fly

beyond the proveable, it will, one day,
meanwhile the man of rain sits
on the edge of the bed, he suggests

a flick of the brain from flesh to rain,
from solid to flowing, I try to comply,
a needle is gossiping in my blood,

you dirty old thing you dirty dirty old thing.
Well, proveable enough, let the gossip flow,
the man of rain is smiling,

I know that smile, he's taking the side
of flesh right now, backing the way it is
supporting the way we flourish and rot from day

to day, that's the secret, out in the open,
but nothing's out in the open, not completely, his smile
supports that too, it's a necessary style,

he always has mercy on style which must
exist if flesh is to continue
its long adventure through bone and sinew,

itself, as it is, now. Let me lie here and think
till I sleep or imagine I sleep a wink
and fly or imagine I fly when flesh

                would have me sink.

21

There's no edge, only a new place with
one side veering away into nothing and
Mary Moroney is kindness itself, all care
loving care, turns over that body anytime
day or night.

Colours of the left leg, cut from ankle to groin
or groin to ankle if you prefer, I like
ankle to groin for reasons I'll not go into here,
invade the head and capture
three major cities
with the convinced skill of Oliver Cromwell
my old foepal for whom I received
a whack on the jaw on O'Connell Bridge
the night after I mentioned to Gaybo
Oliver had a lot going for him
and we could do with a visit now.
He'd show the killers how to behave so he would,
he'd take the shine off their bliss,
he'd lay down the law, the Lugs Branigan.

Black yellow red brown and
a vaguely disgusting white
are the colours of my left leg.
They hurtle into each other like dirty footballers,
you'd swear my colours wanted to knock each other out,
I was white once, or as white as the next Paddy,
the only thing to do when you're backward is
let yourself fly, I'm blueredblackyellowbrown
            and I don't mind it at all
so don't give it a thought if you see me cry.

I never thought I'd see the day
when I'd cry like the rain
and not begin to know why.

Truth is the tears I can never explain.

Say I'm buried, say I'm on show somewhere,
on exhibition in Merrion Square,
a postmodern explosion of latent rebellions,
Handy Andy from New York would enjoy me
and I haven't even been bombed
or expelled from my province

to become a sly colonising refugee
with a genius for eliciting sympathy.
I haven't cut off my ear
or jumped off a bridge
or distinguished between essential and obvious
because here you could take these labels
turn them upside down for a laugh
and find the battle of the colours
going on in my skin
in that room in the Gallery
where they hang masterpieces
like Judas moving in for the kiss
discovered in old Jesuits' bedrooms
or Big Houses down the country
the IRA forgot to burn
or was it the other lads?
Someone will burn them some day,
                don't worry your head.

Black yellow brown red
blood on the pillow

a woman in my bed
where did she come from?

It was like a tractor going over your body,
says Shirley Love
with the angeltouch.

Massey Ferguson was my favourite tractor,
treacherous bastards tractors are,
plough you into the ground in no time at all
when you wouldn't be looking
with nothing but the green green
grass of home for company
and a trickle of red, you wonder
a moment what is the source of red,
red red who called it red,
woman nowoman in my bed?

Eyelids fall.

The colours are even clearer now
and a few new ones
have joined the company.
These new ones were born in the mind of snow
but they never honoured me till now.

O the colours of pain
are enough to make me dance
at a feis in a field
between Asdee and Ballybunion.

Dance, sing the colours, dance
till he comes, man of rain
whose colours the rainbow envies.

He looks at the colours of my left leg,
touches them, they start to change
into the colours of each other,
Jews into Arabs, Arabs into Jews,
Ulster Protestants into Ulster Catholics
and vice versa, making new colours,
no words for them, not yet, no words
needed they flow
like trout like eels in the Feale,
there is no edge, only this new place

where I am real, real

        as my colours
           in late October
               with leaves falling

        and Dermot Gillespie
           in the next bed
              breathing,

        against all the evidence

           breathing.

22

Come into the ground with me now, he says.

I follow.

I'm in my father's grave, the man of rain
picks up a bone and hands it to me.
'You love that, don't you,' he says
'It always loved you.'

I hold my father's bone in my hand.
A fair ould worker when he wanted to be,
could take a faulty clock to pieces
and put it together again. Perfect.
His hands on her dark head. Singing.

When first I saw you on the village green.

Fixed tractors too. Massey Ferguson.
In the earth all this time. How long? Strong bone.
Damp earth. Isn't it always raining
in North Kerry, that's where the snipe
wear wellingtons and swallows from Africa
swim through the summer.

I see his other bones now.

The man of rain stands silent by.
'Whenever I hear McCormack, my bones are fit to sing,' he said.

My father's bones are fit to sing.
I hold them in my hand.
I smell. Inhale. Hail, full of stories.

His life electrifies my darkness,
Scrolm Hill, the Civil War, America,
whiskey in Ballybunion with Jackie Boland,
the pouring, pouring stories.

A man must fight the hours his heart is lonely.

Bones and stories.

It's raining in my father's grave.

Blue Shannon light accommodates the rain.

I run my fingers over the bone, it's
cold to the touch, it warms my heart,
have another Gold Flake,
sixty a day, is it any wonder
I need the pace-maker, Bridie, is it
any wonder I cough my heart up
every morning, the mad thumping, but I'd
rather one Gold Flake than a
fortnight in Florida. They'll kill
me yet, I s'pose. The ould heart.

Come to me e'er my dream of love is o'er.

I can't stop them, not that I'd want to
but the bones in my hands are singing.

I'm following the man of rain
round and round my father's grave
inside deepdown inside
through his bones, deep within his bones.

Deeper than Ireland, wider than America
is this grave,
here's my journey now, I have my guide,
I follow the man of rain, he moves
like the summer of '55 every moment
bright and warm, touching me
without touching me, leading me
through the dark inside of my father's bones,
dark passages of laughter love smoke
stories phrases like the night in the kitchen
'I wish to Christ I was dead,'
and I never asked why,
why did I never ask why?

Nor will I ask why
his bones are singing now

I will never ask it of myself
I will never ask another human
I will never ask the air or the earth to explain.

I'll follow the man of rain
leading me through my father's bones,
the roads within,
the games, the wars, the ways of neighbours,
the scars that might say something
of what I've done, people I've hurt
been hurt by, strange places I've been,
believed I've been.

When you were sweet, when you were sweet sixteen.

He'd two daughters, six sons, I'm walking
through his skull, its mountains
glens valleys narrows caves
in Ballybunion where a father and son

195

went to explore between tides
and never returned though a car
was waiting to take them home.

I climb the walls of a cave in his skull
and hear the wild white horses
bellowthreatening a few yards away, it seems.

Once upon a time, his dreams ran through this cave.
If my dreams met his,
here, now,
how would they get on together?

Would they talk to each other?

I'm climbing now and come upon
three gates, I open each one
and am able for the mountain
taller than his forehead
when I saw him first.

Darkness next, I go through that
flicking now and then the lamp he gave me
to see if the cow had calved in the shed.

The skull is the least dead road I've travelled,
nothing but surprise
behind where used to be his eyes.

I look and see the eyes
of the man made of rain
looking through my father's eyes.

Love shines through death,
kisses it with those eyes.
Death has its own answer,
its only answer.
Love kisses death again, again.
Death disappears
in the eyes of rain.

I'd love to turn on my left side
but cannot.
I might as well be nailed to the sheet
damp with my sweat.

Lie there in the arms of pain.
Could this be forever?

He's gone.

Father.

Son.

Why can't I lie on my left side?

Where are you, man made of rain?

23

Beyond all wonder is a wonderplan
combining blue and white
with the raucous threats and curses
of the night

Shadows scale a red wall
a man calls for peace
a boy and a girl kick down a door
in Thomas Street

Inside my skin four rows of birds
prepare for flight
Wherever they go I wish them well
I'm glad we met

Beyond all wonder is a wonderplan
I'll see it if I will
Jack Kilready is a dying man
so are we all

dying into wonder beyond wonder
beyond blue and white beyond peace
beyond killers of peace beyond
loss beyond all fear of loss

24

The poison in my body
is the poison of my time.

Kill the trees, kill them here, anywhere,
feed the poison to the paper,

feed the paper to the eyes,
feed the eyes with ugliness.

Killing follows killing follows killing.
The only thing to fear is healing.

Young murderer licks sweat off my thighs
devours the checkpoint with his eyes.

Feed the eyes feed the eyes.
Someone's in for a surprise.

Soldier is nearly twenty-three,
bit young for hell or heaven, too

old for earth, earth's poison
raving through me this stone afternoon.

Bullet wipes away young man.
Murderer licks my sweat again
keen to glut himself on poison.

He can never get enough, failed murderous glutton.
Where is she? Would she recognise her son,
very pretty lad assassin?

I'm poisoned father poisoned brother
murdered man and his murderer

together we've betrayed the sun
the sun's revenge is heaven's poison

my own

25

The accent crawls, colonising the loch,
practising itself in the still
evening.
        Slithery as a snake, rooted as a rock,
it knows how to whine, flatter, beg, kill.

26

Hacked, bruised, foul. 'What is flesh?' I asked the man of rain.
'A kind of everything waiting to be nothing,' he said.
'Great worker, best servant on earth, dustpoem,
lovething, vivid presence in the process of vanishing.'

'Where does it vanish to?' I asked.

He smiled, started walking.

I wanted to rise and follow quickly
but something heavier than the world prevented me,

whispering, Stay, you cannot do without me.

27

'I've never seen you before,' I said,
though I knew I had.
On the hill of blood.

'That may be true,' he said, 'but you see me now,
this cold blue bright day.'

His eyes' cold blue light is
what history should be,
so clear
it makes fleshcomplexity look sad.

Have you been here before, I wondered, will you
be here again?

He read my silent wondering.

'I haven't much time for tenses,' he replied.

My flesh is hot and thick.

Past, present, future. The three-card trick.

Greyhound racing in Glin.
'Pick your card,' the gambler said.
I did and as I did
I knew I'd lost.

Three cards on a table
in a field where the hounds
neck in for the kill. Three cards.
Past, present, future.
The hare's cry is with me still.
No cry like the cry of a gentle creature.

Another gambler said, 'There's a fourth card
you can learn to play.
There's always another card.'

The eyes of the man of rain
outshine the light of the cold blue day.
I throw all the cards away.

He opens up the late October sky.
Windy. Every leaf that flies and falls

is a hare's cry.

I don't propose to go on about cries
but I've been hearing a lot of them lately,
mainly from within.

They need to be heard, I'd say.
But most leaves blow away
or are carted away
to a hole outside Arklow
in the Garden of Ireland.

I'm walking among the cries
buried in the Garden of Ireland.
Nobody gets in touch, nobody writes
to the cries or inquires after them
like 'Is it true you nearly died?'

The cries are shy. If such questions were asked
they'd hardly be answered.

Maybe a cry is question and answer all in one.

The loneliest cry I ever heard
was from an Indian woman
who'd lost her handsome, arrogant son.

No, not quite the loneliest.

Thy will be done.

How lonely was God
when he decided
to make a man

who'd cry
like that?

28

Major operations on the body
operate the mind.

At twenty past four
the godesses let their waters flow.
Stories of long ago.

The black bar ramming three white clouds
is a wound gone underground.

Up on the ditch he set me
when I was nine,
stuck his hand up my trousers,
his black eyebrows scorching me
his tongue licking his turfy lips.

'Did you bring me any black Bendigo tobacco?' he asks.
'I love it, 'tis the devil to cut though I have
the wickedest little knife in the world.'

His hands are calm and mad.
Sit still on the ditch, don't scream,
his black eyebrows fester with rats.

Paddy Brolley traps me between his legs.
He's eighty years of age, I'm eight,
he's laughing, his knees bang me,
manipulating,
coddin' is what he'll call it
if I start screaming.

'Now I have you trapped.
You'll never escape.'

More than half a century later
I'm trapped between his legs.

His old penis twitches like a rat in his grey trousers.

His laughter is a cage as well.
Paddy Brolley is a bit o' hell,
the bones of his knees are digging into my eyes
my mind is bleeding, he's laughing, why
is blood always surprising,
is the pillow drenched, are the feathers protesting?

What can I do
but let blood flow
like memories of long ago
that are the living now,
madcap antics, love, hate, rage,
rob Collins's orchard, run, hide, eat
the apples under the bridge, quick,
there's a comin' tide.

Tonight, I'm trapped in a cage.

No coddin'.

Mindbleeding never ends.

What's half a century between friends?

Now is then, then is now,
no such thing as long ago.

In the stillness of the night
in the prone silence of the body
I know
the fierce uncontainable flow

of the gentle eyes
of the man of rain.

It is part of me tonight,
this high springtide of blood
lifting in its rising hands
images
I cannot hide.

How much have I hidden?

How much have I lied?

Give me the courage
to rise and flow with the tide.

I can't see him but I know
he's standing out there
in here
in the darkness
in my mind

at my side.

29

The man of rain walks the streets of Dublin.

Shadows are candid beside him, behind
and before.

O'Connell Street of the crimes he loves,
drinks it with his eyes,
seagulls crapping on the Liberator.

The Liffey is bullockthick.
How can it ever flow like him?

Beaten children beaten women freezing men
murdered prostitutes and their crying parents
seek refuge in the cool lucid nowhere
visible through his skin.

As he walks, the unacknowledged victims
walk through him.
Dignity lives in his welcoming rain.

Shadows gather to salute, pay him homage,
solid bodies walk unresolved,
trapped in their solidity.

So they live, the bulkythick
and the flowing inescapable nothings
walking through each other.

If I cannot say what I see
have I seen it?

If I see it
do I believe it?

If I believe it
do I twist it
with my scarred mind?

I can only give the smithereens I find.

The man of rain walks the streets of Dublin
like a giant flower
the unacknowledged generations
have slaved to create.
This flower is a human poem
the trodden streets can read.
This poem is the hope of doorways
the whine of midnight traffic
the midair scrawks of seagulls
can you spare me fifty pence, sir, please
and may God bless you and yours forever.

Only in nowhere may I plead for nothing.
Dublin is a buzzing nowhere.
Strange how the flowing blood can freeze.

Fifty pence, sir, please. Please.

The human poem turns away from the lit streets
to walk the dark graffiti
of menace longing condemnation and despair.

I follow, place my trust in nowhere.
Nowhere takes it, fondles it like a small red ball.
Nowhere, the only home that welcomes all.

The tree at my window is October.
I spread my fingers in the hospital air.

Mary Moroney, love and care,
turns me on my side

from which perspective I see
    the man of rain
      the giant flower
        the human poem

    walking through Dublin
      as Dublin
        walks through him.

30

When light sets eyes on rain one anxious evening
it loves and marries it against all the odds
as someone crippled in a bed of pain
is calmed-caressed by inescapable gods.

31

The man in the next bed
to Dermot Gillespie died
this wild flying October afternoon.
All of a slap, Gillespie was a different man
talking of his days in the army,
a gun in his hand,
knew how to use it.
'Know your enemies,' he hissed,
'Men are menaces if they're not disciplined.'

'What's not escape?' I asked.

'Nothing,' said the man of rain.

Nothing is the Four Courts, the Five Lamps,
the Nine Daughters' Hole, the spawning frog
in the bog, the gift of tulips,
the Ten Best Books of the Year.

What year, for God's sake? Why don't I
ask October? I do.

'I'm John the Baptist to the month of the dead,'
October says. 'This one is dying out.
So am I, ever since they named me.
October. I have my own colours.
I have a feeling for lovers, they come
and go through my cool rooms,
my testy fields, my melancholy words.
They stroll willingly into my nets,
some of them I capture forever
as if their presence in my colours
would soften the blow for the dying year,
one more dying year, like an old envelope
blown hither and thither through the streets
or along the edges of the canal.
No one will ever know what it contained.
All the dying years love
to have their hearts caressed by rain.
It feels like praise or cool forgiveness.
What do the dying years remember?
What do I, October, remember?
I like to think my colours touched November.'

I kissed October.

I reached out my left hand to the man of rain.
Some of my fingers were frozen.
Were they dry or bleeding?
Stones or feathers? Alive or dead?

'You'll never escape October,' he said.

32

I looked into his crying eyes, how can
the rain be crying?
It is. Rain sheds itself, sheds tears as well,

the tears are running down his face
yet do not fall to earth.

This helps me to talk, he said.

Me too, I said.

Talk to me, he said.

I'm crying because I'm not afraid,
I said, and I thought I would be.
Fear came to me last night
and slept beside me.
Please let me stay, it said,
please let me lie with you
and live in you,

I want to thrive in you,
to make my own of you,
don't throw me out,
I'll have to spend tonight in some stranger's heart,
I like your heart, bad an' all as it is,
let me take up residence there,
I'll be a decent tenant, I'll earn my keep,
pay my way, what does your old heart say?

I'm a callous bastard at times.

Get out of here, I said, out of my bed,
out of my heart, g'wan, take to the roads,
hit the streets, find another heart to live in,
you're not welcome here.

You should have seen the face of fear,
all black passionate disappointment,
black as oily scrags of sand
on Sandymount Strand.
Fear doesn't like me anymore,
since I sent it slinking out the door.
It's left a deep space in my heart.
I'll put music there instead,
I'm crying, I can't stop crying,
you're crying too, man of rain. Why?

There are only so many ways to die, he said.
The way without fear is good.

I dislike evictions but I evicted fear
from my rain, what you call blood.
This eviction tells me who I am.
I'm a man made of rain, simply that,
only that. My rain is music, can you hear it?
I'll put music in my heart, you said.
It's already there.
Listen. Open your deep space.
Let your music out, let my music in.
The world is a closed shell.
Prise it open with your tears.
Fear is hell, get out of hell.

His eyes were pouring now, no longer crying,
he was rain that doesn't cry but pours
understanding on the frozen
witness of our fear.

Let my music in, he said again, let
my music fill the empty space,
will you let it in?

I'll try, I said, and couldn't explain
the sudden shiver in my stomach, the quick
nail in my forehead. Had I told
the truth? Had I lied?

The wall of my chest opened, bloody unholy door.

I went inside.

33

I want to tell him I've been robbed of words
but none exist for me to say.
Waking this morning
I could name nothing.
Name. Nothing.

What's the meaning of dulcet, Scruffy?
Scruffy Grace never heard of dulcet.
He'll pay for it.
Four on either hand.

Scruffy. Dulcet. Scruffy Grace.
Words so strange they paralyse your tongue.

Four slaps on either hand.
Slaps.
Shlaps.
Four shlaps on either hand
burning the line of joy, the line of sorrow.

Frig him, and his dulcet,
Scruffy spits after school, cooling
his hands at the fountain, what do I
know about dulcet, a lot o' bloody good
dulcet'll do me on a London buildin' site,
I never heard anyone around here
sayin' dulcet this or dulcet that,
dulcet father or mother
or bread or butter
or creamery-milk,
to hell with friggin dulcet,
let me outa here.

Scruffy got outa there
and hit the London building-site,
pick and shovel in the outcast light
and thirty quid a week, a fortune.

Fifty years on, it's all I have :
Scruffy Grace. Dulcet. A fortune.

I can't even say them.
They say me, over and over
and over.
The flesh becomes a word.

What's an eyelid? What's a fingernail?
A human face?

What's a pick? What's a shovel?
A cement factory in Houghton Regis?

There, at the foot of the bed, the face of rain
            looking.

Somewhere in my brain, I say words:

        face

            of

                rain.

I recognise

            the face

               of rain.

34

My mind ran away from me
            down the hill of blood
and I ran after it
            calling 'Come back! Come back!'

but my mind turned and laughed in my face
as it joined a fox in a merry dash
on a sudden green run of the hill.
Then it turned and ran towards me,
laughing all the while because that
is my mind's style if it can be said
to have a style.
'You silly old lump of cotton wool,' it said,
'Why should I bother to live in you,
you damp old house full of stuffy furniture,
you've no idea what fun it is
to escape from you
and run in the living air.
So many sprightly minds are trapped in the heads
of tedious old things like you.'

            I couldn't answer that, I was
mindless at the time, still am
            but I have something else –

a driven thing, a force, a rip, a kick,
a lick, a bite, a wandering, a honing-in,
a taste for things hurtfully sudden and quick

and the heaven-hellish out-of-it
            view of things

you get when you're bloody sick.

35

There's an irony at work I cannot fathom
shining in the sunlit pigeon shit
dripping from the battlements of the castle
where all is useless that is not a plot

or part of a plot. This clean winter day
can't stop the stink of treachery
filling the city: treachery of the dead
against the living, then turn it round,

history is now. Right. Wrong. Sing dumb.
There's an irony at work I cannot fathom.

You never had a penny so let your kingdom come.

36

Amor stares at the long black rib of
        hair on the floor,
at the big black suicide slab near
        the Gallery door,
at students passing. Which of them
        will come home
from a birthday party and hang herself
        in her own bedroom?

37

'Gather yourself, we'll go to the cold,' he invited.

'It must be blue,' I said.

'Why do you put a colour on everything?' he asked.

'There's nothing without a colour,' I replied.

'The cold I'm going to show you has no colour,' he said.

We sat in Saint Stephen's Green, calm as you like,
but the Green and everyone in it
lifted into the sky
and there was Dublin below, far below.
I saw me getting off the train at Kingsbridge,
it was nineteen fifty-four, Manning murdered
the nurse in a field near Limerick
but John the beggar told me fifty years later
Manning didn't mean it, he got carried away
by heaven between her legs and strangled her
and was hanged, the last man to be hanged
by the law in Ireland, hanged in the Joy, John the beggar
played handball with Manning the day before
he got strung up, and all Manning wanted
was a prayer over his limestone grave
which John gave to God before he was released
to stand on the Halfpenny Bridge with his cap
in his hand, the cap stretched out, his head down,
the most humble bleedin' man in Dublin, he said,
that's what they love, the bit o' humility,
that's the boy to stir their charity,
well by Jaysus they have their man, if it's
humility they want I'll give 'em capfuls of it
and I made thirteen pounds and four pence
the first day I stood on the Halfpenny Bridge,
more than many's the Civil Servant made in his office,
beggin' the eyes o' the passers-by, my head down,
my hands cold, my heart warm at the thought
of what turned out to be thirteen pounds and four pence.
For some men, prison is the start o' common sense.

Never commit a crime again, Manning said,
never rob a tourist or steal timber from buildin'-sites,
beg your way to a sound sleep every night
and when you lie between a woman's legs
try not to strangle her or you'll finish up
in a limestone grave and who
will throw an ould prayer to God for you?
From the edge of my grave I beg you be wise
and you'll never feel the cold of an ould judge's eyes.
I looked down into Dublin, I thought I saw
pain and laughter in the eyes
of the man made of rain

but I wouldn't swear to it.
Down there, Dublin was a star in the womb of time,
it was having a hard time being born, remember
the man who said Dublin
is an Empire's abortion, but to me 'twas a star, just then,
shining below, so far below,
the only star whose light
shone upwards
on men, women, children,
shone upwards
like a stray, impossible prayer from hell.

One day you see a woman, one day you don't,
she vanishes, you never even knew her name,
I saw the girl from the Isle of Wight
on a bicycle in Ship Street,
then she was gone into a bath
shoving a clothes hanger up herself,
I'd cherish her name if I knew it, I think the greyfaced man
on the cobbles was the father of what
the clothes hanger tried to polish off,
but the girl died instead, her blue eyes
laughing still
in the guinnessy smoke of O'Neills.
Suppose she can feel, what is it she feels?
How cold is she now, after thirty years?

When I asked these questions I saw them sinking
into the eyes of the man made of rain,
ice now, but kind for all that, kind ice
if that's not too much to swallow,
the kindest ice you'd ever dare to touch,
it was entering me, this cold
was taking me over, so cold, pure possession,
so cold I didn't feel cold any more
and never would again, it seemed,
I didn't even think of it, you think of it only
when you're humancold, or halfcold,
or cold enough to shiver or weep,
that's when you feel it, that's when you say
'I'm cold'.

But I was not.

Gone beyond it, gone
into
blue, I would say.

A bit like the kind of goodbye
you will never describe to anyone,
but let me say there was a white door
and herself
and goodbye
and splitting forever and maybe for good
and that walk by the poisoned Irish Sea
gifting cancer to children
like an evil Santa who'll never rest
till the cries fill his blood
and he sinks to rest
like a malignant sun drowned in the West.

How cold is a drowning sun?

Pluck it out of the heavens
drown it in the poisoned seas
of the world of men who never have time
to sit in Stephen's Green
and gaze at Dublin
from an altitude hard to believe
but easy so easy to love.

It was the first time I looked down
at the sun.

It was floundering, gasping,
struggling to light, dying to shine,
drowning.

It was the first time I saw the sun drowning.

'Save it,' I cried to the man made of rain.

He did.

I looked. The sun was over my head.

Thanks be to God, I said, that's the right place for it.

How long will it be
till all the seas
are one poisoned sea

and what'll we call it then?

She's gone forever
behind the white door.

It's cold, this side of the white door,
so cold it's four o'clock in the morning,
five ducks squatting on the dark waters of the canal,
light in the darkness of water a privilege, a woman
talking to herself on Baggot Street Bridge,
a man cycling so slowly it might be
a summer's day with men gathering hay
in a sweating meadow, houses asleep now
in the freezing nightlight, Joe Tandy bundled up
in *Heralds* and *Independents* in the doorway
of Superquinn, the streets unmolested by people
except myself and other sleepless things, the statue
of Oscar Wilde nice an' lazy in Merrion Square,
cold enough for every window of Holles Street
Hospital to be shut tight as tomorrow or
the old judge's mind to Manning all swaddled in limestone,
streets beckoning, opening up like veins
I must go through again and again, cold
as they were in the eighteenth century
of classic beauty, heroic couplets, Penal Laws,
handsome houses becoming perfect slums,
cold of history, cold facts, can't dispute them,
the statues are there to prove whatever
statues prove, how cold is Oliver Goldsmith
this morning, how cold is Edmund Burke,
how cold is the man made of rain?

The edge of the scythe is cold
the lips of my father's corpse are cold
winter mud is cold
the silence of splitting is cold
the white door is cold.

He flowed beside me.

'You can't even shiver,' he said.
'Ill teach you to shiver again.
I'll teach you to weep.
Shiver and weep.
Are you ready to learn?'

'I'm not cold,' I said.

'You don't feel cold?' he queried.

'No.'
'That's the cold I want you to know,' he said.
'The cold you cannot feel
or will not feel
or do not dare to feel.'

'If I can't feel it
how can I know it?' I asked.

'Trust me,' he said. 'Will you trust me?'

'Into the belly of eternity,' I replied.
'But how can I know?'

He smiled. 'When you are me.'

'When's that?'

'How shall we clean the sea?'

'Don't ask me. The thought of it is enough...
to make me... make me...'

'To make you shiver?'

'Yes.'

'You must be cold.'

'Yes. With anger, bafflement, a block
of icy rage'.

'Good. It's time to go back down
to Dublin town, there's no cold like the cold
of not knowing how cold the heart has grown'.

'What are we doing up here?' I asked.

'Strolling through Stephen's Green,' he replied.

'I'd almost forgotten,' I said.
'Where have we been?'

'Looking down at the drowning sun
Listening to the sun's death-rattle.
That's all.'

The man made of rain looked at the sky.
Darkwhite. Coldwet. Sharp blue light,
the kind that makes me feel I'm free,
the sun in its proper place, as far as I could see,
not far, but far enough for me.

He began to walk away.
'Goodbye for now,' he said. 'You'll sleep tonight.'

He swallowed, or was swallowed by
the trueblue light.

38

Many a man carries a lunatic asylum
on his neck and shoulders
and has the gumption to call it his head.
'You could be returning into what they call
the real world,' he said.
'The real people are waiting for you
to judge, advise, prophesy, explain.
That's the goodness of the heart.
The real people know the truest language
and the most effective way to think.
Depart from that, you're in
the provinces of lost,
the diaspora of the bucking moon.
But don't worry, you'll be with
the real people soon.'

There's an irony at work I cannot fathom.
You never had a penny so let your kingdom come.

'I know I'm going back,' I said
'along the Via Blackrockia
via Sandycove and Dalkey
and the waves of Bullock Harbour
to the real world
where the devil has a mobile phone
and God a walkie-talkie.'

'Don't forget to change your trousers,' he said,
'Your arse is peeking out
like an astounded face
witnessing the first copulation
of Adam and Eve
in the shade of the old appletree
in that blameless tempting paradisal place
where they paid no rent
until they stalked each other with foul intent.'

'How do I know the time to leave,
to reach the real world,' I asked.

'Your father'll tell you.'

'He's dead.'

'Your father'll tell you.'

'Will I ever see you again?'
'You will.'

'Where?'

'I'll be pouring down and around
in your bucking head.'

'And how long will you stay
pouring
down and around
in my bucking head?'

'How long would you like?'

'Until the end.'

'The end happened before you were born
but if you believe there's an end to come,
I'll stay.'

'You'll stay? In the real world? Why?'

'Say I could be your friend.'

39

Pain has a weather of its own
Pain knocks at the skull and slips in
Pain smiles at the child and hovers
Pain can be shy and then turn Hitler
Pain aches for a place in my heart
and who am I to deny it?

40

There's a small room between remembering and forgetting
where tulips live longer
than in most other rooms.
I don't own it, it doesn't own me,
it allows me to remember and forget
as I will, as they will.
It is bare and welcoming, in its way,
nobody is ever there to stay, including me.
This is what it means to be free.
Remember that. Forget it.
Free is a million ways, a wild style,
one way is enough for the moment
and would I know freedom if I
met it in the street?

Pain turns memory into a flood
of knowledge and ignorance.
This flood is the reason for the dance.
If I can't answer the question, Who is God?
I'm for the stick.
Children need the stick, Mulcahy said.
It's the stick that makes 'em dance.
It's the dance that makes 'em happy.

Rosie Keogh throws her bicycle
on the side of the road, September blackberries,
points towards the graveyard and says
'That fella Yeats is buried in there.
They all laughed at him around here.
He believed in the fairies.'

Two miles outside Banagher, Corrigan turns his car
and drives back.

The road is wet, he steps on the gas.
''Tis twenty to eight,' he mutters,
'and I didn't get
my Lotto ticket yet.
This could be my night.'

Galvin's wife is half-woman, half-man.
He found out on his wedding night.
He was a sad eejit after that.
Never allowed to forget.
They sniggered at him in the street.

So what if I remember
what never happened
but is more vicious or foolish in memory
than if it had?
Deceives, animates, wearies me as well.
Memory laughs all the way to hell.

I look into the eyes of the man of rain.
I will not say I know what I see.
I will not remember, I will not forget,
I will let
whatever happens
happen to me,
I will let
what I know of the happy dance
lie down with my agony.

After that, I'll see.

41

'Come back! Please come back!' I begged my mind
'And I promise I'll behave.'
'Behave!' my mind spat, 'Didn't I just see you
rambling up and down your father's grave!'

'Is that all you saw?' I asked. 'Yes,' darted my mind,
'I saw what could be seen, it was perfectly clear.'
'There was more to it than that,' I said. 'You sick nut,'
rapped my mind, 'Shut up! I'm getting out of here!'

My mind took off down the hill of blood
running full pelt through the morning.
It looked back once, saw a real sick nut
seeing a bright, informed, frightened thing.

42

I see the wounded sky
    this bluebright morning
        (such cold, such network cold)

and though the sky is bleeding
    the wound, slowly and shyly,
        begins to sing

filling the silent trenches
    above the witnessing counties,
        above my right and wrong,

above money and killing
    and sacredly useless poetry
        faltering into song.

The wound reaches the sun,
    reassures it as it
        hangs trembling

over Dublin and graffiti
    proclaiming
        fiercely secret loving

and gas couplings in Killarney Street.
    The grateful sun accepts
        the wound's comforting

touch, shining, exploring
    corners it has ignored   forgotten
        since Eden morning.

The wound of love's the most living thing
    in mugging streets of greed.
        I watch it bleeding

there where wings come clattering
    to my window,
        raindrops glittering

like jewels flung to celebrate
    the wound's bloodwonder,
        mild thunder in my heart and head

as I move all of me
    to drop on the waiting windowsill
        small bits of bread.

43

'Say I could be your friend.'

I brought that back from the jungle.

'What do you mean?' I asked.

'If your scars are made of fear, tell me,' he said.
'If there's anything you fear to say, tell me.
Pour all you are and think and feel and dream
into my rain. Telling is learning to drown
in my rain. Say I could be your friend.
Mankind. Do you like that word? These words?
Man. Kind. I like to go raining in the jungle.'

'I like to walk the streets,' I said.

'Could be you will again,' he said.
'Why do you like walking the streets?'

'Variety,' I replied. 'Faces. Eyes. Smiles. Half-smiles.
Averted eyes. Thin, wispy perfumes of fear.
Whatever points to something I've met somewhere
in the jungle under the skin.'

I looked at him. For the first time, I looked closely
at his heart of rain.
My heart was beating again
like the hearts of those in the real world.
His heart of rain beat too, a rhythm
planets imitate and stars will dance to,

neglected, far stars dancing
in the high wide stage of the sky.
Anne-Marie loves Buffo. I read that
scrawled on a wall. Ann-Marie is shy.
Buffo doesn't know. Dance with me, Buffo.
Dance with Ann-Marie.

The rain in his heart is not straight down
but slanting, firm, clear and clean.
The rain on Dublin
has a special poison
but the rain in his heart
is the heavens' own rain.

I want to walk in it, I want to walk
through the rain
in the heart of the man of rain.
He looks at me, reads my obvious brain.

'Come on,' he said 'Walk through my heart.'

Ann-Marie is shy. Dance with me, Buffo.

I'm walking through his heart,
a heart my heart says will not harbour lies,
unlike mine.

Such light, such dancing light, such clear skies.
His rain is pouring through my eyes,
tired years are falling out of my eyes,
falling at my feet, the rain falls on them,
God in heaven, swans in the canal,
these years are turning fresh again,
I hope someone comes along and finds them,
in the heart of rain I know I can share
anything with anyone, in the heart of rain
love is particular and fluent, why am I
talking about love, I never knew much
about it for Christ's sake, it's falling
all around, through me, it wants to live,
what's killing it, don't ask, I never knew
much about it, glimpses of love when love
didn't know I was looking, or did it, does love know
all about lookers-on, does it take pity
on eyes that speak impoverished hearts,
on hearts afraid to love, on hearts

that die for want of telling in the heart of rain,
I'm walking now, this heart is endless,
it stretches away as far as I believe
I see, and farther, farther than the suckling
whale making it from warm Mexico
to freezing waters eleven thousand miles away,
farther than that, walking through rain,
cool joy, happy dance, Ann-Marie loves Buffo,
walking through this heart that's beating
for the stars' pleasure and my soul's poverty,
this heart is fun, is lightning, is what makes the Atlantic
wild and mighty for a worker in September
when it's time to say thank you to the sun
for work well done, the harvest won,
I'm walking still, something is having mercy
on me, walking where a dream might flag,
some things are wilder than the wildest dream,

I'm walking in the hills that tap their feet
for dancing streets that I will walk again,
I hope, I hope, this moment living in the heart of rain,
heart of the man of rain, no lies, no lies tonight,
such light, such dancing light, clear skies.

Where is he?

Foot of the bed.

Where am I?

Here. Lying here.

Why am I dreaming of streets?

He's silent now, I walked through his heart,
will he ever speak to me again,
how must he feel, now that I've trampled his heart?

I make to close my eyes, they're already closed.

The tide is in.

Talk to me, man of rain.

I love you.

Anne-Marie loves Buffo. That love
is writ on heaven's floor
on a wall in Protestant Row
off Wexford Street
in Dublin.

Hard to imagine myself walking again
but if I do
I'll study the signs, consider the evidence,
wondering

what did they do with all that blood,
wondering

which way will I go, which street, which road?
Will he be there?
Will he come again?

Will he lead me where
my dreams won't venture?
What is the cost
of being privileged and lost?

        I thank
           the heart of sickness

        for the man of rain

laughing away from me
  returning
    slipping through me
      like a needle
        a word
          morning ice
            memory blitz
          a knife
        with a mind of its own
          to stab
            cut
          and save
            my life

that, after sixty years,
I wonder at
know little about
sitting here
watching pigeons invigorate themselves
beaks working breast and back and wing
before they test the hardy air
of this March morning.

5

Guff and muscle

Men are fine guff and muscle…
OVERHEARD (DUBLIN)

No Image Fits

I have never seen him and I have never seen
Anyone but him. He is older than the world and he
Is always young. What he says is in every ear
And has never been heard before.
I have tried to kill him in me,
He is in me more than ever.
I saw his hands smashed by dum-dum bullets,
His hands holding the earth are whole and tender.
If I knew what love is I would call him a lover.
Break him like glass, every splinter is wonder.
I had not understood that annihilation
Makes him live with an intensity I cannot understand.
That I cannot understand is the bit of wisdom I have found.
He splits my mind like an axe a tree.
He makes my heart deeper and fuller than my heart will dare to be.
He would make me at home beyond the sky and the black ground,
He would craze me with the light on the brilliant sand,
He is the joy of the first word, the music of the undiscovered human.
Undiscovered! Yet I live as if my music were known.
He is what I cannot lose and cannot find
He is nothing, nothing but body and soul and heart and mind.

> So gentle is he the gentlest air
> Is rough by comparison
> So kind is he I cannot dream
> A kinder man
> So distant is he the farthest star
> Sleeps at my breast
> So near is he the thought of him
> Puts me outside myself
>
> So one with love is he
> I know love is
> Time and eternity
> And all their images.
> No image fits, no rod, no crown.
>
> I brought him down.

The Third Force

The third force grows
Between a man and a woman
When their lives mingle more deeply
Than either knows.

They give to each other what they can give.
Beyond that, it seems they live
Giving everything else to the air
Where the third force grows in silent power
Saying Now it is time to cry
And Now it is time to know
Or to try to begin to know
Every consoling illusion
And what underlies conversation
Of rain whipping the night
And the damp pain in the bones
In rooms where others lived
Their given number of days
In their own forgotten ways.

When the third force decides to laugh,
To spread its particular light,
A man and a woman are happy
Delighting in late-night talk
Alone in the smiling dark
Beyond the world of work
Lurking round morning's corner,
An old wolf without teeth,
All impotence and threat.
The third force lives out its moods
In hearts that would reach each other
Affirming or mocking in one
Love or hate for the other,
Forever sure of itself,
Forever getting stronger,
Eating and drinking the feeling
That knots a man and a woman
In ways we all call human,
Each life a definition
Of the most engrossing loneliness,
Lucid within limits,
At home in the sense of loss,

Ignorant, rhythmical, blind
As this verse.
A man and a woman go their ways
Through streets and rooms of blame and praise
Among the blessingcurse.

Correspondence

I began my correspondence with The Bomb
Because I sensed we were two of a kind.
'Dear Bomb,' I wrote in my opening letter
'Did you ever feel you were going out of your mind?

By that I mean did you ever find yourself
In a place or state where your mind was not?
I hope, dear Bomb, my simple question
Will give you bread and wine for thought.'

'Dear Judas,' responded The Bomb, 'How sweet
Of you to write such a candid letter.
My mind, though my thoughts prowl every road,

Is fine. At times, however, I feel a bit of a wet,
Sitting on my arse, waiting. I'd feel better
If I could do what I'm best at. Explode.'

'Be patient,' I replied, 'There are bright sparks in our hell
Who'll give you the opportunity to show your style.'

Consequences

'When a man explodes, be it in poetry or love
Or at the Annual General Meeting of shareholders
Feeling screwed because they've not profited enough
In Foreign Exchange, there are consequences,'

The Bomb wrote in a thoughtful letter to me.
'Such consequences,' went on The Bomb, 'Can be dire,
Spreading ulcers, causing heart-attacks, oodles of hypertension,
Driving sensitive souls to suicide.

I ponder consequences, overmuch, I think,
But it's all I have to do as I squat here
Like a hunk of Sunday mutton

Wondering what well-trained finger will
Finally, acting on the orders of President Fear,
Push the button.'

A Teeny Bit

'If even a teeny bit of me exploded over London,'
Wrote The Bomb one frantic Christmas Eve
On the back of an expensive card,
'Those who'd still be capable of grief

Might see, had they their eyes and
Sufficient thickness of skin and underlying
Tissue, steel surfaces melt, concrete explode,
Fire having a heyday, bridges
And multi-storey buildings destroyed.

And someone somewhere would be overjoyed

To see the tourist industry badly hit,
The class-structure dismantled. Worst of all
Would be the total loss of hope

Not unlike yourself, you miserable shit
When you tried to cope with your treacherous soul
And solved nothing with your coarse rope.'

Saint Augustine on God

What do I love when I love God?
   Not a thinker, profound and wise,
not a bright shock of light
   mesmerising my eyes

not a song capturing my heart
    not flowers and spices
not bread and honey
    not limbs loved all night:

I love none of these when I love my God.

    Yet I love a kind of light
a kind of voice   a kind of scent
    a kind of food   a long embrace

when I love God:

light, voice, scent, food,
embrace of this inner man
whose fire defines who I am
and nothing can put down.

A voice speaks defying time
    a fragrance concentrates no wind can break
a flavour lives no hunger kills
    in a strong embrace that cannot grow weak:

it is this I love when I love my God.

    I asked the earth first, 'Are you this?'
The earth replied 'I am not it.'
    All things on land spoke with this voice.

I asked the sea, pit of creeping things
    without a name. They said
'We are not God, go somewhere else,
    ask what is above your head.'

I asked the winds, the winds replied
    'Anaximenes? He was wrong.
We are not God.' I asked moon, stars, sun.
    'We are not God,' came sharp and strong.

I asked nothingeverything, 'Who is my God
    summoning me with such a call?'
All voices became one voice. It said
    'Who made us all?'

The Sin

Francis Xavier Skinner committed a sin.

It was a big sin, he thought,
A whopper,
An Everest of error,
A mortaller, as the man said,
Thinking of the price he'd have to pay when dead.

Skinner said to himself,
By this sin
I have wounded an innocent God.
I, Francis Xavier Skinner, have offended
The God of love.
That same God
Made everything that has been made.
But I have wounded him.

Skinner, a philosophical chap,
Considered it fit
To congratulate himself
On this extraordinary feat.
I cannot impress my friends, he thought,
But I can wound the God of love.
There's power for you!

And then he wondered,
What has happened to my sin?
Where has my big sin vanished?
Where have all the sins of the world vanished?
Is there a place where they go to hide?
Where does a fugitive sin reside?
Somewhere in hell perhaps
There's a sin-hospital
Where all the sins go to recover
From their conflict with God.
Do sins get bored and tired?
Do they play scrabble, ludo, draughts or dominoes?
Do they like to lie on the ground like winos
Outside a church on a Sunday morning
Begging pennies from respectable ladies
Whose souls are wrapped in their coats
Like mackerel in newspaper, their dead eyes
Old coins in the light, yesterday's news

Garbled in their skin,
Earthquakes shuddering in dandruff?
And then, having rested, do the sins get to their feet,
Amble off into the heart of some poor human
Who'll commit them all over again, as though for the first time,

Adam how-are-you?
And if one sin hurts God
What does he feel like after a million?
In a pretty bad way, I'd imagine,
Licking his wounds
Stretched on the floor of heaven,
Wondering
Is there any end to this damned repetition?
My divine arse is bored
By men who have murdered and lied
And thieved and deceived and whored
Ad nauseam.
I am bored. Therefore, I am.
O for a sin
Original
New
A sin
That will make my heart leap up to itself
My head spin
Down to You
Until I stand in the morning
Of my first creative excitement
On this dear dung-heap of a world
Calling
Cock-a-Doodle-Do.

Thoughtful soul that he was, Skinner wondered
What did that old excited God
Feel like
After my sin.
That shook him, I bet.
That gave him something to think about.

Did it really,
Did my sin hurt
The maker of the grass and the sea
The giver of my every heartbeat
The sweet creator of light
The image-maker in the dark
The fountain of grace and of truth
The first call of the cock in the morning

The last cry of my frightened mind?
Did my sin really hurt
Him?

Now that I think of it
I suspect my creator
May well be amused
By my sin.
Skinner, old son, you're a laughing-stock,
God smiles in the pleasant morning
Frowns in the storm
And if he ever noticed my sin
He was probably touched by its
Smallness, like a little bitchy insult
In a lost conversation.

I wonder, mused Skinner, is it possible
To be anything other than trivial?
Did I create Hell
To flatter my vanity?
How could any sin of mine
Be worthy of that Hell?
Hell is viciously divine!
Hell has such high standards
Though it is a low dive
Where all the unsaveable baddies
Get roasted alive.
Is all
My sinning
My own refusal to know
I am small?
Is there a sin
That God respects?
He must have respected Adam,
He threw him out of the garden,
But I won't imitate Adam.
When a sin is original
Imitation is fatal.
Mortal man is a spit in the wind.
Who cares how mortally he has sinned?

My trouble, said Skinner, is
I'm quite incapable of sin
On an honestly damnable scale.
I'm just another dwarfish vain male,
A puny son-of-a-bitch,
A spiritually juvenile offender.

I'll pray to my maker
To give me the vision
To commit a significant sin.

Dear God,
Give me the grace
To be a true sinner.

I'll be grateful forever.

Yours sincerely in Christ,

Francis Xavier Skinner.

Adam

Two loves were quite enough, herself and God,
(God knows how hard it was to have to choose!)
Green shoots of innocence sprang from the sod,
Wild tendrils whispered that he couldn't lose.
High disobedience roared through his blood,
His heart beat faster, suddenly stood still,
He found another way beyond the good
And little doubts, like puddles, stained his will.
A graceful world snapped, an axis jarred,
Long, shabby fields appeared, the sunlight thinned
In places under skies become ill-starred
Through rage of storm and ice and cold and wind
He, darkly conscious, touched her darkened will,
Grew grim, suspicious, furtive; loved her still.

I Saw a Beautiful Man

I saw a beautiful man and he
Was uglier than me or you
He was a beautiful man because I
Had the eyes to see him true
And then my eyes went blind a while
I saw a mean man standing there
With lips like snakes, his eyes snake's eyes,
Snakespittle dribbling from his hair.

Then I slept, sleep changed my eyes,
My eyes were cleaned, I saw again
The beautiful man
Standing there, happy and wise
For those who had eyes to see.
What strikes his eyes when he looks through me?

Saint Augustine's toe

He heard her pray that her soul
would be so pure 'twould make the snow look black.
She leaned forward and kissed
Saint Augustine's toe.

A hard man, by all accounts, quick
to take a rub o' the relic himself
before he repented and said his prayers.

She's off to get a chicken from the butchers.
Nine mouths to feed, nine bodies and souls
to fight another winter.

A Man of Faith

'Buff,' said Oliver, 'some poor sad prattling priest
May have spoken to you of faith,
Thinking your soul might work towards its best
And understand God's reasons for death.
Your poor sad prattling priest was right, or partly so.
This gutless age sinsickens in disbelief,
Only a man of faith will do, will rise and do
What he must do, be it smooth or rough.
A man of faith is a ready blade
Cutting through the bluster of himself, his time,
Friends, enemies. He lives for what is true
In himself. I am such a man, not more, not less.
Some say my faith is lies, my best deeds crimes.
I believe in God Who believes in what I do.'

Who Killed the Man?

Was he sitting in a car in a suburban street
reading a paper
or did they shoot him dead
asleep in bed?

No, he is trying to cross a ditch
at the side of a country road.
The truck's headlights select him in the darkness
he's dead clambering
a boy clawing a cliff's face for birds' eggs.

'Fling 'im in the back o' the truck, lads.
We'll ditch 'im near 'is 'ome
mustn't let 'im get lost
make it easy for 'em to find 'im
he'll be 'ome, never more to roam.'

Sixty years from now and then
villagers are gathered to commemorate
the deadinaditch.
Each man has a three-pronged pike.
Each pike bears a flaming sod.
There's a smell of paraffin in the air.
It is the freezing sixth of November,
time to march
the black country road
to the spot
where he was shot.

Yes, he was shot, we all know that,
but who killed the man?
March march march
through the dark dark dark
let the speeches be made
(there's a Big Man here tonight)
the prayers be said for the dead
in freezing November.

What is it they think?
What is it they remember?
What is it they think they remember?
The truck, it is agreed, where he was thrown to bleed
was a Crossley Tender.

Or did they fling him in an ass's cart?
A black ass dragged a dead man's heart.
'Sit up, old boy, don't be so bloody dumb,
ride on an ass's back
into Jerusalem.'

No one stands in the cold too long.
Time for a drink and a song.
Killigan names the dead
lifts his beads on high
appropriate rage and grief in his eye
rattles it out
lust in his throat
Mother of Christ
Star of the sea
pray for the wanderer
pray for me.

It is three o'clock in the morning.
Where are the faces the flames
the passionate words in the freezing dark
the paraffin-smell
the pikes the prayers the naming of names
the wishing of souls to heaven and hell
eternity twisted and tickled by time
that crawled slithered slouched shambled ran?

Who killed the man?

Who killed the man?

Baile Bocht

Outside the pub the killer stands
death dumbfounding his victim's eyes.
Dionysiac applause
bombs the Hogan and the Cusack Stands.

Shy

Lar was as shy a man as ever broke bread
Who found it difficult to talk to men;
If you addressed him he turned away his head,
His mouth was dumb, his dark eyes spoke their pain.
You'd hardly notice when he'd come or gone
In any company where things were said,
But sometimes if you walked abroad at dawn
You'd see him striding freely down the road,

Two bounding limber hounds on either side,
Mad for the kill. When they bared teeth and snapped
At each other, growing bolder, bolder
Every second, Lar spoke. The hounds calmed at his word.
Hours later, silent, they returned. Lar walked
At their heads, fox and hare flung on his shoulder.

Needles

An alder twig will bend and yet not break,
The right material to make a cage.
In winter Noonan watched the snow flake
At his window, the sleet spit its cold grudge
At the world. He stripped an alder tree,
Wove the lithe twigs patiently until
A little prison stood in the snow,
Breadcrumbs within. Three birds fell

For the bait. Two he released, kept the third,
A thrush whose heart beat faster than any man's.
Noonan held it in his fist, looked long
And long. Two red-hot needles he shoved hard
Through its eyes, explaining later that
A blinded bird will sing a sweeter song.

The Grip

In Moynihan's meadow
The badger turned on the hound
And gripped.

The hound bit and tore
At the badger's body;
Harder, harder,
The badger gripped.

The men ran up.
O'Carroll shouted 'Quick! Quick! Crack a stick.'

The stick cracked.
Deceived,
The iron jaws relaxed.

The hurt hound bit in fury.
Again the badger
Gripped.
The neck, this time.

No loosening now.
Fangs tightened in a fierce embrace
Of vein and sinew.
No complex expertise, no difficult method,
No subtle undermining, no lying guile,

Only the simple savage style
As the hound weakened, slumped, died.
The white teeth parted
Red with the fresh blood.

The men watched him turn,
Head for a hedge,
Low grey killer,
Skin ripped from sides, back, head, neck.

O'Carroll prodded the dead hound
With a blackthorn stick,
Said, more to himself than to others
Standing there –

'A hundred hurts are bad
But a good grip
Will break the heart
Of the best hound in the land.'

Cock

Dee was small and squat, built all on the ground.
Strength bulged in his shoulders, legs and back.
I watched him take the thick brush in his hand,
Test the long handle, shove the cock's neck
Under it as it stretched on the kitchen floor,
Mutter his guttural words to the bird's weird
Awk! Awk! that choked as Dee stepped on either
End of the handle, his packed weight pressed hard

As a boulder on the cock's neck, the claws
Frantic in his fist. For five seconds he
Stood frozen, eyes fixed on the trapped head.
Then he jerked the red body viciously
Once, twice, three times. It seemed the cock was
Stretched beyond itself. Dee dropped it on the brush, dead.

The Pig-killer

On the scoured table, the pig lies
On its back, its legs held down
By Ned Gorman and Joe Dineen.
Over its throat, knife in hand, towers

Fitzmaurice, coatless, his face and hands
Brown as wet hay. He has travelled
Seven miles for this kill and now,
Eager to do a good job, examines

The prone bulk. Tenderly his fingers move
On the flabby neck, seeking the right spot
For the knife. Finding it, he leans
Nearer and nearer the waiting throat,

Expert fingers fondling flesh. Nodding then
To Gorman and Dineen, he raises the knife,
Begins to trace a line along the throat.
Slowly the line turns red, the first sign

Of blood appears, spreads shyly over the skin. The pig
Begins to scream. Fitzmaurice halts his blade
In the middle of the red line, lifts it slightly,
Plunges it eight inches deep

Into the pig. In a flash, the brown hands
Are red, and the pig's screams
Rise and fall with the leaping blood. The great heaving
Body relaxes for Gorman and Dineen.

Fitzmaurice stands back, lays his knife on
A window-sill, asks for hot water and soap.
Blade and hands he vigorously purges, then
Slipping on his battered coat,

Eyeing the pig, says with authority –
'Dead as a doornail! Still as a mouse!
There's a good winter's feedin' in that baishte!'
Fitzmaurice turns and strides into the house.

The Pig

You, Heavenly Muse, how will you justify
The pig's ways to men?
How will you sing
Of the pig's origin?
What thighs opened wide
To let out that snout
Rammed on a carcase of timeless slime?
When the old sly juices went to work
What womb
Sheltered our little darling?
What breasts
Gave it suck?

Suck, suck.

And on our treacherous planet
What hearts worry for its welfare?

The pig is everywhere.

He grunts between the lovers in their bed
His hot sperm flooding the girl
His dungeon breath rutting into her skin
Where a man's fingers move in what he thinks
Are patterns of enchantment.
The pig's eyes smile in the dark.

The pig's eyes glow with ambition.
He knows that where his head won't go
His tail will enter,
His little corkscrew tail.

The pig sits on committees,
Hums and haws, grunts yes and no,
Is patient, wise, attentive,
Wary of decision (alternatives are many)
When he hefts his bottom from the chair
The seat is hot.
His head is dull
But, maybe, he's just a little stronger now.

The pig knows how to apologise.
He would hurt nobody.
If he did, he didn't mean it.
His small eyes redden with conviction.
Remorse falls like saliva from his jaws.

The pig is bored
But doesn't know it.
The pig gobbles time
And loves the weekend.
The pig is important
And always says 'It seems to me' and 'Yes, let's face it'.
The pig chews borrowed words,
Munching conscientiously.
Sometimes he thinks he's a prophet, a seer so elegant
That we should bow before him.
He is more remote from a sense of the unutterable
Than any words could begin to suggest.

The pig knows he has made the world.
Mention the possibility of something beyond it –
He farts in your face.

The pig's deepest sty is under his skin.
His skin is elegantly clad.

The pig knows might is right.
The pig is polite.

The pig is responsible and subtle.
How can this be so?
I don't know, but I have seen the pig at work
And know the truth of what I see.

The pig has lived in me

And gone his way, snouting the muck
In the wide sty of the world.

His appetite for filth is monstrous
And he knows
There is more sustenance in filth
Than in the sweet feast at the white table
Where friends gather for a night
Talk and laugh
In a room with warm light.

The pig might enter that room
And swallow everything in sight.

But the pig's sense of timing
Is flawless.
His own throat is fat, ready to cut,
But no one will do that.
Instead, the pig will slit
Some other throat.
There will be no blood but a death,
The pig will hump into the future

Huge
Hot
Effective

His eyes darting like blackbirds for the worm
Waiting to be stabbed, plucked, gulped,
Forgotten.

And still our darling lives
As though there were no
Oblivion.

Time for the Knife

'You've a good one there,' Enright said.
Morrissey asked 'Is he right for cutting yet?'
Enright lifted the terrier pup in his fist
Slid the skin back on the gums
Fingered the neat fangs.

Caressing the brown and white head,
He handled the terrier's tail.

'Time for the knife,' he said.

The penknife from his waistcoat pocket
Flicked open. Twenty years of cutting tobacco
Had merely dented the blade.

'Let you hold the head.'
Morrissey gripped the skin behind the ears.

After he'd sharpened the knife on a stone
Enright stretched the tail
And started to cut.

It was over soon. Enright looked
At the severed tail in his fist
And pitched it into the grass.

The terrier pup
Howled as it fled,
Pursued by drops of its own blood
Regular as a pulse of pain.

For a while
It whimpered and cried alone
Like a woman mourning.

When the bleeding stopped
The stubby tail stuck up
Like a blunt warning.

The Tippler

Out of the clean bones
He tipples a hard music.
Cocking his head,
He knows himself sole master of his trade.
Hence his pride.

A goat ran wild
Through field and hillside,
Was tracked, caught, tethered, tamed,
Butchered and no man cried.
And the Tippler got his bones.

All bones dry in the sun,
Harden to browny white,
Mere flesh stripped and gone;
But bones create a new delight
When clacked by the proper man.

Let flesh lie rotten
When the Tippler takes his stand,
Holds the bones between his fingers;
Death has given him command,
Permitted him his hunger,

Made his heart articulate,
Tender, proud,
Clacking at shoulder, chest and head.
That man is for a while unbowed
Who brings music from the dead.

Work

Blood will cling for days to the skin of a goat.
Jackety took the hide in his hands, pulled hard,
Then let it dry. He rounded pliant wood,
Fastidiously chipped and tacked until he got
A perfect ring. Corked wire for the grip
Of a fist and then he stretched the dried skin
Around the ring. He tacked again,
Hard, until the circle was closed up.

He gripped wire in his left hand, with his right
He touched the taut face stretched to breaking point
Knowing, as he tested, the work was good;
He bunched his right fist then and hit
The bottom, top and centre – the tambourine
Echoed the clean, sweet beat of his blood.

Man Making Fire

Wizened branches crackle and burn
And the red flames flicker like tongues
At the gapped hide of burly thorn.

Lately fallen November snow
Recedes from the jubilant circle of fire
Blackening ground where tame grass used to grow.

O man piling branches on to the fire,
Pile branches, pile branches, until the sky's floor
Burns bright with your flame, high flame of desire.

Red flame stretched aloft like the neck of a hound
Surpasses itself in devouring the grass,
In embracing the air, in outstripping the ground.

See how he sweats as he steps near the fire,
Tight fingers of heat contracting his skin
As he urges the flames leaping higher and higher.

And now in the heat that bullies the sun,
The afternoon glories to see how the flame
And the branch-bearing man are made violently one.

He burns like the flame! Like the heart of the fire!
In the core of this wintry miraculous day
He flames like a god at the height of desire!

And it dies; the fire is a dozen small fires;
The man shudders quickly, the branches are ash,
And gloom shuffles in as the evening expires.

The King

During all summer calms and winter rages
And seasons when you'd be hard put to tell
If the next moment would be ill or well
The King kept singing birds in home-made cages.
And in this court of melody he sat
Smiling on coloured singers, his proud head
Aloof from the living, aware of the wise dead;
'Only a burst of birdsong's pure: that's that' –

Pronounced his Majesty. If you loved a bird
He stripped the wall, gave you cage and all;
No money; enough you loved to hear it sing;
When a bird died he hit the bottle hard,
Neglected all the other birds a stricken while
Until he died. He died. Long live the King.

The Thatcher

He whittled scallops for a hardy thatch,
His palm and fingers hard as the bog oak.
You'd see him of an evening, crouched
Under a tree, testing a branch. If it broke
He grunted in contempt and flung it away,
But if it stood the stretch, his sunken blue
Eyes briefly smiled. Then with his long knife he
Chipped, slashed, pointed. The pile of scallops grew.

Astride a house on a promised day,
He rammed and patted scallops into place
Though wind cut his eyes till he seemed to weep.
Like a god after making a world, his face
Grave with the secret, he'd stare and say –
'Let the wind rip and the rain pelt. This'll keep.'

The Swimmer

For him the Shannon opens
Like a woman.
He has stepped over the stones

And cut the water
With his body
But this river does not bleed for

Any man. How easily
He mounts the waves, riding them
As though they

Whispered subtle invitations to his skin,
Conspiring with the sun
To offer him

A white, wet rhythm. The deep beneath
Gives full support
To the marriage of wave and heart.

The waves he breaks turn back to stare
At the repeated ceremony
And the hills of Clare

Witness the fluent weddings
The flawless congregation
The choiring foam that sings

To limbs which must, once more,
Rising and falling in the sun,
Return to shore.

Again he walks upon the stones,
A new music in his heart,
A river in his bones

Flowing forever through his head
Private as a grave
Or as the bridal bed.

Special Thunder

He had to reach the island in the winter gale.
From Saleen Quay he pushed the little boat
Over the rough stones till she came afloat;
You'd swear he could see nothing when he hoisted sail
And cut the dark. Once a grey shape blurred
Above his head while pitchblack water slapped
And tried to climb over the side but dropped
Into the sea, thwarted. In time, he heard

The special thunder of the island shore,
He hauled the boat in, sheltered near a rock
And smiled to hear the sea's defeated roar;
Breathing as though the air were infinitely sweet,
He watched the mainland where the hard wind struck.
The island clay felt good beneath his feet.

The Runner

The truest poetry lies
Just now
On a runner's rainy thighs

While at his head
White rings of breath
Break with his stride.

Winter trees, the windy cries
Of seabirds blown inland
Are witness

To every move he makes.
I wish him well
Whatever barriers he breaks.

He runs towards a freedom
Desired by every man
But always there, ahead of him,

Freedom runs on swifter feet.
He runs with the joy of losing
Yet plucks a sweet

251

Gift from the air.
When he stops
The gift's no longer there.

I think that in his mind
He runs forever
Out of the green field. Now he is blind

With joy, striding a mountain path,
A morning beach
Hard from the sea's creative wrath,

A heavy suburb, a country road
Where rough welcome
Lives in his blood.

Yet even there, or anywhere,
He runs to lose.
On the winter air

Nothing can be seen
But fragile rings of white
Breaking on the green.

All the time in the world

Bell was a hedger, a man of 'might' and 'may'.
Distrusting every glib finality,
He parried questions in his cagey way,
Sidestepped decision indecisively.
'Rain from the north tonight!' 'Ay-ah,' he'd say,
Meaning maybe, and gave no reason why
You should expect him to say yes or no.
Rumoured once he'd cancer and must die

Inside three months. When he went to Dublin
And was back at home within a week
The thing was certain. Death – too plain to see.
MacDonagh dared to ask the brutal question
And got his answer, lazily. Bell took
All the time in the world. 'Could be. Could be.'

That Look

Jack Scanlon heard the scrape at the back door.
The rat was in the yard outside.
He went out front, untied the wire terrier,
Opened the back door, gave the dog his head.
The scraping stopped, no sound for a while,
A tension grew, the snarling started then,
A throaty menace hard and full.
Scanlon stepped into the sun,
Saw the rat cornered near a wall,
The terrier crouched, head down, fangs clean
As knives in the light. Scanlon moved three paces
As if to give command. With a growl
The terrier killed the fear and hate in
The rat's eyes. I've seen that look in people's faces.

A Man in Smoke Remembered

A man in smoke remembered
Lifts his head
From the silence of the dead
And here, beside a fire
Packed to battle a winter,
Lifts a hammer
Takes a tack from between his lips
Thumbs it into place in the cut leather
And beats it home.

What is memory but cutting through smoke?
How well did I know him living?
He lives now, real as rock
In my mind.
His grey head chuckles through smoke
His stories stand up and laugh in smoke
His words are small bright nails
Lit by flames
Dancing in the corner of a smoky room.

He will die alone in a home for the old.
In a garden
Which he chooses to ignore
He sits on a green bench
Glad of a noggin of whiskey.

Leaving the whole crowd behind
Was not as bad a wrench
As he'd imagined it might be,
But he doesn't like the other old people
And complains that they complain too much
Especially of callous families
Who take care of themselves alone
And know how to forget
Long summers, long winters
That put them in an old man's debt.

He will chuckle to the end
And fiercely scratch his head when brooding.
This is the last time I'll see my friend
Until I see him in smoke
Twenty years through the fire.
Again it is winter
And he is chuckling
With more self-delight than ever.
He sits across the hearth from me
For an hour, the smoke
Weaving its own stories around his head.
He rises then and shuffles back to the dead.

A Man, But Rarely Mentioned

They spoke more about the killing frost
Of January than of him.
Every tongue was dumb
When it came to mentioning his name.
The road of agreed silence
Led to oblivion.

Con. Con.

The boy tasted the sad
Syllable in the dark
Until the word was a pool
Where he cooled his fevered mind.
The pool formed from a shy river
Among stones in high ground,
Legends of drownings
Grew like grass at its edges,

Dark stones like unblinking eyes
Stared from the depths,
Revealing nothing.
But the boy knew it was there
He must go for news of the man
Who was rarely mentioned
And then so briefly
He might not have been mentioned at all.

The boy stared at the pool
And said Con, Con,
Until the man
Smiled from a stone
In the middle of the pool
Saying 'Only a loving fool
Chooses to know what is so forgotten
And not, perhaps, without reason
When one considers the stones of fear
Hurled at men and women.
There are worse things than the repose
Of being ignored
Though why this is so, nobody knows
And nobody should know.
I will live in some corner of your mind
Wherever you go.'

The boy took the stone's word with him
Away from the pool,
Something that had been completely dumb
Was no longer completely dumb.
One sad syllable had spoken.
One chain of wrong was broken.

Night Drive

I

The rain hammered as we drove
Along the road to Limerick.
'Jesus what a night,' Alan breathed
And – 'I wonder how he is, the last account
Was poor.'
I couldn't speak.

The windscreen fumed and blurred, the rain's spit
Lashing the glass. Once or twice
The wind's fist seemed to lift the car
And pitch it hard against the ditch.
Alan straightened out in time,
Silent. Glimpses of the Shannon –
A boiling madhouse roaring for its life
Or any life too near its gaping maw,
White shreds flaring in the waste
Of insane murderous black;
Trees bending in grotesque humility,
Branches scattered on the road, smashed
Beneath the wheels.
Then, ghastly under headlights,
Frogs bellied everywhere, driven
From the swampy fields and meadows,
Bewildered refugees, gorged with terror.
We killed them because we had to,
Their fatness crunched and flattened in the dark.
'How is he now?' Alan whispered
To himself. Behind us,
Carnage of broken frogs.

II

His head
Sweated on the pillow of the white hospital bed.
He spoke a little, said
Outrageously, 'I think I'll make it.'
Another time, he'd rail against the weather,
(Such a night would make him eloquent)
But now, quiet, he gathered his fierce will
To live.

III

Coming home
Alan saw the frogs.
'Look at them, they're everywhere,
Dozens of the bastards dead.'

Minutes later –
'I think he might pull through now.'
Alan, thoughtful at the wheel, was picking out
The homeroad in the flailing rain.
Nighthedges closed on either side.
In the suffocating darkness
I heard the heavy breathing
Of my father's pain.

Oliver to His Brother

Loving brother, I am glad to hear of your welfare
And that our children have so much leisure
They can travel far to eat cherries.
This is most excusable in my daughter
Who loves that fruit and whom I bless.
Tell her I expect she writes often to me
And that she be kept in some exercise.
Cherries and exercise go well together.
I have delivered my son up to you.
I hope you counsel him; he will need it;
I choose to believe he believes what you say.
I send my affection to all your family.
Let sons and daughters be serious; the age requires it.
I have things to do, all in my own way.
For example, I take not kindly to rebels.
Today, in Burford Churchyard, Cornet Thompson
Was led to the place of execution.
He asked for prayers, got them, died well.
After him, a Corporal, brought to the same place
Set his back against the wall and died.
A third chose to look death in the face,
Stood straight, showed no fear, chilled into his pride.
Men die their different ways
And girls eat cherries
In the Christblessed fields of England.
Some weep. Some have cause. Let weep who will.
Whole floods of brine are at their beck and call.
I have work to do in Ireland.

I Wonder Now What Distance

I wonder now what distance
a man should travel to die;
across a road into a house
or two hundred miles in a car
or take off across the Shannon in the *Marianne*
through the beckoning evening?

Or it might involve a long day's work
with or without a machine:

257

hands blackened with oil
hair cluttered with dust
he is a search for running water,
he is a worker, he'll be a worker

till the work stops like the brown-faced clock
he bought at an auction for six pounds.
He got it going, it was his pride,
a most harmonious tick all through the house.
Then it gave up, the hands had a crippled look
as though time itself had died.

You made your journey,
it was the right distance for you.
Passing that roundabout, climbing that slow hill,
your body was a house of stifled cries.
The evening opened its mouth and swallowed the traffic.
You closed your eyes.

That's when you saw what you had to see,
your journey being done.
A mountain raised itself from your heart
and shuffled off like a nightmare visitor, hoping
perhaps to impose itself like a shadow of sadness
across the face of the sun

that journeys day into day without complaining,
like yourself at the end, except to say
'I'm very tired, I'd like a long sleep.'
An August morning was an end to weeping.
Peace found you in your sleeping.
Yours, for safe keeping.

Always

It will always go back
To a big man hunched in pain over a phone,
Smoking, waiting for news from Cork,
A brown envelope containing
Stamps of Sarawak,
Talk, on the landing near the room
Where I awoke, sweating,
Of freak weather hitting the South,
A forefinger touching a scar

Like a sign of friendship
Made after war,
The first taste of blood in the mouth.

It will always go forward
To a man standing over a grave
Acknowledging a woman,
A woman standing over a grave
Acknowledging a man,
Both rotten, having remembered
The privilege of being forgotten
By children, friends, the faithful stone,
The patient acre fertilising every sin,
The river joining the sea's voice
Like the pair of them standing at the door of the house,
'You're welcome, welcome! Come in! Come in!'

The Love of God

A smell of bread in the air,
A fiercely gentle light
On the walls of the Regional Hospital
Where he has come to die
After a rough journey,
His mind breaking like his body
As he asks me to stay the night,
Cork accents flashing like hurleys around me
This Sunday afternoon in late August, seventy-nine
Faces of the sick
Cigarette smoke
Gifts of fruit and drink
Nurses white as Holy Communion children
A little transistor music
From somewhere along the corridor
Leading back to the suffering air
And the healthy people
And this pouring
Pouring
Sense of what needn't be mentioned

Bringing to mind
The gracious, pained man in the train
Reading a letter from his son

Rebelling through France and Spain
Against the father's notion of a man.
'He writes to tell me that I'm blind.
After twenty years, I find
My son is a stranger to me.'

And I see her head
Twisted like a dead bird's on the pillow,
Her fingers
Eaten by the years,
Closing, unclosing on the sheet,
Himself beside her
Pleading through his silence
To her silence.

After fifty years, two silences
Deep as the pain of never knowing
The familiar strangers in the head.
Touch the flesh, the bone, the skin.
The woman is gone.
So is the man.

Here come the children,
A crop of innocence
Emerging from the dead.

And I know
As I move among cities
I am part of the ignorant sea
Rising and falling in me,
Waves chasing each other
Like the blackthorn stickbeats
Of the old sailor, Johnny
The Ducker from nowhere,
Hunched against the wind,
Scarecrow in a garden
To keep the good crop free from harm,
Tea, sugar in his pocket,
Fresh bread under his arm

And from his private station
The faithful blackthorn
Broadcasting his coming and going

Nearing, fading

Insistent codes of night dissolved in morning
Seavoices hinting at their lost meaning
The calm aftermath of suffering
Tiptappings of the blind guides of eternity
In the street of the village
Where I was born.

Missing

Would you doubt him? At the first sign of rain
he's out dragging the ladder from the shed
where in the safe weather it had lain
idle. When the sign becomes a downpour
he stands the ladder against the back wall,
climbs the rain and scours the flooded eaves for
what? Sogged leaves, a starling's corpse, a small
ball green-mossed drop from the sky to the ground

below. Soon as the sun finds heart again
he ransacks every corner of the house
for bits of cardboard, letters, all kinds of paper.
The fire he lights seems part of the man
leaping in and out through his face
so intent, you'd think he didn't miss her.

A Glimpse of Starlings

I expect him any minute now although
He's dead. I know he has been talking
All night to his own dead and now
In the first heart-breaking light of morning
He is struggling into his clothes,
Sipping a cup of tea, fingering a bit of bread,
Eating a small photograph with his eyes.
The questions bang and rattle in his head
Like doors and cannisters the night of a storm.
He doesn't know why his days finished like this
Daylight is as hard to swallow as food
Love is a crumb all of him hungers for.

I can hear the drag of his feet on the concrete path
The close explosion of his smoker's cough
The slow turn of the Yale key in the lock
The door opening to let him in
To what looks like release from what feels like pain
And over his shoulder a glimpse of starlings
Suddenly lifted over field, road and river
Like a fist of black dust pitched in the wind.

Blood

He's dead for months now
And every night I see,
While the old, honest darkness
Is forced to come and go
Like a slave who can never be
Set free,
My own blood flow
Out of my mouth and eyes
Out of my chopped limbs
Scattered like branches after a storm.
The storm will gentle but not die.
My blood aches back to him
Lying in his grey suit on the slab,
His right fist
Black with blood that once
Welcomed the blood of Christ,
His body a battleground
Where young men lie dead.

He couldn't give a continental damn
For all the blood in the world.
If the Atlantic turned to blood
And rose to drown the people he loved
And they floated like dolls or twigs
Or broken branches in the worldsea of blood
Bobbing up and down like corks
In the eyes of God,
He'd ignore it all,
Every final cry, every choking call.
Or so the floating ones
Could they but think
Might think.

All the floating dolls will sink in time.
When, with his new accomplice,
The old, honest darkness,
He visits my sleep,
He is saying something
I will never hear
Though once I gathered that
His soul is a shrewd, leathery old bat
Blindly rejoicing in the coldest corner
Of an old church without a roof,
Shocked with starlight on certain nights.
I'd love it if he smiled
But his face is winter
Chilling my dream
Where my blood to its last drop
Warms back to him
So painfully near
So drifting away
To wander, return, bewilder
My blood,
This living fool crying among stones
Scattered rainspots waiting to dry
Bits of foam thrown here and there
Like half-thoughts of the people I love
Or try to.

A Winter Rose

Happy to speak of intertwining briars
Mingling to breed, let's say, a winter rose
More defiantly beautiful the fouler the weather
Till the world knows what its true nature is
But all I see is an old man standing there
His mind blasted, snot and tears in his face,
His fingers freezing into a shape like prayer,
His words falling to earth the feel of ice –
'God rest you, love! God love you, darling dear!'
Fingers unlock, lips shut, he turns from the grave,
Stumbles on other graves, small grassy hills,
He'll come tomorrow, speak, and will she hear?
He'll come, and come, although his mind must rave
To know she's dead, and time is what he kills.

The Names of the Dead Are Lightning

'All my old friends are dying,'
You say in your letter,
Last night the wind cried

Through the house and the rain
Flailed at the streets and trees.
I thought of your loss

Knowing too well,
If I tried for weeks,
Not a syllable

Would salve your wound.
Tice. Joe. Jackie. Gone.
Father, why does the sound

Of thunder make me seek
The darkest room in the house,
Sit and wait for the blue flick

Of lightning over the walls?
You know how I hate loud voices
But this voice called

As though it would not be denied
From heaven to earth, from earth
To heaven. All night I tried

To decipher its tone of cosmic command
But all I found was your letter
Flickering in my mind

The darkest place I know.
The names of the dead are lightning.
Tice. Jackie. Joe.

I See You Dancing, Father

No sooner downstairs after the night's rest
And in the door
Than you started to dance a step
In the middle of the kitchen floor.

And as you danced
You whistled.
You made your own music
Always in tune with yourself.

Well, nearly always, anyway.
You're buried now
In Lislaughtin Abbey
And whenever I think of you

I go back beyond the old man
Mind and body broken
To find the unbroken man.
It is the moment before the dance begins,

Your lips are enjoying themselves
Whistling an air.
Whatever happens or cannot happen
In the time I have to spare
I see you dancing, father.

Oliver to His Son

'I love you, you are dear to me, so is
Your wife but, my son, you have waxed fat,
You are grown thick, you are buried in fatness,
You have exceeded your allowance and that
Is bad, you fall in debt. If pleasure
Be made the business of a man's life,
So much cost laid out upon it, so much
Time spent in it, as rather answers appetite
Than the will of God with which I am familiar,
I scruple to feed this humour.
Remember this: you are my son, therefore be lean,
I will not support your voluptuous blood,
I will help you to clean your conscience,
I love you, I write as honestly as I can.'

Where Women Pray and Judge

After two hundred miles of snow
I walk into the room
where women pray and judge.

We know all about him.

Child of Mary, corpse in blue,
focus of tears and sighs,
love is what I kiss,
and love is ice.

Oliver to His Daughter

Dear Daughter, I write not to your husband,
One line of mine begets many of his.
This makes him, I fear, sit up too late and
Breaks his sleeping peace.
Seek to see your vanity, your carnal mind.
To be a seeker is next to being a finder.
To taste the Lord, first taste your sour self.
Who can taste Him, and go less in desire?

Dear Heart, press on. Let not your husband
Cool your love of Christ, but let the marriage-bed
Inflame your love of God's own Son.
Love most in your husband what bears the image of Christ.
Look on that, love it best, and all the rest for that.
There is no sweeter reason to love a man.

Blood

I drink the blood of God and I feel good.
How would I feel if I drank the blood of man
Or woman? Drink what you will, what matters is the work,
Responsible intensity of that illusion.
Work is what you do, what you escape into
From to be.

Lie on the floor, praise the cooking, do not eat,
Food is death done beautifully
As the taste of her defeat.
When you meet her again she will tell you
Why Albert is such a bore.
She'd leave him but is amused and almost moved
By his capacity to adore
Her while bequeathing her a measured solitude.
Wine, dear God, more wine she pours, thank God,
Drink God, the miracle slides into the blood.
Mike Shay drank two farms in three years
Singing Hail, Queen of Heaven in his cups
And buying pints for all the neighbours.
He drank Cork gin, Powers, Paddy, Teacher's, Jameson Ten, Haig, Bell's
Black and White and protestant Bush.
He pissed good land away day after day
And when it came he didn't feel the crash
But lay on Kiely's floor moaning over and over
'Jesus Christ, you'd never know a man's mind,
A man's mind, never know a man's mind!'
         When Mike was dragged from the river
He got fair burial in holy ground.
O all the blood he sweated into the land
Yet met a fool's end, they said, though he was canny.
         I drink the blood of God and I feel good
And if Scanlon can't find money
For the next bottle this'll be a bad
Morning, no peace of mind for all the early
Drinkers, tired whores in the dawnlight,
The back-of-a-lorry man selling whatever fell
And must rise again like our hope, our hope
Out of our hell.
'How's the body, citizen?'
'Ahr, what's the use complainin'?'
Enter Kirwan
With a bucket containing
One small black-and-white television set,
Silver knives, forks, spoons, walkman, silken gloves.
Bucket empties, money keeps appearing
From nowhere, Kirwan gives to Scanlon,
Dawnlight is the dark about our loves.
My loves include forgetting much of what I see.
My loves involve remembering Magee
Who sailed three thousand miles
To drink whiskey
With a woman whose heart-stealing smile
Spawned legends in honeyed abundance.

If you love a smile how far will you travel
To drink with it? To it?
It could be the style of a she-devil
But you can't wait to be entranced.
Magee's heart danced
When she smiled her possession of all
He was and had, he was a decent man,
He had a giving heart, he gave it gladly,
She took it, ate it, looked around for more,
The queue formed with tragic precision,
No one remembers what Magee had to say,
He drank his dream, she ate it, sounds like folklore,
Legends followed her across every floor.
If someone eats your dream you turn to thirst.
Remembering Magee, I find the night exciting,
The lady smiles and whiskey you're my darling
Though blood waste itself in towns of squandering
And we remember nothing of our manic singing
Or the mingled images the night is bringing,
Old men flushed with youth, young men spilling wisdom:
    From his seat in the corner Mike Farrell is rising
To grab the last bus home and be killed
Stepping off it, fifty yards from his bedsit
And the last chapter of *The Godfather*:
'I hate finishing a good book,
You have to eat and drink in secret.
That's the way to live, boy, good luck and bad luck,
I don't believe it but it passes the time, same as any other.'
    Whiskey you're my darling and when you enter
The blood of certain lonely men
You make them speak as poets did once,
I hear. Speak. Mike Farrell is gone from his corner
And if you ask any of the crowd where he's buried
Every manjack of us will be dumb as a dunce
Yet we keep moving in this loud, lonely dance.
Buy a ticket from that gliding bird
'In aid of sending a child to Lourdes.'
It is our blood we dance through, free slaves of its rhythms.
Dance it! Drink it! Give to the heavens!
'Mike Farrell was hit! Ach! Old men are like children
When it comes to findin' the right road home!'
    Home is where you drinkescape from if it's bad
Enough; the old jockey pours his life into my ear:
'She was all right at first, then she went mad
Or I did or we both did. I couldn't take her.
She devoured me in bed, mocked me in the light,
Her smiles were knives driving into my heart.

Where was the girl I married? Where was I?
Where was the promise we must live and die
For? This was the end, I had to make a start
Somewhere, somehow, I walked away one April morning,
I had to shake herself and winter out of my bones,
I walked, got lifts, begged, slept, boat to England,
Worked, drank my way through a dozen towns,
I came back, here I am, she's down there,
I'll never see her again, I won't forget her,
I'd rather live in this damned bottle than live with her,
The bad blood between us is there forever.'
        Bad blood is poetry. Speak. 'I saw him yesterday,
Fingers tapping the railings of the Green,
Out of it. I said hello, he looked away
And up the backside of Capricorn.
I touched his arm, thin as a withered stick,
I said why are you doing this?
"All that matters is the work," he said,
"Lend me fifty and I won't forget."
        'Veronica tries to watch him, it's no use,
He hits it night and morning, stops only to sleep,
The blood has left his face, he's grey as ashes,
A famished begging stinking self-deceiving little creep
And something of a genius. Shocking novelty. Depth. Scope.
Only the work matters. Where's the bloody hope?
We must do something soon or he's gone.
Who'd think this lunatic was once a composed man?
The changes, he doesn't know the changes he endures.
How can he begin to know the blood he suffers?'
        There are times I find it hard to look at blood.
It's like looking at my own loneliness.
I close my eyes and look at the North Wind,
How it reminds me of women who have ways
Of cutting through man's folly. Or I listen
To myself listening to the voices of the dead
Humming in my mind while this afternoon's rugby
Supporters, wrapped up, are ready for blood
And God is a hip-flask in the hotting-up crowd.
        Somewhere at the back of all this havoc
There's a simple wish to celebrate some love
Or friendship or need to go on a journey
Or pilgrimage beyond doubt and reason and expense,
To arrive at a place where we are bid
Welcome to food and drink, music and dance,
Song and talking into the goodwilled hours.
For this moment, nobody is killing himself or others.
Birds begin to sing when we have done: all men are brothers

When God's blood pours through dawnlight moonlight nightlight
And I am gone beyond men's voices
Into voices from a childhood prison,
No windows, all walls and bars of unreason:
'Kill him, cut out his heart, he's the worst thing
Ever born, here's the knife, hold him down, down,
Cut out his heart, his treacherous heart
That has no respect for human or divine,
Is happy only when causing hurt
To others, look, look at the traitor's blood,
It must foul the streets and foul the innocent sea!'
The walls of my childhood prison are crying red
And every cry is out of me, for me.
I drink the blood of God and I feel good.
I have no voice. I am the voices of my blood.
The voices of my blood force me to be free.

James Joyce's Death-mask

He, in this death-mask, warms the vision like a joy,
For whom the cold of exile was the only place
Where home was art's acropolis; now, passions stem
From fretted skin, the hollow landscape of his face.

Eyeing this mask, I see him bending to life's work,
Some prodigal son who scorned, from love, to claim
A fatted calf, but irrevocably estranged,
Strode lonely down the bright meridians of fame.

Inert, the poem-troubled skin squats round the eyes,
Limp hair, white spike of light that strikes the fervent lips
Which opened once to utter sung whisperings; now,
Harsh yearnings hurt wilfully and cold wind rips.

Away, outside, he sees from his total prison,
The bone-bright life of things that grows remote and dim,
A ring of Being, glinting like sunlit water,
Spurting through stoney clouds, outside, away from him.

And yet those eyes knew life's repeated thunder once,
Tumult of images, city roaring and blind,
Leaped wild through his head with a hard, choking wonder,
Stumbling to expression in dark streets of his mind.

His life-work finished and Ireland still blown by the
Wet winds of fear, his death-face has its own life yet;
Some simple no music, birdsong, nor branches
Breaking with full flowers can equal, or we forget.

The Dinner

James Joyce had dinner with the Holy Family
One Saturday evening in Nazareth.
Mary was a good cook, her Virginsoup was delicious,
Joyce lapped it till he was nearly out of breath.
The Holy Family looked at Joyce who said
Nothing, he was a morose broody class
Of a man, his glasses made him look very sad,
It was next to impossible to get him to talk and
The dinner was uncomfortable as a result.
'How're things in Ireland?' asked Joseph. 'Ugh,' said Joyce.
'What're you writing now?' persisted Joseph, 'I couldn't find fault
With your last book. Perfect.'
                                Joyce seemed to sulk.
'A large work,' he muttered, 'Like the Bible. The sea. My voices.'
'Am I in it?' queried Jesus. 'Yep,' said Joyce. 'Pass the salt.'
'Is it too much to enquire about the rôle I play?'
Continued Jesus. 'It is,' said Joyce.
Mary changed the subject. 'Are there many grottoes to me
In Ireland?' 'Countless,' replied our hero.
Joyce's short answers were buggering the dinner up.
'The Society of Jesus,' queried Jesus, 'How's it going?'
'Who knows Clongowes?' said Joyce. 'Could I have a cup
Of Bewley's coffee to round off this occasion?'
'Why did you leave Ireland, James?' queried Joseph,
'The Swiss, French, Italians are just as lousy
In their ways.' Joyce pondered. 'Crime,'
He replied, 'Of non-being.' Jesus butted in:
'In that case you must have sinners in plenty.
I think I should visit Ireland, sometime.'
'I wouldn't, if I were you,' said Joyce.
'But you're not me,' said Jesus. 'Though there
Are times when you behave as if you were
The Son of Man Himself. You get in my hair,
James, from time to time, with your pretentious
Posturing, sitting on a cloud, paring your toenails
In an orgy of indifference, pissed on white wine.

Though I readily admit your prose is divine
With touches of Matthew Mark Luke and John,
Why can't you be an honest-to-God
Dubliner, go for a swim in Sandymount, spend
Sunday afternoon in Croke Park or Dalyer,
Boast of things you've never done,
Places you've never been,
Have a pint in O'Neill's,
Misjudge the political scene,
Complain about the weather,
Miss mass, go to Knock,
Take a week in Killarney,
Listen to McCormack's records,
Re-learn to mock, jibe, scandalise, sneer, scoff
And talk your head off.
James, you have a block about Ireland,
You're too long on the continent.
In some strange way, James, you are,
If you ask me, bent.'

'But I didn't ask you, Jesus,' replied Joyce,
'It so happens I think things out for myself,
I had to leave Ireland to do this
Because no one in Ireland has a mind of his own,
I know that place to the marrow of its bone
And I insist that people are dominated by your henchmen,
Those chaps in black who tell folk what to think.'

'I beg your pardon,' said Jesus 'These men
Are not me.'
             'Would you put that in ink?'
Asked Joyce.
             'In blood,' Jesus replied.

'This is getting too serious,' Joseph interrupted.

'Shut up, Dad!' said Jesus. 'The matter *is* serious.
It's precisely for this kind of crap I came and died.'

'But you're alive and well, son,' Joseph said. 'You're not dead
And we're the Holy Family. That's what they call us.'

'What family is wholly holy?' asked Jesus.
Joseph looked about him, then at the ground, perplexed.
That honest carpenter didn't seem comfortable.
There was nothing he couldn't do with timber
But this was a different matter.

He said nothing,
Just poured himself another cup of Bewley's coffee.
Mary said, 'Let's finish with a song,
Mr Joyce, I understand that you
Took second place
To Mr McCormack at a Feis.
But that's a long time ago, a long
Time ago.
Though second place is not the place for you
Perhaps you'd give the Holy Family a song.'

Joyce brooded a bit, took a deep breath,
Straightened his glasses gone slightly askew,
Coughed once, then sang *The Rose of Nazareth*.

The Holy Family loved his voice.
It was pure and clear and strong,
The perfect voice of the perfect sinner

And the perfect end to the dinner.

The Blind Man

Dark from birth,
And therefore spared the shock
Of losing light, not having known its worth.
I am aware of darkness round the clock,
A velvet kingdom, limits undefined,
Where touch, smell, ear equip me well.
Fastidiously, I try the noisy grind,
The aimless gusto of external hell.

I walk the inner alleys night and day,
Explore the salty laneways of the blood,
Note weeds and grasses, refuse thrown away,
Deduce what's evil, beautiful or good.
I move down sidestreets of the marrowbone,
Go moodily along its thoroughfare
On which the sun has sometimes shone;
And therefore I am blithe and debonair.

I've been informed of the things I miss:
Birds that steadily attempt the air,
Peculiar tints of whiskey in a glass,

Surprising sunlight in a woman's hair;
Shells half-buried in the sand
Originally spawned at sea,
Nature's gayest finery and
Casual phenomena of every day.

But vision is not simply seeing straight,
And things discoverable without exist within:
My shells and birds are different, yet elate
Me utterly. Images that spin
Within these limits are my own,
With colours, shapes and forms that I create,
Discovered somewhere in the blood and bone –
I only see whatever I can make.

Therefore I accept dark privacy;
I move beyond each voice
Which unaware, asserts I cannot see.
While they claim, reproach, ignore, rejoice,
I go among them, prodding the strange air,
Awkwardly involved while still outside,
Conscious of the things I'm fit to share,
Acknowledging the light I've been denied.

I See

Blind Shanahan walks in my mind tonight.

His eyes are hungry thrushes
Hopping through hedges.
I'd frighten them if I went near.
I'll watch from here.

His fingers play strings of the air,
Rainfingers touching a thirsty field.
The grass quickens with gratitude.
He listens to the wet whispers,
Voices of people he'll never see.

He is wearing the brown suit he always wore.
He is thinking of his brother
Who will soon be going away forever.
He knows it is late summer.

He can smell the definitive dying
Better than anyone.
Leaves are starting to clatter about in his head
Men speak of hay and cider,
Their words caressing his face.

The days are crooked roads.
Light
Is a word he stores in a secret place.

Thinking of his darkness
Is light to me.

I see what I can see –
Bits and pieces to feed my emptiness.

I make but little of it
Yet I can make enough
To see him shuffle down a road in winter.
He walks close to the stripped hedge.
Coming to a bridge
He pauses to listen to water.
It is a peaceful sound
Though he knows it is capable of rage.
His mind fills with that sound.
It has come through invisible fields.
It will find an invisible sea.

He moves on,
Untroubled by failing light,
Every step a step into another sight.

Blind Shanahan walks in my mind tonight?

Moloney Sees Through a Blind Eye

'A farmer's wife was waked in Sixmilebridge,'
Moloney said, 'and I came staggerin' home from hedge
To hedge and side to side o' the road,
Needless to say, teetotally scuttered and mad in the blood.
(The corpse's left knee
Was very crooked and stiff, and we
Had to break her leg with a brick in order
To fit her into the coffin.)

Comin' home, I lost my way,
And between hoppin' and trottin', I went astray,
Stumbled through meadows, fields and caves,
Byres and boglands, dykes and drains,
Through hilly places, moors and glens
Where thistles sprouted and yellow whins,
By marshy patches, fort and lot
And many a Godforsaken spot,
Till I finished up in weed and sedge
Gapin' through the eye of a bridge.
Slowly there, as I sat and stared
All the forgotten dead appeared
Before my wide bewildered eyes,
Dead friends, dead loves, dead hates, dead enemies,
Forcin' themselves in the crooked light
Into my fascinated sight.
One by one, over watery sedge,
They passed through the blind eye o' the bridge.
There were the shapes of those I'd loved,
Of those approved or disapproved;
Girls found and lost in a night
Grey and cold as the winter light,
Loose women of a lost riffraff
With painted face and belly-laugh,
And one or two whose love I'd won
And who'd won mine. They too passed on.
Passed the shapes of men I'd fought,
From whom I'd learned and whom I'd taught,
Men that moved me for the airs
They'd worn at weddings, wakes and fairs;
Hucksters, farmers, labourers, lads,
Noted blackguards, printed cads,
Laughin' topers, fools and tinkers,
Tug-o-war men, famous drinkers,
Scrappers, matchmakers, busy rhymers,
Snotty widows and double timers,
Three-card-trick men and crafty knackers,
Spalpeens, thatchers and bonham-spladers;
Healers and quacks I used to know
But for all their cures, they had to go;
Fiddlers and ballad-makin' rakes,
Corner-boys with their smart cracks;
Soldiers, many a man and boy,
The lost makers of history,
Faces out of the Civil War,
Staters and Republicans mixed together,
Irregular and Black-and-Tan

Rubbin' shoulders as they passed on;
Faces I'd known from cradle to grave,
Faces I'd looked at only once,
Faces I'd seen as a child, and then
Faces that crowded my days as a man;
Some so long dead I could hardly know
And some who'd died but a year ago.

So moved, before my startled eyes,
The dead into their mysteries,
And left me starin' at the bridge
And I spraddled in moss and mire and sedge.

     What could I do
But pick myself up and stumble through
The night, makin' my way as best I could
With that nightmare in my blood
Through nameless pathways in the dark.
Don't ask me how I managed to work
My way to threshold, stairway, room and bed,
But with the grace o' God, I managed to come
To the safety of a livin' home.
The livin' are changed by the dead,
I know, though I can't say how;
But I am different now
From what I was then.
Never will be the same again.

     It simply brought me face to face
With the fact that I must take my place
In darkness and a final shade
Somewhere in that huge parade;
No longer humble, no longer proud,
But one of that silent midnight crowd
I'd seen when I was forced to lie
And gape through a bridge's big blind eye.'

Kind eyes

Over Dublin the full moon
strikes the heavens dumb
enlightening the kind eyes
of the man who split the atom.

An OK Guy

So much depends on a TV appearance.
It's true it's true it's absurd.
I practised for days but clean
Forgot how my beard
Stuck like a watery turd to my chin
And what a seedy sneaky voice I have
And darting ratty eyes
Infecting the light of surburban paradise.
No one believed me, I was dressed in lies.
And yet in spite of these disasters
I might have come across as an OK guy
Were it not that at a vital moment
I picked my nose. The whole fucking nation
Rang the station and said I should be crucified.
Today a blob of snot on my forefinger
Recalls an agony on which I shall not linger.

According to *The Moderate Intelligencer*

This evening, about five of the clock,
The Lord Protector set out for Ireland
In a coach with six gallant Flanders mares
And a life-guard consisting of eighty men:
Ireton, Scroop, Horton, Lambert,
Abbott, Mercer, Fletcher, Garland,
Bolton, Ewer, Cooke, Hewson,
Jones, Monk, Deane. And others.

May God bring Cromwell safe to Dublin
To propagate the Gospel of Christ
Among the barbarous, bloodthirsty Irish
Whose cursing, swearing, drunken ways
Dishonour God by sea and land.

Visit them, Oliver, like God's right hand.

The House I Built

(i.m. Jonathan Swift, Founder of St Patrick's Hospital, Dublin)

Last night, in sleep, I built a house. My dreams are true.

This morning, sitting in my bed, I had a fit of giddiness.
The room turned round and round a minute or two.
The fit passed, leaving me sick, yet not plunged in sickness.
I saw Dr Cockburn today, he promised he would do
his best for me, send me the pills did me such good last year.
He also promised me a healing oil for my ear.

For months now, I'm in a bad, dispirited way with deafness,
giddiness, fluxes. Will I ever be able to leave this house?
And what can I do for people who suffer like this
or worse?

'The Bedlam of Paris might be a good plan for that you intend
to found.'
              'It is truly worthy of your great soul.'
'Your heart to bestow is joined in you with a head to contrive.'

I saw what was needed, I worked for that to the end.
The end?
              Cancers? Leprosy? Falling sickness? King's evil?

Sickness struggles to own the world. I want you to live.
Live, do you hear me? Half-living is a safe hell.
The house I built is for souls who would be well.

Courage

(i.m. Larry Kelly)

And yes, old dying friend, it's best
to cultivate
a ludicrous largesse of spirit,

show a cocky smile in the face
of dissolution.
I never knew the source of courage

until now.

You know me when I say
it grows from your decay,

flesh flagging towards the box.
Your laughter,
absurd and admirable,

flowers from cankered roots
and is a deeper thing
than I have ever heard from mouths

that do not taste the worm
budging through the blood.
Why is the judgement of rotting lips

impossible to dismiss?
Is this
the only true authority?

Calculators, crawlers, pigs and slaves
abound, you say,
and they will always have their way

until their way fouls to its end,
abrupt or gradual.
Therefore you smile, my dying friend,

and though the terror touches your heart
and every day the ice advances,
the deeper chill

lies in your quiet words.
Last night you stood
at the bottom of the steps

resting for the climb.
I had nothing to say.
You were taking your time

when I saw that courage was something
chuckling and grey,
easy to miss, impossible to follow.

Then you gathered your coat about your throat,
coughed
and went away.

The Loud Men

And how O God shall we learn to cope
With the loud men?

Yes, you have a point to make
But must you turn your fisheyes on me
As though you were the voice of revelation
And I a thing of stone?
Must you glare like a ghoul in nightmare?
Poke your burning head at me?
Spit in my face?

All I am allowed to see
Is the hysterical foam on your lips,
Your coronal of victory.

Today, in the city,
I saw a child sitting at a bridge.
Her name was Sheila Lehane.
When I spoke to her she whispered.
She had her problem.
Her voice was low and steady.

Her suffering would not allow her
To be loud.

Only bullies shout
And politicians
And bitches with phoney convictions
And bored, truculent men.
A shouting woman, however,
Is the worst of all,
A loud deformity of nature,
An articulate obscenity.

Why do they shout, I ask myself.

Because
Under the noise
There is nothing.

Because
The loud will always win attention
For a while.

Because
They are afraid of silence.
Because
They proclaim their own emptiness.
Because
By spitting in the eyes of others
They run like madmen from themselves.

When I hear a shout
I fear for humankind.

I see a black abyss
Where souls roll and writhe.

I get hell's smell, I know hell's loss,
I feel hell's evil heat.

I walk the other side of the street.

Time for Breaking

When the old man said, watching me
watching the leaves tumble with the river,
' 'Tis like the inside of your head,'

I didn't know for decades what he meant.
In fact, I'd forgotten his words
or consigned them to a corner where they couldn't

be heard until, forty years on, something in me
broke. It was summertime. Not, you'd think,
the time for breaking, but there's no

knowing when the breaking will happen.
Well, the day I have in mind
was sprawled August with other men

who for dreams and reasons of their own
had broken too.
The day started well, the sun shone

on the first shreds of hope for ages,
but towards midday, heaven cracked
in one of its majestic rages

and lashed the well-lashed earth again, again,
while lightning flashed spectacular anger
and thunder forecast in my brain.

I saw the old man watching me
watching the leaves in the river.
Over forty years he stepped slowly

and peered through my eyes.
I don't recall being seen through
so clearly by anyone.

He said ' 'Tis like the inside of your head.'
I hadn't known I'd carried the river in me,
borne it in my blood

these long years. I carry the old man too, closer than ever.
Between us, we make a river, another river,
a laughing angry sunny stormy kind of river.

The Second Tree

My head sore with nightmare –
The seagulls tore the crows to death
Dipped the ripped bodies in the sewers
Of the trembling city
Dropped the shite-caked corpses on my head
Till I was buried, breathing, in a heap
Of bleeding flesh of crows, their features
Fixing in my skin like hateful glances
Thrown like knives across a room
Which for someone must be home
Where he can slip the world off like an overcoat –

I walked, stiffnecked with nightmare,
Under a sky split open like my mind
Out into the small garden at the back of the house.
I closed my eyes, breathing the morning air,
Breathing the innocent air.
I opened my eyes and saw a pear on the ground
Nearly hidden in the grass.
I picked it up and felt its coolness
Thrill my fingers, then my blood, my being.
I tasted it. And I knew,
As though I were another Adam

To whom another tree, a second tree
In some small corner growing unseen,
Was shown by accident
At the moment of his deepest need,
What nightmare hungered for
As it regrouped its battering legions
Of packed, implacable assassins
To savage vulnerable sleep,
The cool, moist taste, caressed by grass,
Of sanity, clear, sweet, miraculously
Normal, so near it must always be easily
Lost.
                              I could have knelt
Before the second tree, but stood in silence
While my mind rejoiced in priceless quiet
Then turned towards a human voice,
Eating the garden's flesh as I entered the house, dumb with gratitude.

A Black-and-Tan

In May, 1957, I met Will Flint
driver of the 657 trolleybus
from Shepherd's Bush to Hounslow, The Bell,
via Chiswick and Brentford
where the gasworks stank
bad as the Liffey
to be redeemed in time
by a sign that said
Come to Kew Gardens
and he told me he'd been
a Black-and-Tan
somewhere in Cork.
'These bloody rebels were everywhere, mate,
'idin' in villages, up in the 'ills,
'idin' in farmers' 'ouses.
Played bloody 'ell with us, they did,
I was lucky to come out alive.
I did some damage meself
but now most of all I remember
the soft women of Buttevant.
Tell you this much, Paddy,
I was never short
of the bit o' crumpet
in the Emerald Isle.

The blokes were out for our skins
but the birds opened up in style.'

Having been reared
to hate the thought
of a Black-and-Tan
the scum of England
more beast than man

I was somewhat surprised to find
how much I liked Will Flint
and his Black-and-Tan talk
warming my heart and mind.

'You've 'eard of the three F's, Paddy,
the three F's for the Irish peasant,
Fair Rent, Free Sale, Fixity of Tenure?
Well, look at the three F's
of the Irish in London today –
Fightin', Fiddlin', Fuckin'!
No wonder you're a race o' bloody wantons!
An' tell me this, mate,
why do you Irish walk our streets
as if you was climbin' fuckin' mountains?
Sometimes I think all you Paddies
shudda stide up in the 'ills!'

Will Flint had thought a little
more than a little.
'I was 'ardly a man
when they sent me to Ireland,
I was a killer
when they brought me back.
Not that it bothers me much.
King an' Country, that's what Flint fought for,
King an' Country, Country an' King.
Well, it must be for somethin'.
I 'ad some good times in Ireland,
drinkin' an' singin' an' lovin',
I'm not complainin',
Then I got 'ome to a small bit o' fuss,
King an' Country looked after me well.
'Ere I am, nearly forty years later,
in the drivin' seat of a bus,
the good ol' 657
goes all the way
from Shepherd's Bush to 'eaven!'

The Grudge

Once upon a time
Someone hit someone.
Conner hit Kelly
Or Kelly hit Conner
In Listowel or Tralee
At Christmas or Easter
Over land or a woman.

One man
Hit another man.

The grudge began.

Cause was forgotten.
Bad blood grew.

Bad blood
Split Conner and Kelly.
It split their families too.

Children not born at the time of the blow
When Conner hit Kelly or Kelly hit Conner
Were taught to hate each other
From the word go.

The grudge gripped both families,
Possessed their houses and fields,
Snaked through their words
And always, always
Lived in the hearts of Kelly and Conner,
Of their children,
Of their children's children.

Within each house
The grudge was stronger than anything.
The grudge proved love a weakling,
Respect, an idiot,
Co-operation, a sick fantasy,
Help, a crime.

The grudge grew stronger with time.

Kelly died.
Conner died.

Their children died.
Their children's children died.

The grudge blossomed in strength and pride
And by Christ, by the dead
The grudge thrives
In every living heart and head

Descended from Kelly and Conner.

Some who have felt it most deeply
Have said
It's a matter of honour.

Do you know what strength is?
Strength
Is the grudge,
The force that severs and divides,
Nourishes ignorance
As though it were the weakest babe of all,
Tutors the young in hatred,
Teaches them slogan and cry,
Refuses to die.

The grudge grips generations.
The grudge refuses to die.
The grudge stole from the soul
The secret of immortality.

The grudge laughs
In its strength and pride.
Taking its sustenance
From human blood.

The future is full of human blood.

The future is the grudge's best friend.

Both houses know the grudge cannot end.
Pride. Honour. Strength. Blood.

Ah, thank God. Thank God.

What Use?

'What use is that language to a man out of work?
A fat bastard of a teacher rammed it down my throat
For eight years before I could quit
That school where I learned nothing
But Sorrowful, Joyful and Glorious Mysteries
And answers to questions I never understood
And that damned language brings tears to my eye;
Every time I struggled to say a word.
Can you see me facing a foreman in England
Equipped with my native sounds, asking for a start
To prove I can use my hands
Like any other man from any other land?
That language should have been choked at birth
To stop it wasting my heart and mind.'

Old Soldier

'I'm eighty-eight,' he said,
   trenchtwinkle in his eyes,
'and though I fought in the worst o' wars
   I'm barkin' lively.

Slogged in the Kimberley Diamond Mines,
   sang on Fiddler's Green
and never, never would accept
   the notion of a has-been.

The years are old, my heart is young,
   there's plenty left to do;
strings of a fiddle, words of a song
   keep me feelin' new.

Complainin' gets ya nowhere.
   Old eyes need a sparklin' sight.
Take me for a walk, young friend,
   to see the Shannon light.'

Service

The best way to serve the age is to betray it.
If it's a randy slut slooping for hump
Hide in a dark ditch, wait, waylay it
And land where no one can extradite you.

If it's a moneyman with a philosophy like
'There's only cash and as many fucks as you can get'
Inspire him to talk of Daddy's tenderness
Till his eyes are wet.

Be a knife, bullet, poison, flood, earthquake;
Cut, gut, shrivel, swallow, bury, burn, drown
Till someone senses things ain't as they should be.

If betrayal is a service, learn to betray
With the kind of style that impresses men
Until they dream of being me.

Ask the Children

'That man fought for the English,' he said.
'Why should he sit there
telling stories to children
gathered about his chair,
stories of his wanderings, his wounds, his stupid war?'

'Ask the children,' she replied
'Why they love him.
Ask the children, if you dare.
Then sit there yourself and try
to tell them a story
born of your ignorant pride.
Your story will tell them who you are.'

Tail-end Charlie

Tail-end Charlie
Eighteen years of age
Last of the patrol
Was ringed by women's rage

In Leeson Street
Two girls ran
To fetch the executioners
Of this young Yorkshireman

Tail-end Charlie
Could have shot his way out
But women ringed him
He didn't shoot

Came the IRA
They did the job
On tail-end Charlie
The women went home

He had six weeks' training
In the north of England
Was sent straightaway
To the North of Ireland

On his first day of duty
Lost touch with his patrol
Tail-end Charlie
Was somebody's fool

Born in black Leeds
Where life is made of smoke
Died in black Belfast
Where life is no joke

All his mothers circled him
Screaming such and such
Tail-end Charlie
Out of touch O out of touch

The Story

The story was not born with Robbie Cox
Nor with his father
Nor his father's father
But farther back than any could remember.

Cox told the story
Over twelve nights of Christmas.
It was the story
Made Christmas real.
When it was done
The new year was in,
Made authentic by the story.
The old year was dead,
Buried by the story.
The man endured,
Deepened by the story.

When Cox died
The story died.
Nobody had time
To learn the story.
Christmas shrivelled,
The old year was dust,
The new year nothing special,
So much time to be endured.

The people withered.
This withering hardly troubled them.
The story was a dead crow in a wet field,
An abandoned house, a rag on a bush,
A sick whisper in a dying room,
The shaking gash of an old man's mouth
Breaking like burnt paper
Into black ashes the wind scatters,
People fleeing from famine.
Nobody has ever heard of them.
Nobody will ever speak for them.

I know the emptiness
Spread by the story's death.
This emptiness is in the roads
And in the fields,
In men's eyes and children's voices,

In summer nights when stars
Play like rabbits behind Cox's house,
House of the story
That once lived on lips
Like starlings startled from a tree,
Exploding in a sky of revelation,
Deliberate and free.

The cries repeat themselves

Crackling fun above our heads, seagulls wheel about.

David then: 'A thousand years from now
someone will stand under these black cliffs
and hear the same wild cries.'

The evening tide is going out.

I look at David. Seventy years
pour strength into his words,
laughter through his eyes.

Everything dies yet nothing dies.
Why is everyone no one? No one, everyone?
The cries repeat themselves. The wild, wild cries.

Roger Boyle

The Mass was finished, the priest gone, Roger Boyle
stood in the sanctuary alone
holding by a string the black bag
with his surplice and soutane.

He remembered the smell of wine on the priest's breath,
the talk of God's body and blood.
He wanted to get drunk on the wine.
That October morning, he did.

Stumbling through leaves and chestnuts
down the avenue leading to the main road
Roger Boyle mumbled to the trees
'I'm drunk on the blood of God

and the river is drunk and the bridge is drunk
and so is the sun and the leafy air
and the people stuck into their work
are drunk with Godeverywhere.

And the cold rooms of the school are drunk
and the big grim-eyed man
with the stick in his hand, and my friends' fear
when they stare and listen, trying to understand.'

He came to a roadside fountain,
he watched the water flow,
'O saving water of the world
I know what you know.'

He looked at the grass of Bambury's field
still and morningwet,
'I won't forget this moment, grass of God,
till you forget.'

He turned to the calm river,
the creek, the unchanging mud,
'O mud and river and creek
we live in the blood of God.'

He went to Bambury's hayshed,
he lay in Bambury's hay,
while the calm river flowed past
he slept his God away.

He woke, he sat, he stood, he felt
the hayshed shake
but could not say what his heart felt
now that he was awake.

But it did

(a drama)

A summer's day: an old man sits in the shade,
leathery effigy chewing the cud of dream –
a quiet drama privately staged in his head,
greyed by things that are, saved by things that seem.

A dog lopes into the street where an oily bitch
sweats as she waits, her steaming tongue hanging out.
He circles, smells her, circles again with such
deliberate care, it seems his heart is in doubt.

He mounts of a sudden, expertly spraddles the brute,
his head at her back, scaring the busy flies.
The old man's drama suddenly switches to youth,
the dogs' rhythm increases, he closes his eyes.

In the shade of the castle, the meadowscent was sweet,
the bitch that he mounted then he cannot recall,
the pure daylight, freedom, summery sweat,
rising desire he believed would not end at all.

But it did... and he opens his eyes to the day,
to the dogs that do it, unconscious of living or dead;
a woman passes and turns her eyes away,
he watches, knows there is nothing to say,
the vice of dream tightens his dying head.

A Bottle

This is a strong old house, made of stone.
Not the kind you might easily label.
The white-coated chemist, a silent man,
has worked all day in the small
room with the smells of (is it health
or sickness?) filling his head.
He moves intently, almost, it seems, by stealth
till the work is done. In from the red-eyed
winter day where the wind and the rain
vie with each other to humiliate the town
shuffles the farmer, old and strong with caution.

If his body were all pain he'd give no sign.
A few words with the chemist and he's gone,
his pocket bulging with a bottle marked Poison.

Columkille the Writer

(from the Irish)

My heart is jacked from writing.
My sharp quill shakes.
My thin pen spills out
blood from my stormy lakes.

A stream of God's own wisdom
flushes my hand.
It blesses the waiting page.
It blesses where holly is found.

My thin pen is a traveller
in a world where books are waiting.
Who dares to see? Say? Who bothers to listen?
My heart is jacked from writing.

What Else?

Be with me Brendan of Ardfert when I
Question words. Song and speech like mine were cast
Aside when, stung by treachery,
You killed a man. Brendan, was it remorse
Made you confront the problematic sea,
The gruff distraction of the wind until
You breathed the cold air of sanctity?
I see you searching with a passionate will

The changing waste at feet and head,
The constant abyss. What reassured you?
Glint of leaping fish? Arrogance of birds?
The sea's tempers? All that has been said
About your lonely strength and rage is true.
What else subdues the sea or masters words?

Sebastian

The arrows harass him like winter pains
frequent and grim
and yet it seems that he ordains
they riddle him

as if they did not split the air
whistling for blood
but that their heads are buried where
Sebastian would.

One angry shaft
explodes inside his groin –
grotesque, excruciating part
of a sure design

in which he twitches, writhes, succumbs
with gasps that seem to bless
the point of all such martyrdoms –
man's nakedness.

His consummating fall
proves his mortality well;
destruction proves him, most of all,
indestructible.

Light Dying

(In Memoriam Frank O'Connor [Michael O'Donovan])

Climbing the last steps to your house, I knew
That I would find you in your chair,
Watching the light die along the canal,
Recalling the glad creators, all
Who'd played a part in the miracle;
A silver-haired remembering king, superb there
In dying light, all ghosts being at your beck and call,
You made them speak as only you could do

Of generosity or loneliness or love
Because, you said, all men are voices, heard
In the pure air of the imagination.
I hear you now, your rich voice deep and kind,
Rescuing a poem from time, bringing to mind
Lost centuries with a summoning word,
Lavishing on us who need much more of
What you gave, glimpses of heroic vision.

So you were angry at the pulling down
Of what recalled a finer age; you tried
To show how certain things destroyed, ignored,
Neglected was a crime against the past,
Impoverished the present. Some midland town
Attracted you, you stood in the waste
Places of an old church and, profoundly stirred,
Pondered how you could save what time had sorely tried,

Or else you cried in rage against the force
That would reduce to barren silence all
Who would articulate dark Ireland's soul;
You knew the evil of the pious curse,
The hearts that make God pitifully small
Until He seems the God of little fear
And not the God that you desired at all;
And yet you had the heart to do and dare.

I see you standing at your window,
Lifting a glass, watching the dying light
Along the quiet canal bank come and go
Until the time has come to say goodnight:
You see me to the door; you lift a hand
Half-shyly, awkwardly, while I remark
Your soul's fine courtesy, my friend, and
Walk outside, alone, suddenly in the dark.

But in the dark or no, I realise
Your life's transcendent dignity,
A thing more wonderful than April skies
Emerging in compelling majesty,
Leaving mad March behind and making bloom
Each flower outstripping every weed and thorn;
Life rises from the crowded clay of doom,
Light dying promises the light re-born.

Oliver to a Friend

All things work for the best.
You wish to hear of me. I am the man
You have always known, a body of death and sin.
I struggle to be honest
As I exalt the Lord and abase the flesh.
I have seen the Lord, I have prevailed,
I share the goodwill of Him who dwelt in the Bush,
I am not deluded by this world.
You are troubled. Call not your burden heavy or sad,
If the Father laid it on you, He intended neither.
Go evenly through foul and fair weather
And know all fleshly reasoning is a trap
To make you say 'heavy', 'sad', 'pleasant', 'fine'.
Dare to be human; you'll be divine.
Dear friend, I dare to speak of spirit,
Such spirit as the world fears to know.
Quit your fleshly reason, seek to touch
The mind of God shown in the chain of Providence.
I say again, submit, let that spirit teach you,
The spirit of counsel and of might,
Of wisdom and the fear of the Lord.
He will lead you to what pleases His eyesight.
If you fail, good heart, to bear your burden well
You shall hardly bear the burdens of others.
I have done, I, a poor looker-on
At the workings of that spirit in this world.
Suffering? Men bring it on themselves.
Therefore, be fearless. My soul loves you, young man.

A Man I Knew

(i.m. Patrick Kavanagh)

1

'I want no easy grave,' he said to me,
'where those who hated me can come and stare,
slip down upon a servile knee,
muttering their phoney public prayer.
In the wilds of Norfolk I'd like to lie,
no commemorative stone, no sheltering trees,
far from the hypocrite's tongue and eye,
safe from the praise of my enemies.'

A man I knew who seemed to me
the epitome of chivalry
was constantly misunderstood.
The heart's dialogue with God
was his life's theme and he
explored its depths assiduously
and without rest. Therefore he spat
on every shoddy value that
blinded men to their true destiny –
the evil power of mediocrity,
the safety of the barren pose,
all that distorted natural grace.
Which is to say, almost everything.
Once he asked a girl to sing
a medieval ballad. As her voice rang out,
she was affronted by some interfering lout.

This man I knew spat in his face
and wished him to the floor of hell.
I thought then, and still think it well
that man should wear the spittle of disgrace
for violating certain laws.

Now I recall my friend because
he lived according to his code
and in his way was true to God.
Courage he had and was content to be
himself, whatever came his way.
There is no other chivalry.

Raglan Lane
(after Patrick Kavanagh)

In Raglan Lane, in the gentle rain, I saw dark love again,
Beyond belief, beyond all grief, I felt the ancient pain,
The joyful thrust of holy lust, I stretched on heaven's floor,
One moment burned what the years had learned and I was wild once more.

The years' deep cries in her sad eyes became a source of light,
The heavy gloom and sense of doom changed to pure delight.
And as we walked in joy and talked we knew one thing for sure,
That love is blessed togetherness and loneliness is poor.

Then I grew rich with every touch, we loved the whole night long
Her midnight hair on the pillow there became an angel's song,
Her happy skin, beyond all sin, was heaven opened wide
But as the dawn came shyly on, I slept, and she left my side.

Why did she go? I'll never know, nor will the gentle rain,
Her up and go was a cruel blow, and yet I felt no pain
For I had known her body and soul in my own loving way,
So I lay and thanked the God of love at the dawning of the day.

A Real Presence
(in memory of John B. Keane)

There comes a time when words have said their say,
You rise and walk, alone, the banks of your loved river
Surrendering to music God has sent your way
Beyond the mouthings of the smug and clever.

This music flows from silence before words are born,
Wings at home in freedom, a bright, unpoisoned sky,
Heard later when bells tell of thoughts forlorn
And words are found for all who have to live and die.

You found words for love and lust and cunning greed
And polished men whose hearts and minds are power
And lonely men and women in their bypassed need
And gentle souls who see, and try to care.

The stars above the Feale became your words
And you are waiting now for what the night may bring
And while you see the death that you are moving towards
You raise your head to heaven and begin to sing.

I think that you were most at home in song
Clear and ringing through the Atlantic night
Where, for a moment, right defeated wrong
And stoneblind ignorance became sympathetic sight.

Late August evening near the cliffs. You're there with Mary,
You're flying, singing to the merciless, generous sea,
You're gone beyond your pain into a no-words-needed beauty
And a hushed place cherishes a real presence,
Laughing, lovable and free.

Late Yeats

Our greatest poet was worried
    rather late in life,
'I can't have sexual intercourse
    with lover or with wife.'

A friend said 'Go to London
    for a monkey's juicy glands.'
'My sexual future,' mused the poet,
    'lies in Eugene Steinach's hands.

Steinach's operation
    will renew my sexual power,
my poetry will be rammed with life
    as I near my final hour.

A poet's life is poetry
    his blessing and his curse
and should his penis shrink and droop
    so will his verse.

Verse-making and love-making
    inspiringly connect.'
Then love and verse exhorted Yeats,
    'Erect, old man, erect!'

Was Steinach's op. successful?
    Yeats, when he came through,
believed his penis hardened.
    His poetry hardened, too.

The poet became a singing Will,
    ladies grew uncouth
for the youngold man who'd not accept
    the body's stinking truth.

And as rotten death iced nearer
    with all its rotten wrong
the poet loved with his dying breath
    and spilled his living song.

Penny

'What the hell use is poetry to anyone or anything?
Why persist in bullshitting about the dark night
of the soul? What is your purpose, man, what
is your purpose?'
                                    Ace was dumb,
the economist kicked him in the guts and spine
and told him to study money.
                                    Ace crawled home
and studied a penny
    bright and shiny
undulled as yet by the fingers of men,
    very small like Ace's self-esteem.

The penny made him remember himself as a child
when a penny was fun, infinite fun.

He remembered two pennies covering a corpse's eyes,
men praising the corpse when alive.
He saw pennies drop into an outstretched hand,
words of blessing rise, clear and sweet
beyond the world of beggary, loss, lies,
into the surviving skies.
He saw pennies on the side of a street,
himself and others playing pitch-and-toss.
Where were they now? He began to brood
on the loss of friends, the loss
of pictures in his shat-on head:

Matthew Farth who lost every tittle o' sense
thanks to his martyr's obsession with women;
Dabbler Coote who spent long years
finishing a never-finished self-portrait;
Fisher Lynch who spent his nights
poaching salmon in rivers and lakes;
Maggie Denny who lived in a caravan
and filled it with flowers for Saint Martha.

Where were they now? Ace
pressed the penny against his face
and smiled.

                The smile eased his pain.
There was nothing to explain
with pictures like that for company.

He smiled at the pictures. He was free
as he dared to be,

and grateful for a penny.

Not a word

The greatest poet who ever lived
never wrote a word

but was overheard
to say

Death of a Strong Man

That night, as always, he spoke of cattle,
The pint glass snug in his great fist,
A man whose name for strength had travelled
From his own parish to the tip o' Dingle.
On the way home, he was cut down,
His massive promise become sudden loss,
It took him four days to die and then
His friends put up a commemorative cross.
Now, in the city, seeing grim
Headlights tigering through night,
Luminous eyes that flash
In midnight dark, I think of him
Who left the pub's comfortable light
To be broken and remembered on the roadside grass.

A Tale for Tourists

Mr Patrick Healy, a grumpy old man
Who lived alone
In a small, thatched house
Such as nowadays a tourist might call
An authentic expression

Of a dying culture
Was considered a most insulting son-of-a-bitch
By his various neighbours.
They decided to teach him a lesson.
One night, while the old man
Slept with the resonant soundness
Of a whiskeyed batchelor,
They coaxed his most familiar possession,
A black ass, master of the gigantic fart,
Into his kitchen.
Dismantling the ass's cart
They lugged this also into the kitchen
And, in a chuckling tick,
Tackled it to the ass's back.
Though I didn't personally witness it
Mr Healy's consternation on awaking
Was said to be of mythical proportions
Comparable to an enraged god
Forced to stare
At a shackled beast there on his kitchen floor.
(Don't imagine I am unaware
Of gods pottering in their kitchens.
Why, I can scarce keep them out of my hair,
Scruffy divinities, heaven's greasy elders
Abundant as dandruff
On my helpless shoulders.)
All I can say now
Is that it would be most salutary
For your ordinary decent citizen
Suffering from boredom
To awaken
And find an ass in his living-room,
An ass, perhaps, with a loveable face
Such as the citizen's wife once had,
And teeth quite incapable of going bad
And crooked rainbows of breath
And beautiful delicate feet
And a succulent bit in its mouth
And a shine on its dark coat
And a simple, eternal, wise
Question in its trapped eyes
'Master, what are we doing here?'
Mr Healy had no answer
Though it is said he laughed to think
His ass could bring him such surprise
All of a May morning
Braying him out of sleep

With a loud, long, intimate warning
Such as might herald an earthquake
Were asses trained to bray
When such catastrophes are on their way.

Mastery

Five hounds obeyed Dowling
In the walk from the village to Callaghan's Cross
And from there to the Cross of the Wood.

Bran, Shannon, Carrig Pride,
Brindle Killer, Ballyline Boy,
Light at his heels.

I liked Dowling, what he did he did well
And knew the time to dare.

This or that hound sniffed the air
And followed the master.

A usual scene,
Epic in its way.

Dowling stepped with authority,
Expected to be obeyed.

He was.
He had a way with hounds,
An eye, a voice, a touch, a secret skill.

At the Cross of the Wood
Bran broke and ran.
Dowling could not tell the reason
But ran too
And failing many times to get the hound in line,
Angered.

Bran played with Dowling's anger, so it seemed,
Leaping beyond his grasp
Again, again,
But not, one time, his boot.
Pain in the hound's side
Changed the day.

There was an end to play
When Bran turned and leaped at Dowling's throat,
Fangs whiter than sunlight
Stained in no time at all
With the master's blood.

Shannon, Carrig Pride, Brindle Killer, Ballyline Boy
Got the scent Dowling had taught them to wait for.
They snarled in for the kill.

Dowling had trained them well.

It seemed that in return they liked their master's flesh
And tore it from his thighs and shoulders.

He cried and screamed and cried.

The tearing
Stopped as suddenly as it began.

The hounds slunk off into the wood's daylight dark,
Wild dogs now.

The master was found, cared for, cured.
On some parts of his body
Flesh would not fill again
Obeying whatever law the flesh obeys
When it has survived the kill,
Failure of the eye, the voice, the touch,
The secret skill.

The Wake

The grey peace of a day-old death
Lies on him in his bed,
His bridal, breeding, dying bed;
No movement now, yet I
Here kneeling, seem to see him stir,
As if the swaying of his soul
Into eternal life
Could in an hour beget
A pulse that moves him yet.

The wooden Crucifix is in his hands.
A pillar book of prayer prevents his jaw
From sagging to his chest.
The Memorare and Confiteor
Support his chin.
His final dress is brown,
The brown of stagnant water
In an old bog pool.
Beside the bed of death,
A blackened table holds a candle blessed
That flickers on the greyness of his face.

They come and kneel in ones and twos,
Pray at him, for him, to him
Lying there,
Depending on their way of prayer.

This evening
They will walk behind him
To Church and priest and holy water,
And bare their heads
And search the earth
With eyes averted from his clay.
And he will stiffen for a day
Deep in the quiet gloom
And presence of his Maker.
A few will mourn him in honest prayer,
And some, in porter-prayer,
Will drink him high to Heaven's gate
And far beyond.

Still now, the whipping tongue behind the grey-blue lips
And still the head framed in its white, new lace.
But oh! how grey, how ashen-dead the face.

I rise.
His woman, red-eyed,
Holds forth a mug of drink.
I shake her hand
In murmuring
A felt and unfelt sorrow.
I take the proffered mug.
I drink.
She moves away.
He sleeps.

Between Sky and Stone

Knee-deep in the river the man stood.
Deliberate in everything he did
The few words he said
He seemed unaware of the expectant crowd
On the bank. Shyly the boy moved towards him
Not even a small disturbance in his wake
Till he stood, head bowed, before the man
Who sprinkled water over him and spoke
Words of blessing drifting like riverbirds
Back over the water into the middle of
The people shifting in anticipation
Of a changed boy returning among them,
The air itself charged with tongues of love,
Flood-promise in the heart's desert, touch of a man
In the river standing between sky and stone.

A Peering Boy
(for Louis le Brocquy)

Men, horses blacken the plain
Where blood will spill.
Sunvertigo, knifewind, spasm of rain
Nurture and kill.

'Of course I don't believe in ghosts
But I wouldn't like them to hear me say that.'
A traveller who fears Cain more than most
Stares at the moon and lifts his hat,

Explores Connemara of the stony arts
To come, in time, to the sea.
Where's the meat? Famine hearts,
Sauce of hostility.

On. Belong. Leave. There are worse things than being
Cut off. Here's a condemned man
Congesting himself to find an opening.
Peer, dear man, at your pain.

Finished vision is a peering
Boy behind a door
While a man creates a bird, a cat laughs
And Lazarus comes up for more

Of the same, heartened by what
He found in the coldark, had to leave
For the promising, troubled future –
Adam and Eve,

Her heel, descending, ready to crush
Whatever cramps her style,
His tears mingling with hers, with the leaves,
With the rose-pink angel's maybe smile.

If You Were Bold Enough
(i.m. William Scott)

Hardly an outdoors man:
Flickering candle, domestic gold,
Bottle, basin, pot, pan:
        Slowly the shapes take hold

And will not be forgotten.
        Eggs, lemons, grapes, pears:
The man walks through the kitchen,
        Wanders among stars.

A girl sits at a table, war flares,
        The man leaves France;
Blue fish, herrings in a bowl, a jug of flowers,
        His kind of permanance.

You might say, if you were bold enough,
        A black-yellow bottle contains it all
But who's as bold as that? Look at
        The Blue Lady looking at the Nile.

To Rembrandt
(after Osip Mandelstam)

Like a martyr of light and shade, Rembrandt,
I have gone into a numb time
My burning ribs are not protected
By the watchmen there
Nor by the soldier
Sleeping under the storm.

Forgive me, brother, master,
Father of the green-black darkness
The eye of the falcon-quill pen
The hot casks in the midnight harem
Disturb to no good the tribe
Frightened in the furry twilight.

If our enemies should take me
And stop me talking to the people,
If they should rob me of all in the world,
To breathe the truth and open the doors,
I will not be silent again,
I will not stifle pain.

Milk

I

Three men
On a morning in early summer
Tipped a lorryload of poisoned whey
Into the Line river.

The water opened
And gulped it down.

It was a white poison.
The river swelled with the
Evil milk,
A snowy vein of death
Piercing the land's body.

All through the land
Seeped the scum in a murderous rut,
Through fields and
Meadows waiting to be cut,
Past villages and townlands
Into the sea.

II

Everything died in the milky river.
Brown trout, eels, fluke, young salmon
Perished, every one.

White bellies to the light
Fish floated down the river
Corpses jostling in the tide.

In the summer morning
Poison entered the sun,
Riddled the light
On land and sea,
Possessed the invisible stars
Turned to dust in the air
Dropped like a gentle malignant shiver of snow
Into the hearts of three men
Standing on a bank
Of the Line river.

III

Men working in the fields
Saw white bellies of fish.
Pain jabbed the hearts of some.
They waded in as far as they could go
Collected the bodies in bags
Returned to the banks
Spread the fish in the fields –
Row after glittering row.

Strange to see
Fishbodies
In the rivery grass,
Men bending over them
Incomprehension in their eyes.

Looking back at the river
They saw countless trout
Try to leap from the water
As if wanting to be alone,
Preferring to die
In an alien element
Than in their poisoned own.

A few fish reached the grass, gravel, stones
The air pressing on every side.
They stirred, leaped, flickered in the sun
And died.

IV

Milk of peace, milk of human kindness, sign of the fish –
The fields were strewn with dead metaphors.
Language had fought a pitched battle and lost
And now the choicest of its soldiers
Lay corpsed in the sun,
Their hearts yanked out and flung at random on the grass.
What grass would grow from these abandoned hearts

Would be sour as the words of a man
Whose days were black pits
Of disappointment.
Light that might have been a light of love
Circled like a bird of prey
Above the fields
Where nothing could be done or said
To halt the carrion light
From ravaging the dead.

V

The men who poisoned the river
Seemed hardly to know what was done.
Would they know what they did
If they poisoned the sun?
When they dumped death into the water
What did they do or say?
They turned their backs on a job well-done
And walked away.

VI

Later,
People walking through or near the fields
Were forced to drink the stench.
Implacable as cancer
It pierced their clothes and skin
Lived there
White and vile as leprosy.

The whiter, the viler.

It seemed to many women and men
That God's air
Would never be clean again.

VII

In time
Fishbodies would be clay and grass,
Pain in the men's eyes
Lessen
But the river will never
Recover
Its own creatures rotting in light.

The river
And the land it flows for
Will not forget
The summer of poisoned white.

Prodigal

(after Osip Mandelstam)

I shall leave this hyperborean land
To satiate the vision of a destiny's end.
I shall say 'selah' to the chief of the Jews
For his crimson caress.

Land of unshaven mountains that remains obscure:
Scrubs of bristle pierce, lodge.
And fresh as a clean fable
A green valley sets the teeth on edge.

I love military glasses
With their usurious powers of vision.
Only two colours in the world are unfaded:
The yellow of envy, the red of impatience.

Treasure

He bleeds to death at the corner of William Street.
If this chalice were restored in time
He might drink God's blood from it,
Stagger up and go home.

Cover him with a bronze basin,
Lay him in the ground.
Let him rest in the darkness for a thousand years.
Treat him skilfully when he's found.

Let the sensitive people
Dole him out among their expert friends.
Let him enliven lethargic committees,
This most exciting find.

Let exquisite instruments be brought to bear
On the bones and skull.
Remove the dirt without damaging the bones.
This treasure belongs to us all.

The Hurt

Jack Ahern was gored by a bull
One day in deep winter.
He was sixty-two. For three years after he sat silent
Staring into the fire,

Graffa turf stacked brown and black
Reddening in the hearth, reddening in his eyes.
He stared at fire, a man of fire
Turning the colour of ashes.

Every night of these dying years
He washed his feet
In a chipped enamel basin,
The flesh dark and white by firelight.

The bull had mauled his breast.
His hand hovered at his heart
As if seeking to touch it.
All he ever found was the hurt

Rending his body that had worked the fields
And rarely been ill.
Now he read in the fire's eyes
How he'd never be well

Till the grave released him
From pain so unshareably his own
Daylight was a gulf
Between him and everyone.

There was a fire with its own life
Never the same from second to second,
There was a man trying to understand
Why this hurt had happened

On a darkening winter afternoon
In his favourite meadow.
He'd cut hay there for forty years
And not suspected his sorrow

Waited its proper moment.
Were all his days a waiting for this?
Why, when he tried to see,
Did his heart know the world was

A Hereford bull horning the air
In its red rush
To pile on a tiring man,
Mangle his flesh,

Roar off like a winter storm
On its blind way,
Not knowing what it had broken,
What lay

Bleeding and gasping on the grass
Where love was willing to work
Till horns and hooves
Pounded it into the muck

And it was borne in pain by other men back into the house
To rest but not recover, between bed and chair,
Seeing the infinite shapes of hurt reach out,
Recede, renew themselves in eyes, in fire.

Immediate Man
(i.m. Chearbhall Ó Dálaigh)

If, in the course of a journey
That covers more than half a country,
Small though that country be,
And there is this opportunity

To see, as if for the first time,
Lakes that glint back at you for a name,
Fields that together create a wild home
Till the world is a particular room,

A child thirsts because all this
Is bigger and deeper than anything she knows
Or can know during years stretching like stations
Ahead of her into treachery and promise

Mingling,
Is it not a heart-lifting
Sight to see a laughing
Prince of a man rising

From his seat in a crowded train
And go, immediate man,
To return with solace for one
Who, undistressed in a moment, will never forget him?

'The fields and the lakes have names, dear,
And every rock, mountain and hill,
And don't worry if the stations come quickly or slowly
Or there are too many hurrying people.

Take your ease and consider them all,
Think of the names and know what you feel.'
He gets off at Killarney, this man of style.
Over the years, she has mentioned his smile,

His greyhound words, his wise eyes,
His contemplative hands' impulsive ways,
The sense he transmitted that we are witnesses
To stations, fields, lakes we should name and praise.

Six of One

1 *The Barbarian*

Applause he craves, music he loves, plus conversation
Plus working lunches plus the idea of progress
To which his days are a studied contribution.
The damned are a vulgar lot and he'll not bless
Them with enlightenment though there are some
To whom he'll show his sweetest disposition,
Even invite into his mind's kingdom
Where wisdom like a golden brooch is seen
Mesmeric as the thought of his own origin.
To accept one's true function is the problem.
Instruct the ignorant; ignorance is a sin.
Civilisation being the urge towards self-control
He makes articulate the pitifully dumb,
Dark souls lit with the glow of his own soul.

2 *The Expert*

The area is limited, it is true.
His knowledge of the area is not.
Right from the start, he knew what to do
And how to do it. All the fish he caught
Were salmon of knowledge and not once
Did he burn his thumb although he touched the fire
Of minds zealous as his own. God's a dunce
When the expert pronounces in his sphere
For he has scoured the fecund libraries
Till each one yielded all its special riches.
Prometheus, overworked and undersexed,
Files in his mind the succulent clarities
Knowing, from the ways of pricks and bitches,
Living is a footnote to the authentic text.

3 *The Warriors*

First, the leprechaun, gritty and sincere
Although his fairy rhetoric might spill
Like heaven upon all heads staring here
Till they felt clonked by some cosmic bible;
And then yon moon-faced fat above the beard
Blowing its dust across the helpless stones
Splutters to be heard, and will be heard
By all who see these two as paragons,
Warriors furring from the visionary north
To execute their comprehensive plan,
Improve the shabby towns, re-write the laws,
Assert for good their quintessential worth
Thus re-discovering heroic man
Pregnant with honour in service to The Cause.

4 *The Missionary*

Dear Souls, I am here on behalf of God.
My mind is made of His light.
I'm ready to shred my flesh, shed my blood
Doing His work among you. It
Is clear that all your gods must go
Back into the darkness from which they came.
I tell you this because I know.

You, your women and children will know the same.
Pray, O my brothers, for humility
And courage to surrender to the true.
Each man is a star, his soul is bright
As anything the heavens have to show.
Heaven's brightness flows to you from me
And on behalf of God I say, that's right.

5 *The Convert*

Reason, king of reasons, reigned alone.
There could never be another
Pretender to the throne
Of understanding. Mary, God's mother,
And other sweet begetters of the divine,
Together with all antics of the magic dark
Within the heart, were unquestionably fine
Illusions, especially when seen to work
For simple mortals. And then, one day,
In the broad sun, reason upped and slipped away
Restless, perhaps, for different air and food.
Our reasonable man felt quite distrait
And shocked admiring friends who heard him say
(He meant it too) 'Thank God! Thank God!'

6 *The Savage Ego Is a Circus Tent*

The savage ego is a circus tent
Containing the beasties and the people
Clapped together into a violent
Belch in the middle of a field.
Innocent eyes, as ever, widen at the sight
Of brave man swallowing fire;
Daddy is a surge of lost delight
Finding that tigers are what tigers were.
Elephants, snakes, the man on stilts,
Clowns, Fat Woman, mountain of happy lard,
Vivid fliers defying sternest laws
Replace the solid world that melts
Until no heart can ever again grow hard
Nor anything be heard except applause.

A Short Story

'For *Hunger*, a short story by James Stephens,
I am bid eleven pounds!'
The auctioneer
With fat red-faced finality
Brings his hammer down.
I think how Stephens
Suffering, remote,
Trudged Dublin streets,
Brooding on the singers and the wise,
Wolves of hunger prowling in his heart,
Sorrow in his eyes.

Heigh-Ho

Judas Iscariot is buried and dead
Heigh-Ho buried and dead
And the heartbreaking worms work to nibble his head
Heigh-Ho nibble his head

Judas Iscariot has run out of cash
Heigh-Ho run out of cash
O give him a choice of the nail or the lash
Heigh-Ho the nail or the lash

Judas Iscariot has run out of hope
Heigh-Ho run out of hope
And he's casting his eye on this rogue of a rope
Heigh-Ho this rogue of a rope

Judas Iscariot would make a great cry
Heigh-Ho make a great cry
But he knows in his heart he'd get no reply
Heigh-Ho get no reply

Judas Iscariot with silence is one
Heigh-Ho silence is one
Questions and answers can't tell what is done
Heigh-Ho tell what is done

Judas Iscariot swings from a tree
Heigh-Ho swings from a tree
O he was the bad one the good ones agree
Heigh-Ho the good ones agree

Judas Iscariot grins at his doom
Heigh-Ho grins at his doom
Where did he come from? Out of what womb?
Heigh-Ho out of what womb?

Judas Iscariot is hanging alone
Heigh-Ho hanging alone
And no one can say where Judas is gone
Heigh-Ho Judas is gone

But I met an old goat who said Judas is well
Heigh-Ho Judas is well
And as long as that's true there's hope left in hell
Heigh-Ho there's hope left in hell

The Ovens

Six o'clock of a May morning,
He rises with nothing to say
Except the silent sentence he passes on himself
To attend the ovens all day.
But first he takes a peek at the May sky
Notes the old working sun
Faithful to its slavery as any man.
He shuffles in to the ovens then.
He knows each one better than his wife
Who lies abed and modestly snores.
The ovens wait and seem to beckon
As they have beckoned for fifty years.
He opens, one by one, the high iron doors.

The Kill

Quick on the turn, the brindled bitch stretches
For the twisting terrified fur;
Half the field to go, the hound reaches
Nearer and nearer the tiring hare –
Tired of eluding the death in the slender
That bears implacably down
On its back, the hare twists frantically
Again – then as hound's teeth crush bone,

Draw blood, it cries like a choking child
And is ripped asunder as two men
Pant to the scene; one calms the wild-
Eyed hound, rubbing the sides, the long backbone;
The other (in case the hare is still in pain)
Breaks the warm neck. They move to the hunt again.

John Bradburne

Your truly balanced man is a dead man.
Bring the old coach out of retirement
To steer the lanky youngster in the rain
Running to see what it means and has meant
To puzzled daylight and more puzzled sleep;
Or let that other aspire to his African cave
And pray for bees in his room to keep
Neighbours away who worry because he must save
His solitude and work towards three white flowers,
Three drops of blood, three wishes; the last will be fulfilled
In his coffin with newspaper under his back.
Your balanced man will likely come to power,
Mention, sometimes, John Bradburne at the Wailing Wall,
Fighting the red ants, loving the heart of the rock.

Failure

Who can match
The green undulations of the plant on the window-sill
Or the cat's shadowy movement
Along the whitewashed wall?
Merely to stand where man-planted rocks
Oppress each other in the sun,
To see a girl in a green raincoat
Caress the sand with vague eyes
Is to taste the failure that is the source
Of all our celebration.
Who will understand the desolation
That is the father of all our fun?
A man wearing a full red cloak
Bearing a long brown staff
Is walking across the sand
In the direction of Dún Laoghaire.
There are small pools, impertinent tides
Mimicking the horizon.
Horses will come shortly, thunder
Silver watersparks to a mid-air heaven,
A rat will dart from the rocks
Into the sun, run back, lacking trust
In crust of foam or shell or shipwreck,
Old women with milkwhite feet
Will lie in the grass, drinking summer.
I will look at all this, loving it
As I have always loved it,
Feeling the failure rise like the tide,
Waves wasting their perfection
On my ignorant shores.

Islandman

The use of a persona in poetry is not a refusal to confront and explore the self but a method of extending it, procuring for it a more imaginative and enriching breathing space by driving out the demons of embarrassment and inhibition and some, at least, of the more crippling forms of shyness and sensitivity. A persona, though apparently shadowy and elusive, can be a liberating agent. It/he/she can provide friendly company in loneliness and give dignity to desolation.

Through an act of sustained and deliberate indirectness, it is possible to say more completely whatever one has to say. It is one of the fertile paradoxes of poetry that one can be more candid by engaging less in frontalism and by listening more keenly to the voices of the personae in the wings. A persona embodies not only some essential, peculiarly bewildered aspects of one's self but also, one hopes, something of everybody. I don't know why, but I'm convinced that the persona, obliquely manipulating and orchestrating the monstrous yet magnificent energies of egotism, is capable of revealing what the poet at any given moment believes he knows of reality in such a way that, for example, horror is presented with a grace, and therefore a precision, only rarely available to the mere self. Like a courteous host, the persona introduces the self to itself and lets the dialogue begin and continue unimpeded. (Other individuals at the party may crash in, of course. Such interruptions must be endured and allowed to expire before the dialogue can resume.)

We are all occasionally turned to stone by what we witness, think and feel. Out of that selfstone, the imagination moulds and coaxes a persona who, entering poems and animating them by his presence, is seen and felt to be a creature of flesh and blood. The cold of stone is imaginatively caressed into human warmth, surely one of the transfiguring graces of poetry. (It can happen the other way round too, and be no less a transfiguring grace.) My islandman is as real to me as the people I meet every day because he *is*, in fact, these very people, but without their disconcerting ways, arbitrary opinions, puzzling eccentricities, transient yet upsetting incursions into the mere, messy self which nevertheless remains the truest if murkiest source of poetry. The persona helps me to see through and under these necessary distractions to the essential humanity of people and therefore to come into contact with what I hope is my own. It is possible, and necessary, to hope that we are beginning to be more human. Poetry insists that we, with the help of the liberating persona, allow ourselves to dare become ourselves, for a time at least. The persona appears to want to make the self more fluid, multiple, articulate. It is like a shadow that darklylightly stresses the validity of the substance.

There may be simpler and more effective ways for a poet to do this. I'd love to know them because I want to love every heartbeat, every musical second of happiness and grief, boredom and fun and the usual no-man's-land of viable and reasonably rewarded half-being, permitted between stoneself and definitive dust. Whatever forces help one to love this frequently muted music of time are to be welcomed by imagination and intelligence, body and soul. Whatever or whoever you are, be with me now.

The following poem was written during a year of depression. One shouldn't make too much of these things; but a small room became for me an island in a fairly remote part of the Shannon estuary. I met the islandman there.

I will try to speak of the island
As though
My words were clear
As a field of snow

Covering the green centre, dark edges,
Patches of blue mud
Cracking in summer into zigzag lines
Suggesting the directions of my own blood.

I hear the old men talk like prophets
Of heaven and hell;
When the tide is out I take in my hands
An empty shell

Knowing the flesh the sea has made
Splits the sky
In a white, ragged,
Ever-hungry cry

Echoing voices I hear insist
That nothing fills
This gouged world
Of empty shells.

Wherever I look, nothing but fragments
Hints of battles
Hints of men praising God
Hints of power to behold the daisy.

Fragment in a world of fragments
I watch an eel's body
Make letters in water
Before it vanishes in gravel,
Old, black, literate snake
Despairing of men.

My heart, my hands are empty.
The sea itself could not make them full.
In its gravelwater world
The snake is whole.

I take a fistful of wet seaweed
And squeeze till my fingers seem to meet.
The loneliness of my own life
And of the lives of others
Drops at my feet.

When I stand in the ruined castle
I hear again the banquet clatter,
Laughter of women and men

Dying out over the Shannon
That covers the mud,
Grey veil over the face
Of a disappointed god

Whose hope dropped from the battlements
Into the mud below.
Buried in blackness there, hope hears overhead
The river come and go.

Three miles from the island
Is the graveyard where I'll
Go down.

What I know of the world
Is buried there.

My people
Plucked the sea
Worked the fields
Created their own angels.

From my own door
I see the bones

Of the old church
Full of holes, like lost centuries.
Put the wind's mouth to those holes –
You have music to make Tice Nugent
Lay the strings aside.

On summer evenings
Old bones shine
With a brightness that hurts my eyes
As if God, for his pleasure,
Made a bonfire of the dead
Or tried to blind himself with human loss.
I could not hear such music
See such fire
Anywhere but here.

The last time I leave the island
It will be nothing to me.

Was it ever anything
But my own eyes
Fondling its body?

I know
Children's laughter grows deep green grass
Women's hearts fatten the rat
Old men's anguish satisfies the fox
And the backbone of a lively boy
Gives a fertile tongue to the clover.

Why am I furious at the sight
Of broken things,
At wrecked hearthstones, smashed walls?
They hurt me like wrongs

Planned before I was born,
Reminders of a state
That deepens my sense of injustice,
Nourishes my hate

But cannot reconcile me
To the blade betrayed by rust,
The door rattling in the abandoned home,
The bullet in the gull's breast.

There is always this hope in being still,
Listening to the wind,
Letting troubled eyes look their full

At the crab's progress.
Here is your scuttling builder of cities
Full of a proper fuss and purpose

Though rarely escaping the mud.
If I bend down I can see the tiny marks
His claws have made

On the blue surface, thin creeks
The river will fill in time,
Streets awaiting the works

Of their appointed architect.
I am filled with admiration for the crab's blueprints
And regret

That first wave,
Dream-wrecker, smasher of cities, gift-bringer,
Purge, law, bully, fresh grave.

Do not speak to me of sacrifice.
The summer tide
Allows the dancing flies
Their brief ecstatic life

And flows calmly
Still...so still,
A clean vein of peace
That could swallow all.

'Move! Move!' the sea says
'Like my greenest pits and furrows.'
'Dare' says the island, 'to accept
Your own repose.'

Between sea and island
Pools and stones
The battle is always won and lost
In my own bones.

Every time I walk the shore
The shore is changed from what it was
Before the sea came to cover it.
These changes are written in cold places,
Pools like my own eyes
Staring at the castle gapped in the sun.
The changes go on and on.
I endure them as the shore endures the sea.
My eyes sympathise with sea and shore.
Sea and shore ignore me.

If I ever learn to make what I feel and see
As whole
As the island appears to be
I shall recognise
The roots of sadness behind people's eyes

And link them with my own.
Till then
I let a feather drop from my fingers
And watch it flutter down
Between a broken shell and a broken stone.

Cursed be the hand that splits the island
Making *they* and *we*,
Forcing bits of my own heart to drift off
Into the sea.

Thought of the bodies that have trampled the island,
Gone out and back, are dead
To enrich the grass the rabbits nibble
Hurts my head.

Silent old island, you absorb us all
In age or youth.
We crawl on your skin like flies a while
To find your mouth.

Listen, the island is not dead
Although debris drifts in
Like bits of lost mythologies
Mingling with shingle, scraping rock and stone.
Evidence of death converges
On even the greenest corner of the island.
Somewhere the ghostly stations
Despatch their messengers with poisoned omens.

That is why I rise to fight the death
The shackled sea is forced to bring.
Strange waves of strength muscle my will
When, following the brief designs of my own breath,
I pause to hear a blackbird sing
Or watch a fox illumined on a hill.

The months of the year
Are twelve moods of the maker.
My blood does not resist them
But tries to surrender
To pit and mountain.
I endure his dream, he mine.
I never wonder, in the worst of nights,
Why the morning was so fine.

Looking out across the sloblands,
Muck-reaches, muck-depths,
I see the years are steps through the muck,
Footprints before and after
This body that I see
Dragging towards water.

Water is music and murder,
Purge and threat.
Staring and listening
I return to myself in it,

Ungraspable presence,
Weapon of storms,
Killer of the inappropriate,
Sly inquirer,
Breeder of forms.

It is said the island will sink in the sea.
I find that acceptable.
Insatiate silence devours
Every desperate syllable.

If those scoundrel seabirds that I love
Ever learn to sing
They will enchant the heart with the music of water
– The king.

I crack a match in the dark.
Every ghost that I can name,
Guard and prisoner of the heart,
Concentrates about the flame.

Seabirds that break my sleep
Before full morning
Crying and barking in the sky
Pierce me like stabs of memory
That will not leave me until I die.

One is the cry of a nightmare child,
One is remorse, one is the cough
Of flesh half-rotten,
And one is the cry of a girl in the dark,
All words forgotten.

Sometimes I sense the world's filth
Converging on the island.
The sea is a slave
With a foul cargo on its back.

I have created this myself.
What is now returning
In a horrid, drifting ooze
Emanated from my own heart.

Why should I blame the sea,
Mere vehicle for my own crime?
It is my curse
That no matter where I look
I see my own face, hear my own name,
Find mocking mirrors everywhere
Accepting my blackest oath, my truest prayer.

I will not blame the sea
But I wish the sea were free of me
That I might face the threat the island suffers
From evils drifting night and day
Out of hearts like mine.

It is the heart
That has fouled the sea.
I can no longer stand apart
In vigilance or worry.
The sea whispers 'I am your guilt,
Because of you, I am obscene.
I am the foulness that you dreamed.
How will you make me clean?'

If the sea around me were to become
A sea of blood lapping the island
In an endless rhythm of accusation
I would understand.

So much has been murdered here,
Youth cut down in a moment,
Children...the old.

The story will never be told.

I think sometimes the sea knows it,
Crafty old hoarder of tales
And one day...one day...so burdened
With what it knows

The sea will rise

Changed to a sea of blood

And wash the island in a red rhythm of accusation.

No one will remain untouched
By that rhythm,

It will enter the lives of all
Who have walked the land.

And we,
Witnesses, killers, reporters
May understand.

Though it was a warm summer
It took weeks for the whale's carcase to rot
As it lay there on the shore.
Every day the gulls ate

The flesh, hacking and rending
Till there was nothing but bones.
Now when I walk that way
I still find bits of the whale

Scattered in weed or bad grass.
I hold in my hand
Clues to a death I shall never solve,
Knowing little even of land

And so much less of this bone
Darkest fathoms could not keep
In their grasp, but surrendered
To gluttonous beaks to rend and rip.

This evening I can barely tell
The sea from the land.
I can make out the seabirds returning
Almost touching the sea's ground,

Heads low as though in gratitude
For the covering night,
Wings dipping the spindrift
Blowing darkly across my sight

In this light where everything
Becomes everything else.
When I close my eyes the beat of the waves
Is my own pulse.

I see the nettles
Clean and wicked after rain.
They trouble me. I'll never see them
In this light again.

I have heard it argued
This is not really an island.

If I had eyes to see
I would know it was one with the mainland

Bulking between my eyes and the sky.
My answer is no more
Than the sound of a sparrow scratching in gravel
Here at my own door.

One evening I discovered the sky
Was an arena like my own heart.
Creatures ate each other there
For the sport of the watching gods.
When I closed my eyes I heard each cry

Filling my heart with its own pain.
This pain was like no other I had ever known.
It belonged to the sky, the grey and blue reaches.
Out there it lived and extended towards me.
Now it is my own.

When the sun pays attention to the island
Casting a special light on the stones
I am conscious of drawing breath somewhere
Between stars and skeletons

– All hidden.
Held by what is concealed
I could wonder forever
At the world revealed

By the sun's attention.
Between sky and slime
My eyes touch things as though
For the first time, or the last time.

I stroke the ferret's golden head
With my right hand.
Accepting the gesture, he gives no sign
Of what he has found

Down in the darkness under the tree
Or what he has left for dead.
My fingers drink the purpose
Of the golden head.

I bend among stones.
Two hours ago the tide was full.
I see the packed bones
Of the rabbit's skull

Ready to shed the skin.
Terror lives in the dead eyes.
I touch the wet fur with my fingers,
With my dumb cries.

Those who live alone
Should die alone.
Every wave that breaks on the gravelled shore
Is a lonely man

Scattering the last bits of himself on the land.
The sea tries to suck him back again
But he has broken himself into countless pieces
And gone down

Among the gravel creatures
That share their home
With pieces of shipwreck, weed, bone, timber,
Disintegrating patterns of foam.

Names of martyrs never die,
O'Scanlon, Hanrahan, O'Shea.
Every meadow in this island
Gives a good crop of hay.

Many will have spoken to you of the fragile
Gift of the days.
Because I know the smell of the death-bed
I know the meaning of praise.

Because I have knelt at the head of a corpse
And kissed its face
I have taken seaweed in my hands
In a dripping place

And pressed it to my lips.
I have lifted stones
And rubbed them over my flesh.
I have gone

Out at night to look at the tide
That cannot rest.
Cattle shifted in a nearby field
And a bat crossed

Inches over my head.
There was a legend of spiders in the air
And I knew their art would astonish me
If I reached another summer.

Most of this happened
Under a chill glitter, a silver blaze.
In the common light I shudder
At the gift of the days.

There is nothing that has not been given
But how does one receive
Fresh wetness on an upturned face
Or the hot crust of a white loaf?

Or the images in a winter fire
Filling the house with their own
Suggestions filtering
Through to the crouched bone?

Flesh is a clumsy receiver,
Graceless and dumb.
The shadows help it on its way
To what it may become.

If I become an old man
Mumbling how hard it is to bear the days
I think I will spend the winter
Looking for suntraps in out-of-the-way places

Like this old man I know,
A craggy old boy trudging along
Making sucking noises with his lips,
Complaining

About the yahoo sun, never around
When it is wanted most.
'This island is a crazy dream
And the sun is a ghost!'

All the strength of the sea
Worked
To drop at my feet
This patch of shrivelling foam.

I spend myself
Again and again
To make this island
A home.

Though it spawned me, reared me,
Led me by the hand,
I wonder indeed if I know anything
Of the island,

If my life is a long ignorance
Suffered alone,
An impotent trek from door to road
Over mud and stone,

A movement, idiotic, repeated,
Under similar skies.
The island's answer is silence.
The island is wise,

Granting, as always, the days
That appear to belong to me,
Permitting all creatures who wish
To set out to sea.

Let the nightmare bring what it will,
Make my own evil
Grotesque as possible,

Resurrect the dead to accuse
Me of indifference or neglect,
Present a face whose hope I wrecked,

Point out the source of the fright
I feel in a sleepless night,
I will wait in the dark for the first light

And rise
To taste an egg
That lay all night
In warm ashes.

Traces of neighbours who visited me
Are now no more
Than the track of water
Leading to my door

A friend makes of an evening
When for reasons of his own
He leaves the outer cold
To share my hearthstone.

Having said his say
He stands upright
And (is he a memory too?)
Becomes the night.

The sea's music affirms
What at best I have half-known.
I turn deaf ears to it for the most part

But now and again

It coincides with a music I find in myself.
I hear
'My glittering green is your power to move,
My spindrift is your fear,

My roar is your blood's emphasis
On what you can hardly face,
A cosmic push towards nothing,
Green weed like a necklace

Round the world's throat that whispers
Always back to me
How those on land live to reject
The insights of the sea.'

The plague of ignorance spreads forever.
Five drowned pups in a bag
Barely shift in the water.
My body is a wet log

Hacked from roots years ago,
Left to rot in the rain.
Bag and log
Know little of pain

And the water heaves like a heart
That cannot stop.
The water tries to lift the bag
But that grotesque shape

Is grown immovable as the island.
Bag, log, water, heart –
The sky is a face
Drinking the whole hurt,

Petrifying everything in sight, and out of sight.
There is not even a cry
Only a bag of death
Under a stone sky.

The sea's presence is everywhere in the house.
When I sleep
I am one with the most fragile and monstrous
Beings of the deep.

When I awaken
I consider the four walls that enclose me.
I am not mistaken.
I have been taken from the sea.

My blood is seabreath,
Seapresence my mind.
I live as though it were something else
I hoped to find.

This dream returns.
The island is running, running through the sea
But whether in pursuit or escape
Is beyond me.

It devours leagues, unable to stop
And beckons me to follow.
Swallowing the seadust
I rise and go

Where the island plunges
Whalebacked through hiss and roar
To sprawl in the amused light
Where it lay before

The frenzy summoned it
And the island answered the call,
Beckoning me. Now I wonder
Have we moved at all.

Rouse the drowsy gods.
Nail the island into the sea.
Is it fixed?
Brother, there's no guarantee.

No rock that I know
Is so sure
Of itself as to claim that the sun
Will shine on it tomorrow.

On this particular patch, the gods
Were not proved wrong
But inadequate.
Let them sleep again.

I try to imagine a man who can
Endure it all.
Everywhere I look I see him
Stumble and fall.

The raving poems of sleeplessness
Make the cock's greeting to the day
Tame as the lips of a communion-child
Learning how to pray

To the god who hovers over sleep
Yet never comes awake
To face the human consequence
Of his mistake

But sends those boiling images
That make the slavemind work, work,
While unshuttable eyes
Devour the dark.

When will we permit the sea in the head
To flow as it will?
The moon has laws but no theories.
It sends out a cold, golden call

And hangs in suspense for the answer
We fear to give.
I would release the sea in the head.
I would let it live,

Pour through the brain's darkest caves,
Out through the eyes,
Touching the distant skin of other
Minds and bodies.

Who will say which is more real –
My hands on the sea,
The strange flesh or the hurt roar
That is part of me?

Who will say which is more felt –
Loneliness
Or the desolation written on stones
When the sea withdraws?

I have learned to live both night and day
Uncertain of day and night.
This beautiful island is poised forever
In a dubious light.

I drink from a cracked cup
With white and blue stripes,
Walk for an hour
Where the world comes to a stop

And an evening tide
Shyly returns
Over the waiting muck.
Beyond this, a lifelight burns

Stronger than the light in my own window.
Towards that light now I set my face.
Seagoing wings in the darkness
Put disappointment in its place.

The wind that cuts the island tonight
Would galvanise the dead.
It snatches boats from the sea
Pitches them into my own blood
Scoops up waves, spits them
Into the stars' faces,
Lashes anger on the heads
Of island homes.

What is going on in the hearts of those
Standing still in the presence of this rage?
Where is the hawk that ripped the starling
At my own door yesterday?

Where are the white birds that know the humours
Of the smaller winds
And display their craft with a lightness
That lifts you out of your flesh?

Now, in the presence of this fury,
I am more remote from an understanding of calm
Than I have ever been.
This is an assault on what I have learned of peace
A cosmic attempt to destroy what I know, have been told,
Received in the homes, gleaned from the white birds.
I will hold. I will try to hold.

The island is made again.
Not everything is lost.
My heart is one with this morning's
Hoar frost.

I will try not to betray this moment
Despite all I have bought and sold.
I could never rise early enough
To live the cold.

Island,
Thank you for the straw of knowledge,
For standing by while I learned to cope
With my own ignorance in an ignorant world.
The best I will ever do is grope

Like a blind man through dark and light,
Huffing my way through words
And their worlds that will never be still
But send me slithering through muck
Without the grace of an eel

In a shallow pool.
I am never impartial as you are
But am glad for what I have found
Of a story told in the air
Between the sea and the land.

The bread of doubt my heart has eaten
Grew in your grass,
Fears that beat in my chest and head
Flared in your mud.
Whatever I know of the living and dead

Was whispered first in your trees.

The turning tides in my blood
Roared from your shore.
Like you, I am all, I am nothing.
There is nothing more.

My voice has the sound of your streams,
Secret streams, streams any traveller might see.
Out of your deepest springs, out of your buried stone
It came to me

The colour of rocks sunning themselves after rain,
Ripped feathers blown to the shore,
Hot bread to the touch,
Sharp, bright weather,

Curved beak savaging the shell
Pitched like innocence on the mud,
The man, the hound, the fox
Meeting in my blood.

Its hunger was your best gift,
Hunger that cannot die,
Hunger that increases the more it feeds
On what should satisfy.

It knows and lives with its own lies
And would speak what is true.
Out of your first silence it came.
It speaks for you.

He Left Us

Not much point in wishing he was different.
He went the road he chose to go
or had to.

He left us
a mythic ribbon,
a story told

boating on the Shannon
with congers revelling in their own flow.
a bright blue morning

between Christmas sunlight
and Easter snow.

The Bell

At six o'clock on a summer evening
   Danny Mulvihill rang the bell.
It could be heard out in Lislaughtin
   And down in Carrigafoyle.

The fields heard it and were still
   As Michael Enright's mind
Lulled by a field of wheat
   Goldening the ground.

Under the bridge the river calmed
   Its lifeblood towards the sea;
Touched by the bell the river kept
   Its depth for company.

At the height of the bridge Jack Jones stood alone
   Hearing the two sounds,
Through his blood flowed river and bell
   As through the summer land.

Then beyond the river adventured the bell,
    Beyond the silent man,
It lingered over every weed,
    It entered every stone,

It celebrated its own life,
    Its sense of itself as a friend
To even the midges and the briars,
    It praised its own end

Which, when it came, was hard to tell
    Since there remained on the air
Presences like happy ghosts
    Summoned from near and far.

Fool

'As great a fool as ever walked God's earth,'
They said, noting the uncouth gaping face;
Derision was his legacy from birth,
The playboy, clown and jester of the place.
In spring, he took a murderous blue blade
And muttering his usual foolish words,
Fingering in meadow, field and glade,
He slit the throats of new-born birds.

When he came home, dead fledglings in his hand,
He strode past those whose eyes were mockery;
Small bodies became bleeding trophies and
Lifting them in his right hand, the fine
Blade in his left, he'd cry exultantly –
'The birds, the singing birds of spring are mine.'

Killing the Winter

One rainy day in late November
Red gathered his builder's traps together;
While the Atlantic boiled in wicked weather
He shaped a small boat, killing the winter
With creation. In the first days of spring
He gave her a dandy finishing touch
With blue paint. 'God but she's the sweetest thing
Red ever made!' Clancy said as he watched

Red launch her proudly at Saleen Quay.
Clancy knew boats and hardly ever praised
But even if he'd wished he couldn't hide
Envious admiration as he saw
Red facing the Shannon, the white sail raised,
Blue beauty thrusting on a lively tide.

Spring

Curtin spent the winter in the County Home
And drank and whored and gambled in the spring;
I met him once, the black days coming on,
He told me straight that he was going in.
'Last night,' he said, 'I left a farmer's house,
The moon was up, a wicked light abroad,
The innocent roads were turning treacherous
And ice, you know, is the pure cruelty of God.

Well, soon enough, I'll meet the men who fail
At everything poor Christian men esteem.
Down-hearted villains! You should hear them sing!
Homeless as crows, yet they keep body and soul
Together. Just like me. Know what I mean?
The winter within walls. And then – the spring!'

Heat

MacDonagh sat and watched the summer dust,
Fixing his eye on a dry-as-powder stone
That through long years had stood the weather's test.
At his back, the implacable sun
Burned in the blue, withered the roadside grass
And where it willed, dispensed a savage life
That doubtless would in time be perilous
And lost. But now all seemed to thrive

In the high heat. White dust with his finger
He lifted, let it fall finely to the ground
Where on the stone he saw a tiny fly
Converge on a fellow creature, dart, linger
As though undecided, probe, touch, mount,
Stick to its back and lie there silently.

Loss

It was hard getting the bull on his knees
Then on his side but Jim Creed and Bob Flynn
Knocked him, tied the thick legs, held him down.
Fury began to burn in the slate eyes
When Xavier Canty came with rope and sticks.
He stood a while eyeing the trussed bull
And said 'The divil has balls as big as rocks
But no matter.' Canty bent, took the full

Scrotum in his fist, weighed the great globe of power,
Went to work with knot, stretch, thrust, cut and pull
Till the rich bloodlumps soaked into the grass.
He knelt at the bull's side for a full hour.
The other men still gripped the legs. The bull
Roared in the agony of loss.

Design

Mathematics? Formal logic?
Easy. What frightens is following a path
Where nobody has walked. Let me be quick
To say I welcome Cain's treachery, Christ's wrath –
Parables of what has happened for the first time.
But treachery and wrath are dead
Till the idea of anger or a crime
Beyond imagining howls into my head.

There is no difference then between
The skulking murderer in the woods,
Innocent brotherblood staining his hands,
And those squalid thoughts that I have known.
Legacy of men? Nightmare of the Gods?
A design that nobody understands.

6

Savage civilities

Moments When the Light

There are moments when the light
Makes me start up, fright
In my heart as if I feared to see
Unbearable clarity about me.
Once, on Portobello Bridge,
I had the sudden privilege
Of seeing light leap from the sky
About five o'clock on an autumn day,
Defining every visible thing,
Unseen by one among the moving throng;
Road, bridge, factory, canal,
Stained swans and filthy reeds, all
The set homegoing faces
Filling motorcars and buses;
Then I knew that energy is but
Unconsciousness; if moving men could
See where they are going, they would
Stop and contemplate the light
And never move again until
They understood why it should spill
A sudden benediction on
The head of every homegoing man.
But no one looked or saw the way
The waters danced for the visiting light
Or how green foliage glittered. It
Was ignored completely.
I knew the world is most at ease
With acceptable insanities,
Important nothings that command
The heart and mind of busy men
Who, had they seen it, might have praised
The light on Portobello Bridge.
But then, light broke. I looked. An evening glow.
Men go home because they do not know.

Pram

On the Liffeybed a pram
lies like a broken marriage.
Not even the all-knowing Liffey
will ever know the full story.
                    Overhead
gulls scream for bread,
for anything, this cold day.
Maggie MacDonagh begs on the bridge.
Thousands shiver homewards.
No one looks her way
but that won't stop Maggie
begging the air that doesn't give a damn,
her eyes deeper than the river
housing a broken pram.

The Hole

A wizened little old lady
Raised the alarm
(God between us and all harm)
– A smallish hole has appeared
In a road in Ringsend
And since the first moment
It was seen by human eyes
Is getting bigger all the time.

A local who considered himself a blasphemer
Said it reminded him of the mouth of God.
This outlandish image was reinforced
When a shirt factory fell into the hole
To be followed by a Corporation horse
Twenty-three humans
The body of a church
A betting office
Seven pubs
And a well-known greyhound-racing stadium.

The hole widened and deepened
Like the thought of history
In a scholar's mind.
It was a mouth with a cosmic appetite
Yet all the time remained
Silent and polite.
Strangest of all, the hole
Became increasingly magnetic.
Things and people formed
Into the most orderly queue
To fall into the hole.

You know what? said a distinguished member
Of the Church of Ireland,
A most thoughtful member of the queue,
After years of viable anguish
I feel that I have finally saved my soul.
It is a divine privilege
To fall into the hole.

Civil servants, priests, police,
Assiduous devotees of nightclubs
Sportsmen with an eye on records
Superbly articulate members
Of radio and television
Critics looking like green chickens
The Government followed by the Opposition
Students emptied of protest
Bishops and journalists and the cool people of science
Not forgetting the professors
Stooped with paradox and dichotomy
At various fascinating stages of decay
All
Dropped
Into the hole.

Latest reports say that the hole
(Hereinafter referred to as The Mouth)
Has begun to speak
After a period of incoherent mumbling.
It represents an appetite, it says,
(Thus confirming my original suspicion)
And would wish to be constantly fed.
It will swallow everything living
And even the more edible dead.

This thought seems more ungraspable
Than terrifying,
Though terrifying it undoubtedly is.

As for myself, I have so far
Avoided the queue.
You?

The day will come, I suppose,
When I must slip into that queue.
As well as myself, I shall offer
This poem
By way of tribute to the hole
Or The Mouth, if you prefer.
Down and down and down
I will fall,
Madly waving my tiny irrelevant poem
At all the great irrelevant poems
In the nowhere tumbling darkness,
Falling and falling and falling
With every cherished enemy and friend
Towards what we might all
According to our individual philosophies
Call
The end.

Our Place

The murders are increasingly common
In our place which certain of the old songs
Celebrate as a changeless pastoral heaven.
Due, however, to some folk's sense of wrong
Nothing is right nowadays. I must confess
I've become a bit of a callous bastard
Myself. Sipping the latest atrocities
From our one good paper shows how little I care.

Consider, for example, this morning's gem:
Two youths, both about sixteen, and said
To be savagely bored and out of work
Battered an old man to death in his bed.
Making his sister lie in a style of some shame
They pinned her through the neck with a garden-fork.

Johnny Gobless

Gaunt, ungracious in the rain,
fingering a silver chain,
he goes stalking up and down
blessing the unwieldy town.

Madness glitters in his eyes,
weight of sacred sympathies,
and from his lips explode, like birds,
flocks of rapid frightened words.

I think of lonely William Blake
who did a world make, re-make,
who hounded truth until it cried
and laid its head against his side,

whose discontent was made and given
by the amazing hand of heaven,
whose deep divine unhappiness
could only bless, could only bless,

as now this gaunt disordered man
in holy madnesss, knows he can
bless the city in the rain
fingering a silver chain.

Who but poet or madman could
affirm that all there is, is good?
Or with the truth of passion tell
that heaven holds out its hands to hell?

The Fool's Rod

The city, built in mire and mud,
is refuge for the poor and mad;
the busy man and watchful God
suffer the lash of the fool's rod.

And in the streets, the madmen ply
their holy trade of asking love
with alien eyes, while high above,
shrill seagulls, snowy scavengers
of air, lope, swerve, bank, plunge, make light
of all beneath their marvellous flight –
sewers that rattle, sink and slide
into the fat outrunning tide;
madmen shuffling past blithe lovers
who smile and perfectly rejoice;
past glittering windows, showy flowers,
past silences and small endeavours
and everything without a voice.

Corroding silence is the worst,
has wounded many a noble heart,
made splendid rage and sorrow start
from good Jon Swift, the city's son
and indignation's paragon,
who, loving bitterly, was first
to fight that silence tooth and nail,
to pour the lava of his rage
into the soul of every age,
to break the rod that caused it all.

How strange it is that madmen sing
in sidestreets, rifling litter,
seeking something worse or better
than a passing glance. O may they bring
their queer heart-scalding song
into all armoured hearts, old, young,
indifferent, and may they
give the brutal world that vision
that earns them pity and derision –
lost kingdom gained incredibly,
stretched fields that thrive in sun and wind,
some loveliness whose origin
is built astoundingly within
the deep elysium of the mind.

I name the names of Dublin's mad;
Red Biddy, laughing at the doom
that calls through laneways of the Coombe;
Johnny Gobless, whose heavy tread
is total gluttony for God;
Mad Meg in whose dishevelled hair

the Holy Spirit set a star,
and who, 'tis said, at one time had
such surpassing beauty, all men
who witnessed it were there and then
changed inwardly; Nostromo, tall
and bearded, maddest of them all;
the only mad you'd ever find
who'd spit at rain or clout the wind;
old Zozimus, whose gamey life
became an act of faith in strife;
the Fop, a gentleman from hell,
a defiant rose in his lapel;
Mad Peggie, lifting up her skirts
to remind the world where life spurts
from; then, grabbing one of sixteen
children, cavorts along the street
till at Whitefriars she stands to greet
the Virgin, heaven's fertile queen;
Bang-Bang, who aims the loaded gun
of his defiance at everyone;
and all the nameless ones who talk
to beckoning angels as they walk
the streets with frantic mouths that could
express the marvellous folly of God.

Gibbering tattered souls pass by
raising their strange and distant cry
for something lost in air or ground
that may be sought but never found,
as they, poor souls who crave and moan,
are always seen but never known.
The city, built in mire and mud,
is refuge for the poor and mad;
the busy man and watchful God
suffer the lash of the fool's rod.

A Parable of Pimlico

A kind lady of poorish Pimlico,
Lonely, developed the unusual custom
Of feeding a rat that dared to her door.
Bread, mainly. The rat ate every crumb.
The kind lady relaxed into her chair
Feeling, almost, that she had found a friend.
The rat scoffed offerings with rattish care
Darting the odd glance at the lady's hand.
The lady sickened. The rat nipped to her door
And crossed the ready threshold for the bread
She owed him. But hunger owned the place.
Pimlico neighbours didn't visit her.
As she lay weak, weaker, and yet not dead
The rat sniffed at the hospitable face.

In Dublin

'Swearing, cursing, fighting, drunkenness,
God's Holy Name dishonoured and blasphemed
To the scandal and grief of all good men,
Obscenity the Devil would be hard put to dream,
Nothing but contempt for the laws of the land
And the known articles of war –
I will change the ways of this reeking town
For the good of the Irish poor:

Let the buff coat, instead of the black gown
Appear in Dublin pulpits; God knows it is
Meritorious to use two swords well.
Silence St Austin and Thomas Aquinas,
Let Protestant honesty come into its own.'

He stabled his horses in St Patrick's Cathedral.

Crossing the bridge

When the old lady stopped Ace on O'Connell Bridge
and asked 'What is a poem, Mr de Horner?'
Ace was flummoxed. The old lady went on,
'Whenever I hear or read a poem

I feel as if I'd a friend somewhere
who surprises me in the strangest ways,
I see pictures in my mind which I
haven't seen since childhood days,

I hear music sweet as my father's fiddle
in the house I was born in down the country.
But, Mr de Horner, when I read your twaddle
I'm listening to the squeaks of a lost and lonely

soul. You do have a soul, Mr de Horner,
don't you? Don't you? A soul? In spite of your jingles?'

                    Ace lowered his head.

'A soul,' he murmured, 'A soul...' He trailed off.

'Thank you for telling me all that,' the old lady said

and crossed the bridge into one of the jungles.

Bewley's coarse brown bread (unsliced)

There are days when Ace
can't begin to be human
till he feeds the seagulls

worrying the Liffey. He buys
a loaf of Bewley's coarse brown bread
(unsliced), plods through the eyes

of Westmoreland Street, turns left
at O'Connell Bridge, heads for
the wall, breaks the bread,

starts to feed the shrieking
creatures of whatever heaven
hangs over scuttery Dublin

like a letter begun by a fallen
angel with a nice writing style
millions of years ago, still

being written by hordes of
angels and demons, manky chancers,
chatty conmen, parodists of love

and hate, parodists of parody itself. Alone
at the wall, he watches the ravenous
birds come into their own,

breaking the bread from the generous
waters of old mother Liffey
(how she flows for you for me for all of us!)

and slowly, like light stealing
through the overcoat dark of a winter morning
a feeling, a small real feeling

of being human invades old Ace (hard
enough to come by these days). He feeds the birds
till the sign of a smile crosses his face.

Not for the first time he thanks
the insatiable gulls. Soon he'll walk
past restaurants shops churches banks

more human with every step.
(Would the gulls eat him, properly prepared?)
Who knows their ferocious snow? He may let it rip

tonight, find something new in this parodyplace,
this black pool of cynical skins
and quite unoriginal sins,

some new slant on the gathering dark,
gossip lighting up living and dead,
the fabulous power of coarse brown bread

bobbing on the river
slowly creating the sign of a smile
auguring a hurt unkillable style.

Hunchback

Day after twisted day, I carry it on
My back – this devil's hump, this mound
Of misery sprung from the roots in
My body's clay, grotesque companion
Of my wildest dreams. I have to bend
Beneath it, flame and rage
Because distortion is my closest friend,
The faithful ally of my youth and age.

Along the quays I walk and watch
The seagulls climbing in their flight
Or skimming the slow Liffey. Such
Perfection hurts my blood. In broad daylight,
My ugliness gapes like a wound while I,
Hands rammed in empty pockets, see
White miracles of grace on every side.
They circle to astonish and torment me.

Torment eats my heart. I see small ships
From Hamburg, Copenhagen. A sailor
Gamecocks on an upper deck. My lips
Form silently the names – *Regina*,
Honor Belle. Ships are women, queens
That ride the ocean, plough the sea,
Leaving the white foam of unrest where they have been,
Hacking hard voyages from port to port in me.

The outside world explores me but I
Am unknown territory, a secret river
Of obscure source, uncertain estuary.
I flow through time that time may yet deliver
Me from myself, my sense of well-made
Manhood from monstrous flesh and bone.
Creation preens itself, neat planets are displayed,
Jupiter wheels above me. I move alone.

The Liberties, Townsend Street, Stephen's Green,
Stations in my shuffling odyssey
Of old, appalling loneliness and pain;
While girls grow up and boys put out to sea
And women shape new histories in the womb,
I walk the streets of failure day and night,
Watching the symmetries life must assume,
Easy ships at anchor, able birds in flight.

O shapely world that I'm compelled to see
But be no part of, I move
Through your designs deliberately.
I feel a certain love
For what I see but cannot linger on;
Wet pavements shine at night, clean church-bells ring,
I stand where multitudes have come and gone –
The parody best proves the real thing.

Eating a star

Ace and Kanooce strolled across O'Connell Bridge
Liffey chucklingsobbing underneath
like a secret history of women,
enough to take your breath

away if you studied it
but what dog or poet has time for that?
Kanooce and Ace were passing Eason's Bookshop
when Kanooce stopped, stared at

Madonna, star of sex, on the cover
of a not inexpensive book in the window.
Kanooce leaped, sank his fangs in the goddess,

tore her to pieces, began licking her
pieces with a vigour to induce vertigo
in onlookers. (There were many). Poor, dizzy, pop-eyed Ace!

Poor poet! Poor dog! Poor star of sex!
Poor star of all the seas!

Liffey slides on, slimey with secret histories.

Ambulance

Shrieking on its mercy mission,
The white hysterical bully
Blows all things out of its way,
Cutting through the slack city
Like a knife through flesh.

People respect potential saviours
And immediately step aside,
Watching it pitch and scream ahead,
Ignoring the lights, breaking the rules,
Lurching on the crazy line
Between the living and the dead.

A Visit

No.10 bus to the Park.
The conductor gives his promised shout.
I enter the house of the mad.

A late March day. The sun
Warms my back as I go in.
They sit, stand, walk, stare. Are alone.

No sharing this loneliness.
Unrelatedness
Is the skin on every face.

Unrelatedness.
I'd like to smash through this,
But find only an abyss. An abyss.

I've come to see a man.
I find him in the garden.
Flowers flourish all about him

But he is withering now,
Failing away from me.
I am stupid, cut off. How

Can I suggest a link?
I can neither speak nor think.
He speaks though, his eyes sunk

In his head.
Something about dolls he has made.
All around, the unreachable mad.

He has painted pictures too.
They cover the walls of his room.
Maybe I should see them sometime?

Yes I would. What are they about?
He can't say that.
I'll find out.

So.
After silence, I must go.
What else can I do?

As if I'd never been he sits there.
Mad flowers bloom everywhere.
Men and women stare at me. They stare.

Dream of a Black Fox

The black fox loped out of the hills
And circled for several hours,
Eyes bright with menace, teeth
White in the light, tail dragging the ground.
The woman in my arms cringed with fear,
Collapsed crying, her head hurting my neck.
She became dumb fear.

The black fox, big as a pony,
Circled and circled,
Whimsical executioner,
Torment dripping like saliva from its jaws.
Too afraid to show my fear,
I watched it as it circled;
Then it leaped across me
Its great black body breaking the air,
Landing on a wall above my head.

Turning then, it looked at me.

And I saw it was magnificent,
Ruling the darkness, lord of its element,
Scorning all who are afraid,
Seeming even to smile
At human pettiness and fear.

The woman in my arms looked up
At this lord of darkness
And as quickly hid her head again.
Then the fox turned and was gone
Leaving us with fear
And safety –
Every usual illusion.

Quiet now, no longer trembling,
She lay in my arms,
Still as a sleeping child.

I knew I had seen fear,
Fear dispelled by what makes fear
A part of pure creation.
It might have taught me
Mastery of myself,
Dominion over death,
But was content to leap
With ease and majesty
Across the valleys and the hills of sleep.

The Black Fox, Again

Sixteen years ago, I saw the black fox
For what seemed the first and only time.
But last night it came back.
There was a countryman, a beggar,
Sitting on the floor behind a hall-door
Drinking whiskey from a tin-cup
Chained through a hole in the side of his mouth
Crying his eyes down and out
Because he knew he would never again know
Who or where he was.
He had beautiful slim wrists
But his face had gone dirty and cruel
With broken, red eyes
And when he said 'Give me a pound now
Because you'll be giving it to yourself,'
I gave him what money I had
And felt myself unburdened of myself.
'Turn around now,' he said, 'And look

At the corner of the half-empty shed.
If you don't look, I'll wish you dead.'
I did.
There was the black fox
Back from eternity
Fixing its quiet eyes on me
But more indolent than before,
Less consciously magnificent, more piercing
And wise in the way it looked at me.
'Why have you come back?' I asked
'And why do you look at me like that?'
The black fox did not speak
But moved its eyes and sides
And I knew the dogs were coming
In all their howling might
From all the quarters of the days and nights
To kill the black fox. That
Was the moment when the black fox smiled
As if no creature had ever been defiled
By any other
And shifting its sides in a quicker rhythm
Like an instrument played by invisible fingers
Became the beggar with the face of a child
Who had no fear, for the time being,
Of dogs tamed or wild.
The dogs flocked, the beggar-child played
With heads and necks and fangs and tails
Then drove them into the shed
With a word I scarcely heard
And locked it.

As the bolt homed
Like a final thought in any simple head
The black fox faced me again,
Directed me to the hall-door
Where the young man with the cruel face
And the broken, red eyes
Complained and drank, drank and complained.
The tin-cup, chained to him,
Was always full, always drained.
The dogs were howling now.
My eyes sank deep into the black fox's eyes,
Saw dogs and chains and children and killings,
Long streets with pavements made of cries
Of those who'd journeyed far to their despair,
Deliberate women inventing faces

They might live in for a scented while,
Old men shuffling out of themselves
In frayed gaberdines of pain
Into scarce patches of sunlight
Like fresh-minted pennies, glittering.

The black fox,
Quiet, indolent and wise, went round
The far corner of the shed and vanished.
I was back out of its eyes.
The young man vanished too
Rattling his cup and chain.
The dogs had turned to silence.
The shed had no door.
The bolt had failed to become a shadow.
I shivered a little, feeling the emptiness
Wrap itself about me
Like a cold embrace
Of fingers reaching from a lost
Forbidden place.

Clearing a Space

A man should clear a space for himself
Like Dublin city on a Sunday morning
About six o'clock.
Dublin and myself are rid of our traffic then
And I'm walking.

Houses are solitary and dignified
Streets are adventures
Twisting in and out and up and down my mind.
The river is talking to itself
And doesn't care if I eavesdrop.

No longer cluttered with purpose
The city turns to the mountains
And takes time to listen to the sea.
I witness all three communing in silence
Under a relaxed sky.

Bridges look aloof and protective.
The gates of the parks are closed
Green places must have their privacy too.
Office-blocks are empty, important and a bit
Pathetic, if they admitted it!

The small hills in this city are truly surprising
When they emerge in that early morning light.
Nobody has ever walked on them,
They are waiting for the first explorers
To straggle in from the needy north

And squat down here this minute
In weary legions
Between the cathedral and the river.
At the gates of conquest, they might enjoy a deep
Uninterrupted sleep.

To have been used so much, and without mercy,
And still to be capable of rediscovering
In itself the old nakedness
Is what makes a friend of the city
When sleep has failed.

I make through that nakedness to stumble on my own,
Surprised to find a city is so like a man.
Statues and monuments check me out as I pass
Clearing a space for myself the best I can,
One Sunday morning, in the original sun, in Dublin.

Herself and himself

They're driving in
from the cricketing fields of Dublin
past the Five Lamps, Empress Lane
and the Corner of the Talkers
where you'll still get wind
of the bombing of the North Strand
in a war we were no part of
or so we thought. It isn't always
we know what wars we're in.

There's shopping to be done,
young mouths waiting for baker's bread.
She knows the shops, the men and women
behind the counters. She knows himself too.
On a tough journey, a few words will do
to ensure the future will be fed.
She does the shops, gets what she wants,
they have two creamy pints together
then hit for home
between the worked fields and the sea,
herself and himself
words and silence
peace and war
you and me.

Lost place

Wouldn't it be nice to have a wee cottage
in Wicklow or Connemara
where I could go and meditate
on the sheer evil of Dublin

but dammit I'm part of the evil scene
as I watch the magpies rise
to the topmost branch of a winter tree
defining the horizon.

The country has come to the city
and will never again escape
to its pure pagan grandeur.
Civilisation is rape

and as we rape each other
with our tongues minds eyes
we have plans for our children.
We'll make 'em classy, rich, wise

as a guy with a black leather bag
at a traffic lights, a phone to his ear
airwaving the present, structuring the future.
There's nothing to fear

but this odd eruptive desire
for a cottage in a lost place
with silence for a strolling companion
and a clean wind in your face.

Whether I follow a wall splitting twenty fields
or sit in a rattling house by the sea
there are many things I have to say to silence.
Silence has many things to say to me.

Good Souls, to Survive

Things inside things endure
Longer than things exposed;
We see because we are blind
And should not be surprised to find
We survive because we're enclosed.

If merit is measured at all,
Vulnerability is the measure;
The little desire protection
With something approaching passion,
Will not be injured, cannot face error.

So the bird in astonishing flight
Chokes on the stricken blood,
The bull in the dust is one
With surrendered flesh and bone,
Naked on chill wood.

The real is rightly intolerable,
Its countenance stark and abrupt,
Good souls, to survive, select
Their symbols from among the elect –
Articulate, suave, corrupt.

But from corruption comes the deep
Desire to plunge to the true;
To dare is to redeem the blood,
Discover the buried good,
Be vulnerably new.

7

History

History is a cyclic poem written by Time
upon the memories of men.

SHELLEY

The Lislaughtin Cross

The Lislaughtin Cross is now in the National Museum in Dublin.
On the upper portion of the shaft and on the two arms of the front
there is a Black Letter inscription in Latin which in translation reads:
'Cornelius, son of John O'Connor, captain of his nation, and Juliana,
daughter of the Knight, caused me to be made by the hand of William,
son of Cornelius, June 4th, 1479.

William O'Connor was made when he made me
That others might adore
God of field and road, shore and river.

Some thought that I was made to be destroyed,
Burned the holy Abbey,
Murdered the calm men of God.

My rescuer ran until his terror and exhausted heart
Forced him to drop me
In the waiting earth of Ballymacassey

Where I lay three hundred years,
My golden body sinking
Deeper into the blackness,

A sun
Pitched into a dark
Waiting to cradle men,

A midnight not expecting morning,
The stillness of two hearts
Entered in each other.

A man named Jeffcott
Found me with his plough.
O see me now

Lifted from that lightless place
Where I understood the dead
And the blunderers above my head

Thumping to and fro
Building and breaking their worlds,
Bursting with get and go

Until they sank into the blackness where I lay,
Inviolate.
I stand now, polished in the light,

Saved from a repose
Impossible to speak of.
I lay so long at the heart of love

I am content to stand in this arranged place,
Upright, immaculate
Prisoner behind glass,

Hoarding in myself the touch of hands, of eyes,
The cries that cannot cease,
The black peace.

Lislaughtin Abbey

Flashing starlings twist and turn
    in the sky above my head,
while in Lislaughtin Abbey lie
    the packed anticipating dead.

Silent generations there
    that long had bent the knee
endow the Shannon with the grace
    of reaching to the sea.

Swollen by the rich juice of the dead
    the Shannon moves with ease
towards a mighty union with
    Atlantic mysteries.

But though the river sweeps beyond
    each congested bone,
its currents do not swirl towards
    a resurrection,

any more than starlings do
    that, fearing death this winter day,
create small thunder in the sky
    and shelter where they may,

ignoring green Lislaughtin where
    subtle shadows pass
through shattered altars, broken walls,
    the blood of martyrs in the grass,

into the ground that winters well
    and blossoms soon or late,
preserving patient multitudes
    who are content to wait

till they at last disturb the stones,
    the fox's lair, the starling's nest,
to cry out with the howling damned,
    to wonder with the Blessed,

to hear the word for which they wait
    under the coarse grass
the meanest blade of which assists
    in what must come to pass,

to see why silent centuries
    have finally sufficed
to purge all in the rising flood
    of the overflowing blood of Christ.

Restless at the gate, I turn away
    groping towards what can't be said
and I know I know but little
    of the birds, the river and the dead.

A Friend of the People

'Mine was the first Friend's face Ireland ever saw,
Little as it recognised me,' Oliver said.
'I came equipped with God's Fact, God's Law.
What did I find? Not men but hordes
Full of hatred, falsity and noise,
Undrilled, unpaid, driving herds of plundered
Cattle before them for subsistence;
Rushing down from hillsides, ambuscadoes,
Passes in the mountains, taking shelter in bogs
Where cavalry could not follow them;

Murder, pillage, conflagration, excommunication,
Wide-flowing blood, bluster high as heaven,
Demons, rabid dogs, wolves. I brought all to heel
Yet my reward was sibylline execration.

Glancing now at my bundle of Irish letters
(A form I think I have perfected)
I see a land run by Sanguinary Quacks
Utterly unconscious of their betters.
Do you think this disease could be cured
By sprinkling it with rose-water
Like a gift of perfume to a flowering daughter?
What could I do with individuals
Whose word was worthless as the barking of dogs?
I addressed the black ravening coil
Of blusterers at Drogheda and elsewhere:

"In this hand, the laws of earth and heaven:
In this, my sword. Obey and live. Refuse and die."

They refused. They died. These letters are fire,
The honest chronicle of my desire,
Rough, shaggy as the Numidian lion,
A style like crags, unkempt, pouring, no lie.'

My Dark Fathers

My dark fathers lived the intolerable day
Committed always to the night of wrong,
Stiffened at the hearthstone, the woman lay,
Perished feet nailed to her man's breastbone.
Grim houses beckoned in the swelling gloom
Of Munster fields where the Atlantic night
Fettered the child within the pit of doom,
And everywhere a going down of light.

And yet upon the sandy Kerry shore
The woman once had danced at ebbing tide
Because she loved flute music – and still more
Because a lady wondered at the pride
Of one so humble. That was long before

The green plant withered by an evil chance;
When winds of hunger howled at every door
She heard the music dwindle and forgot the dance.

Such mercy as the wolf receives was hers
Whose dance became a rhythm in a grave,
Achieved beneath the thorny savage furze
That yellowed fiercely in a mountain cave.
Immune to pity, she, whose crime was love,
Crouched, shivered, searched the threatening sky,
Discovered ready signs, compelled to move
Her to her innocent appalling cry.

Skeletoned in darkness, my dark fathers lay
Unknown, and could not understand
The giant grief that trampled night and day,
The awful absence moping through the land.
Upon the headland, the encroaching sea
Left sand that hardened after tides of Spring,
No dancing feet disturbed its symmetry
And those who loved good music ceased to sing.

Since every moment of the clock
Accumulates to form a final name,
Since I am come of Kerry clay and rock,
I celebrate the darkness and the shame
That could compel a man to turn his face
Against the wall, withdrawn from light so strong
And undeceiving, spancelled in a place
Of unapplauding hands and broken song.

The Limerick Train

Hurtling between hedges now, I see
green desolation stretch on either hand
while sunlight blesses all magnanimously.

The gods and heroes are gone for good and
men evacuate each Munster valley
and midland plain, gravelly Connaught land

and Leinster town. Who, I wonder, fully
understands the imminent predicament,
sprung from rooted suffering and folly?

Broken castles tower, lost order's monument,
splendour crumbling in sun and rain,
witnesses to all we've squandered and spent,

but no phoenix rises from that ruin
although the wild furze in yellow pride
explodes in bloom above each weed and stone,

promise ablaze on every mountainside
after the centuries' game of pitch-and-toss
separates what must live from what has died.

A church whips past, proclaiming heavy loss
amounting to some forty thousand pounds;
a marble Christ unpaid for on His Cross

accepts the Limerick train's irreverent sound,
relinquishes great power to little men –
a river flowing still, but underground.

Wheels clip the quiet counties. Now and then
I see a field where like an effigy
in rushy earth, there stands a man alone

lifting his hand in salutation. He
disappears almost as soon as he is seen,
drowned in distant anonymity.

We have travelled far, the journey has been
costly, tormented odyssey through night;
and now, noting the unmistakable green,

the pools and trees that spring into the sight,
the sheep that scatter madly, wheel and run,
quickly transformed to terrified leaping white,

I think of what the land has undergone
and find the luminous events of history
intolerable as staring at the sun.

Only twenty miles to go and I'll be
home. Seeing two crows low over the land,
I recognise the land's uncertainty,

the unsensational surrender and
genuflection to the busy stranger
whose power in pocket brings him power in hand.

Realising now how dead is anger
such as sustained us at the very start
with possibility in time of danger,

I know why we have turned away, apart
(I'm moving still but so much time has sped)
from the dark realities of the heart.

From my window now, I try to look ahead
and know, remembering what's been done and said,
that we must always cherish, and reject, the dead.

A Small Light

The best histories always partake of the legend-making or legend-debunking faculty, and both legend-making and legend-debunking are legend-making, because a debunked legend will always establish itself in another form. In the world of legend, refutation is a form of re-birth, just as the essence of myth is its unkillability. One "truth" dies, or is killed off, only that another be born. Legend grows through the cracks in factuality, like grass through concrete. Even the most "objective" historian is compelled to look at his material through his own eyes, so that no matter how convincing, through style, tone, sustained rational assessment and intellectual urbanity, his own illusion of "objectivity" may appear to be, his story must remain his story. The word says so. History. His story.

Therefore, it has always seemed proper to me to blend legend and history so that poetry is, literally, fabulous fact. The fact is inseparable from the fable. Ireland is, among other things, a land of old broken castles, great gapped edifices standing alone in a massively suggestive silence, a resonance of ruin. There are stories in the old walls, stories changing, forgotten, reviving, legends like lights on the battlements. They give life and warmth to the cold, broken facts of history. The stones have their stories and, like all storytellers, they need an audience.

I am indebted to Charles Smith's *The Ancient and Present State of the County of Kerry* for some of the facts about Carrigafoyle. For the fragments of legend, I am indebted to many people, living and dead. The poem is the monologue of a prisoner, O'Connor of Carrigafoyle, who, wrenched from his community after his castle was captured during the Cromwellian campaign, was executed in Tralee. The legend adds that he was offered his freedom if he would swear to abandon his people and his faith. Naturally, says the legend, and with the courage of an O'Connor, he refused. The poem deals with isolation and connection, belief and disbelief, distance and affinity, certainty and doubt, loneliness and love. It tries to suggest the long consequences of a single moment of treachery. It concerns the spirit of a man haunting, and being haunted by the spirit of a place. Today, the idea of community is vanishing fast; what we witness for the most part, in the efforts of those who try to create them, are, however admirable the impulses behind the efforts, sad parodies of community. This has the profoundest consequences for everything and everybody, including poets and poetry. It helps to explain that curious sense we all sometimes have of living in a world that is a ridiculous parody of intelligent, coherent living.

The sense of connection, when it occurs, feels like a stroke of great good luck. But with whom or what does it become even momentarily possible to connect? Is the much talked-about poet's "solitude" an absurd state of severance in an increasingly frantic and fiercely trivial world? Is the contemporary poet, by definition, a part-timer, one who with a grateful sigh settles down to try to write when the fierce trivialities have for the moment been coped with? He is so often a voice without an audience, an endured oddity, an articulate freak with oddball values, a stone, a severed head, a voice in a void. Needless to say, I have no solution. That's one fact, at least. If I had a solution, or the ghost of one, it would probably bear a disturbing resemblance to legend. So I'll have to console myself by offering this poem to the memory of a man, a story, a people, a ruin, a river and, of course, to your factual and legendary self.

1

A girl betrayed me
With a spurt of candlelight.
Almost sixteen hundred years
Have died since the birth of Christ.

The windows of my castle are thin
But wide enough
To let the signal be seen,
The bright dying of love,

A treacherous flicker
In a black mass of stone,
An adequate answer
To a brutal question.

Soldiers are rough men.
They love to break and burn and kill.
A small light led them to me.
A small light is all.

2

What is a man's faith?
Something he'd die for?
Here in Tralee jail
I want to praise my river.

My river kissed the cold stone
Of my castle, night and day.
My river has kept faith.
It follows its own way.

Born in the northern hills
Strangers to my eyes
Its conviction deepens
The longer it journeys.

Over the mud it flows,
Over the swamps of grief.
On the far bank a small flower grows.
Its name is belief.

I have seen it reflected
In restless water.
The flower was firm,
The shadow, a shiver.

3

My castle is built in a small island
Defended on the land side
By double walls

The outermost having square flankers
The inward
Round bastions

Built in the infancy
Of the art of fortification.

It is a pleasant place,
I had not thought to meet defeat there.
This ruin
Is a monument to my disgrace
Which I accept
As I accepted my glory.

Let the river whisper my story
To the stones on the shore, hearts
Dumb because they have sinned,
To the reeds, girls waiting
To be hit and ridden by the wind.

4

Language stinks on the air,
Every word a putrid breath.
I hear the river
Breathing underneath.

I love my people
My people love me.
We will be split now,
No longer free.

The river gasps in pain.
Foul words
Are battering my brain;
Words of seabirds

Sharp and clean
As polished knives.
The life I must surrender
Is much the same as other lives,

A fling of weed from the sea
Greening a wall,
A nest in a winter tree
About to break and fall,

Bits of mud and twigs
Showering from the sky
In a hail of words,
Each word asking why.

5

A rat, ambitious at my feet,
Dares the plate.
Sir Rat, you are welcome to the food
I cannot eat.

I fed my people
As well as I could.
All they have now
Is the thin wafer of God

Circling their lives
From beginning to end,
A white sky binding
Horizon to horizon,

Roof of the world
Foundation of heaven
Sun and moon
And bread of salvation

Containing every cry
Every buried pain
The suffering at the centre of an eye
In the head of a man.

God's poverty is deeper than mine.
I can cry out
But He must be silent
About His plight.
Where is His voice tonight?

I sleep with a sated rat.

6

There is a swamp now
Where apple orchards were,
Tides cover

The gardens
As though every flower in creation
Must always be under water.

Are they drowned or growing,
Growing into something else?
I put my ear to the river's pulse

And hear the mud
Breathing its life away.
Every god is buried

And finds his life in hiding,
A mud-flower under water
Like a drowned dancer

Swaying in mime or parody
Of an old, incomparable
Skill,

A shell under a skin of sand,
The same shell sinking, sinking,
Stillness flowing

Through the ghosts of apple trees
Groping downwards through summer shadow
Like families

Flat under stone,
Their names abused by sun, wind
And the maniac rain.

7

Her face
Stares
Through iron bars
At a man
Attending to the end of his affairs.

Her face
Is love that never happened
And never can
Though the next prisoner will see it
Part of his portion as a man.

Her face
Recedes into the darkness
Like a nightsound.
One foolish drop of moonlight
Falls to the ground

At my feet
Revealing nothing
Except her face that is not here
Where I sit, knowing nothing,
Happy as any prisoner.

8

Is there anything more respectable
Than a judge's face
High on his bench?
I'm in a state of criminal disgrace

And must pay.
'Hang, draw, quarter him!'
Death is a mathematical problem.
I shall attempt the sum

And offer an answer
Which, if not right,
May be examined by the unborn
With the help of a small light.

If I fail, do not remember
The travesty of dying cries.
There are solutions
Other than the sentence in a judge's eyes.

My lord is in his little heaven.
I must look up to see him where,
Chewing judgement like meat, he sits
In his ignorant, high chair.

9

I know the dejection of beasts
Stuck in winter muck,
A man's blue fingers clawing
Periwinkles from a rock,

Strangers up to my door
Pleading cold and hunger
Hammering at my heart
For more than my heart can offer.

I carry death about with me
As other men carry money,
A secure burden
Customary

As eyes opening to light
However small
Stealing through a chink in my prison
Until I feel

Death is an ordinary slime
I scratch from my skin
When I believe I am clean,
No longer diminished by sin

But calm outside a door
Closed on terror,
My fingers fit for love,
My heart a home for strangers

Beating again
Like the tide washing my castle,
A kiss no drunken rape
Can make less than beautiful.

10

It was a dream
Nobody has died
All have faded away.
Gentlemen! My head!

Dream-packed, it drops in the dust
With openclosed eyes.
It will sing its own song.
Only the dead are wise

And patient
And waiting
Untroubled by blood.
Listen to the song
Of the growing dead

Rising like a morning mist
Out of the mouth of my river.
It is gone in a moment
And there forever,

A small light in the private dark
Of the increasing dead,
A small light like a treacherous thought
In a girl's head.

Shelley in Dublin

On the Irish Sea, the wind
Booted Shelley and his company
Off course, up into the North of Ireland.
Although exhausted, Shelley did not delay
In Ulster, but struck for Dublin
Where his mission would begin.

In Mexico, a priest,
Miguel Hidalgo,
Had led a revolution.
In a room on the first floor
Of number seven Sackville Street
Shelley wrote:
>   Earth's remotest bounds shall start
>   Every despot's bloated cheek,
>   Pallid as his bloodless heart
>   Frenzy, woe and dread shall speak.

Some days later, *An Address to the Irish People*
Was published. Now was the time
To fight all tyrants, and Dublin was a city
Whose people had known tyranny
For centuries.
>   'We throw pamphlets out of the window,
>   Push them at men we pass in the streets.
>   It is such fun
>   And Percy looks so grave.
>   Yesterday, he hid one
>   In the hood of a woman's cloak.
>   Dear me, why does it now strike me
>   As something of a joke?
>   Poor ignorant thing,
>   She just kept walking,
>   Knowing nothing at all,
>   Misery huddled in a shawl.
>   I was getting tired.'

Shelley advertised in *The Dublin Evening Post*,
Summarised the address:
Catholic Emancipation,
Repeal of the Union with England,
Political self-education,
New groups to fight for justice.

Above all, he stressed his need to reach
The poorest in society.
'The lowest possible price
Is set on this publication.
It is the Author's intention
To awaken in the minds of the Irish poor
A knowledge of their state.
And he wishes to suggest
Rational means of remedy.'

Shelley never quite gave up
The notion that he'd spill some blood.
Dublin was a brimming cup
And might be offered to a thirsty god.

'Are you slaves
Or men?
If slaves, then yearn for the lash,
Lick the feet of your oppressors
Glory in your shame.
If you are brutes, act
According to your nature.
I say
You are neither slaves nor brutes
But men
And being men, have eyes to see
And realise
A real man is free.
How horrible that you, the poor,
Waste your lives and liberty
To furnish means for your oppressors
To crush you yet more terribly.
How horrible
You swell the rich man's gold,
Giving in taxes
Enough to save you and your families
From sickness, hunger, cold.
You must learn to rage, rage
Because the rich men make you
Make your own prison, your own cage.'

'Futile poet,
You talk of awakening them.
You think you are their brother.
They will rise up
Like Cadmus' seed of dragon's teeth
And eat each other.

You must see
We do not need this slaughter.
We need safe discussion,
Congenial intercourse
At each other's fireside.'

Fishamble Street: An aggregate meeting of the
Catholic Committee.

Harriet and Eliza on either arm,
He walked the foulest lanes,
Beggars, drunkards everywhere,
Up a rickety wooden verandah
To the Fishamble theatre, once a church
Where God had stayed to laugh
In a music-hall with stalls and boxes.
Handel had played there.
Inside, candlelit chandeliers,
Boxes packed with fashionable ladies,
Stalls rammed with boisterous Dubliners,
Dressed to the nines.
Doormen spared no effort to keep out
The stinking lower orders.
Daniel O'Connell spoke first,
Took the crowd in his hand.
The Liberator knew his slaves,
Never put a word wrong.

Shelley spoke then.
'I am an Englishman. When I reflect
On the crimes done by my nation on Ireland
I blush for my countrymen.'

(Loud applause for several minutes.)

'I walk the streets
And see the fane of liberty
Converted into a temple of Mammon.
Everywhere I look, I see
Famine, disease, beggary.
I lay my hand on my heart and say
The cause of such degradation
Is the union with Great Britain.'

Next, Shelley spoke of religion
And was hissed.

For weeks, he walked the streets
Of suffering without end.
'I have never known
Human misery until now.
The poor of Dublin
Are the most wretched on earth.
In the narrow streets
Thousands are huddled together,
One mass of animated filth!
And I had dreamed, yes, really dreamed
That I could speak to them.
O madness of the heart and head!
It were easier, far easier
To communicate with the dead.
I found a boy
Starving with his mother
In a hiding place
Of filth and misery.
I rescued him
And was about to teach him how to read
When he was seized by constables
On charge of effrontery
To a magistrate of Hell
Who gave him the choice of the 'tender'
Or military service.
He preferred neither
Yet was forced to be a soldier.
This is war –

Boys kept ignorant, stunted and crooked
Away from their life's due
Fighting for those who know right well
The value of an insult
Offered by a boy
To a magistrate of Hell.

This morning, I saw two constables
Arrest a widow with three infants.
I pleaded, oh how I pleaded.
I was everything my powers could make me.

I said to one constable, 'Have you a heart?'
He replied 'Aye, as well as another man.
But sir, please understand that I'm called out
On matters like this some twenty times a night.'

The woman's crime?
She'd stolen a penny loaf.

She is, however, drunken.
Nothing I can do
Will save her from her ruin.

I close my eyes at night
And walk the drunken streets
Of Dublin, Hell.

Who am I
To have pity for these damned
Who lurch and sway
In the light and dark of nightmare?
Who am I
To have come to this city
Of the beaten dead
Where it is a crime
To lay hungry hands on a loaf of bread?
Who am I
To have committed myself
And every dream of betterment
To the discovery of such waste?
What voice will rouse them
From their long sleep of defeat?
Who will redeem
The condemned streets?
Who will ever make these beggars
See
Their beggary?

Not me.

Who are these people?

O'Connell, fat king of cunning words?
Curran, with his jokes?

John Lawless ('Honest Jack') – him I distrust.

All the others,
Those who talk so much,
Who are they?
Thumping in and out, spewing anecdotes,
Full of plans and schemes,

Good-natured, drunk,
Doing nothing.

How can one do nothing
If one knows one is in hell?

There is a woman, Catherine Nugent,
A spinster with strong republican sympathies
Who works hard to help herself
And others.
Her I understand.

When I inquired if she was married
She replied, 'My country is my only love.'

Catherine Nugent I understand
Though she smiles
As if she were laughing at me.

Why do I think of women
When I reflect
On this city's possible salvation?
Women who smile
As if they were laughing at me.

Nothing remains for me
But to leave this city.
I have done what I can do.
It is nothing,
A spit at morning,
A drunk woman raving in drizzling light,
A pool of vomit in Sackville Street.

I cannot sink down and down
Through the despair of this impossible town.
Nor can I laugh atrocity away.
Nor does my deep, loved, English language have
A single word of hope
For me to say.

My voice is lost here.
I shall hear forever
In my brain
All the demented voices
Of the sick and wretched
In this town.'

'Oh dear
Percy is so depressed
At the failure of his mission
In Dublin.
He is grown sullen of late
And wishes to leave it all behind.
But never mind.
There's so much he can do
At home in England.'

On leaving Dublin
Shelley took with him an Irish servant.
His name was Dan Healy.
He'd worked for the poet
Spreading pamphlets through the city.

Dan Healy was slow but true.
The time would come
When Shelley would ditch him too.

They put out to sea
Into a heavy headwind.
Shelley did not look back.
He stared out and down
Into the Irish Sea
Green and grey and black.

The Saddest News

'The saddest news comes today from Piedmont.
The Lord Protector's heart is hit and riven
By the massacre of honest Protestant people
In the valleys of Lucerna and Perosa and St Martin.
The Duke of Savoy sent his preaching friars
To convert these hearts; they would not be converted.
The Duke sent six regiments, three of them Irish,
To kill and maim and banish. All this is not denied.

The Lord Protector is melted in tears, roused into sacred fire.
Let pity be perennial, let England know
The slaughters done by these missioners of hell;
Let a Day of Humiliation be appointed here
Let help be sent to all survivors now
Let blind Milton write harrowingly well.'

The Big House

The springtide ebbed, green weed on the shore
Lay like evidence rejected by the sea.
Among the rocky pools a small man strode
Gathering periwinkles in a bag.
Waves reflected a grim sky.
A night of packed dark that would explode
In clawing rain cat-footed
Over the Shannon.
               His eyes
Had noted all in a few pools. Finishing
His brief harvest, he walked across three fields
To the Big House, a gapped mask, a racked shell.
He climbed the broken steps, entered, flung
The bag on the cracked floor. Nobody near.
He prowled the windy rooms. They served him well.

Wall

I surround the Big House
hundreds of years old.
Craggy, cracked, indigenous,

I'm close to the Shannon tides,
aware of what it means to be
the line between warring sides.

I saw the Civil War, I was there
the day Eddie Carmody was shot.
A quiet man, Eddie. He whispered a prayer.

Others shouted curses. They swore
they were doing a favour to those
they chose to murder.

One said it was the Civil War
made the Irish grow up, made
men of them. I stood there, undismayed.

Killers will justify whatever they do.
A man must face himself, know the world.
Killing one neighbour can be hard. It's easier to kill two.

In there at my back, among flowers and trees
a cultured man
owns everything anyone sees.

I lack nothing. I know the weathers. I know rage
and easy does it, moon, earth, clouds, stars,
sun, green mossy peace between wars.

I saw Angela Raine drown herself.
I might have saved her. If she'd turned her head
she might have climbed over me instead

of stepping naked into the Shannon.
She went down in no time at all.
The Shannon swallowed her, grateful.

The Shannon rejects nothing: darkness, light,
poison, bird, weed, flower, stone, bone. It tells me
what it means to be pure appetite:

make hunger your friend, watchful and calm,
innocent and clean, waiting and flowing.
Never complain.

Lovers scale me now and then
to find a bed in summer grass.
Only the grass might say what comes to pass.

My silence is my strength. The river talks.
The trees talk. Even the flowers whisper.
I draw the line and witness

changing tides, each dance of shame and glory,
rights of way, who pays the rent, who hoards
and spends. I see the nine sides of the story.

I'm sturdy, vigilant, dependable, old.
What happens, happens. I note the history
of what's never been told.

What's known is a tiny part of what is.
Night and day, year after year, sleepless, I stand
and listen to the river's heart.

Not a word has ever passed between us.
No need for truth or lies.
We are what we are, do what we do,

serving the cause of water and stone.
Killers and killed are deep in the earth,
a ceasefire of bones.

Beatings

Hannify lifted the ash butt and struck
Quilter on the head and back.
For a while Quilter took it standing up
But a blow on the neck
Grounded him. Turning over on
His face, his hands clasped the back of his head.
Hannify's anger seemed more than human.
He hit Quilter till he was half-dead.
Quilter got over it though. For six weeks
He slunk like a hurt cur through dark and light,
Licking his wounds till the strength returned.
On May eve Hannify's sheepdog died.
Five cows were poisoned at a stroke.
No sign of Quilter when Hannify's hayshed burned.

The Curse

The first time I heard the curse in sleep
Was now and a thousand years ago
It didn't assume a pig-shape or dog-shape
Nor was it tarred and feathered like a crow
It wasn't an old soldier talking his wounds
Nor a priest going fifteen rounds with the Devil
It wasn't the smell of blood in killing hands
I'd hardly call it foul

It was more like a small patient hiss
The sound a wind might make trying to be born
A kind of pleading
                    the let-me-have-my-way
Of a child who gets a notion in his
Head to go somewhere
                    only to return
With words like 'I'm back now I want to stay'.

Local History

Pens and pencils conspiring on the desk
The red dog waiting to bite anyone
Who ventures near him without a gun
The boy on the bridge sensing the risk
Of growing up, that is, growing away
From games anticipating the game
That even now he is learning to play
With only the ghost of a ghost hovering about him

Erupted from the serious woman's talk –

The man's footsteps near her made no sound
Though he wore Whiteboys' gaiters in his walk
Up the difficult hillside's frosty ground.
Ignoring her well-meant neighbourly call
He vanished through the estate's orchard wall.

Three Tides

In our very own little civil war
The sea, as employed by some, is an exemplary weapon
Combining an ability to finish a job
With a reliable style of humiliation.
Proper use of such elemental efficiency, however,
Is available only to those who know
The sea's judicial character
In its constitutional ebb and flow.
As it approaches the shore
It nudges, first, a shy, frothful poison
Reminiscent of the slime on dying lips
Prior to that rattle that can still
Shred even the most knitted family
And cause fretful speculation about a will.
This is a slow poison, rhythmically, sensually slow.
Perhaps the stimulating moon
Quickens the pace because our law-abiding sea
Accelerates like a well-executed plan
Of dependable drowning waves, inexorable as generations
Of a fertile Catholic family true to God's
Randy laws, coming, going, coming, going, like sons
And daughters to work or hell or money or England or spawning beds.
Properly judged, a man buried up to his neck in the shore
Will take three tides to die. His brothers (mine too) say
This gives him time to meditate on his mistake
In taking the wrong side in that most uncivil war.
Unlike our manly land, our sea has never lied.
My father drowns to the moon's laws, head to one side.

Freedom Fighter

I am the expression of the people's will.
I am a soldier, not a brute.
I do not bomb or shoot to kill.
I execute.

Call me Mick or Joe or Bill or Pat,
I do what I say.
If careless children get in my way
Can I help that?

My Indifference

'I never saw people so indifferent to life; they continued in the same berth with a dead person until the seamen or captain dragged out the corpse with boat-hooks. Good God! What evils will befall the cities wherever they alight?'

CHIEF EMIGRATION OFFICER FOR QUEBEC

When that brave sailor sank his boat-hook
Into me, I was more dead than ever before.
Not even being hoisted aloft like
A bag of spuds and dumped in the water
Had the teeniest effect on my indifference.
I sank to the bottom with a sodden mind
And lumped there, stone-like, the Paddy dunce
I am. Slowly, as I defleshed, I found
My bones were of a sprightly nature
Apt to romp and frisk on the sea-floor
Frolicking as in a happy dream.
If I could only get myself together
Now, I'd rise to work and love once more.
O bless for me a candle and float it down the stream.

The Prisoner

They came in the middle of the night
And dragged young Lynch out of bed.
He was born and bred in that place.
He was six months married.

They shoved him around the house.
They kicked him on the floor.
'You belong to a secret organisation,
We'll show you what we're here for.'

They took him away.
They gave him a trial.
He got a year in jail.
He was stuck in a cell

Alone.
He'd never been alone before.

He was learning loneliness now.
That's what he was there for.

He had to sleep on the floor.
Sometimes he got food, sometimes not.
Sometimes they placed food before him
But took it away before he could bite.

Sometimes they made him stand
With his face pressed to the wall.
He didn't know how long he had to stand.
He knew the world is a cell.

They left the light on all night.
It scalded his eyes as he lay on the floor.
He cried for a natural darkness.
There was no darkness there.

Times in the light he thought he saw
A happy child;
Times he smelled burning flesh
And wept when the child howled.

Times he felt burning snow
Scorching his head;
Times he laughed at his hands
Veined with white blood.

He couldn't speak or write to anyone.
No one could write or speak to him.
His world was merciless light.
It left him shivering and dumb.

Only the grim skin of their faces spoke
Something about a world outside,
People talking to each other,
A girl who was a wife.

Or was the light only able to lie,
To let ghosts mock his bruised mind?
What were people's voices like?
What was a human sound?

What was the moment of a broken will?
He saw the light, the walls, the door, the floor.
There was so much light fit to kill.
That's what he was there for.

Traffic Lights, Merrion Road, Dublin 4

I

Green orange red
orange green

cars crush by, ruthless
as men wanting to be rich,
Mercedes, Austin, Triumph.

Behind the wheels
faces stern with success
or sour with the possibility of failure.

They stare ahead
seeing nothing on either side,
stiff with the insane concentration of men
going nowhere.

II

Seasons will alter every country
effect a revolution in the buried root
enrich the juice in the thin stem
calm the hysterical sea
with new gold honour the trampled sand.

       Here will be no change
but this quick change of lights.

This change brings silence.

I stand in the middle of silence
like a lost man in a desert
and hear the slaves of history
whining under the whip.

The cars are coffins
trap coffins
bottoms held by hinges at one side
hook and eye at the other.

Disposing thus of dead men
these coffins can be used again.

In this silence the poor do not have coffins
but are buried in their rags.
In some cases
the rags are taken from the corpse
to cover a living body.

Yesterday I saw
five dead bodies
carried through the village in a cart
under a yellow shroud of straw.

A young man reels across my path
laughter boiling in his throat
like a deathrattle,
the fool of hunger.

Captain Harstan
who brought the Eclaire from Africa
told me that on Sunday
he had seen a woman
with a basket on her back
to which was tied
the crooked corpse of her child.

And Dr Trail reported
a father tottering on a road
a rope over his shoulder.
At the other end of the rope
streeling along the ground
were two dead children
he was dragging to a pit.

Mr O'Callaghan of Kilmanus
tells me that corpses
fit well in meal-bags.
Graves are good in ditches
corners of the fields
gardens behind cabins.

Yesterday on the road to Cappagh
I saw a dog
eating the head, neck and ribs
of a man.

Later again
I found part of a human head
gnawed, pocked with blood.
I placed it underground.
In one house
I lifted up a little girl.
Her legs swung and rocked
like the legs of a doll.
Her flesh swam with lice.
Out from the marrow of her bones
scuttled the smell of lice.

It is bad in this place.
No one understands the curse.
Yet word has come that in the mountains
it is worse.

III

I hear the cries of women straggling over stones
or bending in the barren fields,
the cries of men and children too
whose hunger is unknown.
Books will be written
but the hunger is unknown.
Poems will be written, and songs
but the hunger is unknown.
Drunken men will think they tell the truth
statesmen give the bread of explanation
economists suggest solutions
priests wag the finger of warning and accusation
poets celebrate the sacrifice that turns the heart to stone
historians offer facts
wise men nod their theories

but the hunger is unknown.

My brothers will go about the world
in search of money
taking with them
fear pretending to be charm or laughter

insisting on the lie.
Or they'll stay at home
change the barren fields to green
through sunlight rain and hail;

make it nice
and new
and offer it for sale.

Bland reassurances
will calm the blood,
comfort
squat in the bone,
the nightmare melt in the light

But the hunger is unknown.

IV

The light has changed again.
The cars surge forward
like animals unleashed.
Nothing will stop them now.
They'll take the city in their stride.
They drive as though they want to eat it.

It is themselves they eat
to kill the hunger
they do not know they feel
well-dressed, hunched and savage
at the wheel.

Killybegs

1

We drove across the mountains and the bog,
Magenta hypnotic in the fields.
To our left, a glacial lake black with cold
Dropped like a cracked abandoned shield.
You said, seeing a river, it was old:
The oldest river twists and turns at ease,
A proven legend casually re-told.
A younger river, hungry for the sea,

Cuts through the forest, clay and stone.
We watched the crooked meditative path
Sure of its future, glad to be alone.

Most of the time, sunlight is a wraith
In that land, always vanishing. Now
It sprinted through the mountain-range.
There was a change of gods above us. Below,
All the fields dazzled in golden change.

2

Killybegs. Evening. The Pier Bar.
Four old men drinking pints
Turn now and then to stare

At the sea. Up the blue creek
The boats come, rounding the red buoy.
Piratical bands of seagulls croak

Above the foam.
The boats' bellies are heavy with fish.
The sea has given. The boats are home.

In piled boxes, the fish glint.
The sea's secrets
Are hauled towards a shed,

Hungry gulls following,
Cowards all
Till one whips a fish in his beak,
Veers out over the water
Where *Immortelle, Belle Marie*
And *Pursuit* lie at anchor.

The lone gull
Opens his jaws
Swallows the fish whole

Then turning from the pier he
Spreads his wings
For the open sea.

3

Back on the mountain road
The rain pelting.
Hard to see ten yards ahead.

This is a land of loss.
No sign of the river or the black lake.
Only roadside grasses toss and shake.

Even if we could see
There isn't a house for miles.

Suddenly there's a grey heap
In the road.
A mountainy sheep,

Its legs broken. No cry
As it tries to crawl to a ditch
Pushing grotesquely

With its furred back
Neat head
And nervous neck.

We can do nothing. The grey rain
Beats on nothing
But human helplessness and brute pain.

We drive on.
The sheep lies alone with its hurt.
The black clouds hang from the mountain.

A Running Battle

What are they doing now? I imagine Oliver
Buying a Dodge, setting up as a taxi-driver
Shunting three dozen farmers to Listowel Races.
I see Ed Spenser, father of all our graces
In verse, enshrined as a knife-minded auctioneer
Addicted to Woodbines and Kilkenny beer,
Selling Parish Priests' shiny furniture
To fox-eyed housewives and van-driving tinkers.
William of Orange is polishing pianos
In convents and other delicate territories,
His nose purple from sipping turpentine.
Little island is Big, Big Island is little.
I never knew a love that wasn't a running battle
Most of the time. I'm a friend of these ghosts. They're mine.

De Valéra at Ninety-two

To sit here, past my ninetieth year,
Is a joy you might find hard to understand.
My wife is dead. For sixty years
She stood by me, although I know
She always kept a secret place in her heart
For herself. This I understood. There must always be
A secret place where one can go
And brood on what cannot be thought about
Where there is noise and men and women.

Some say I started a civil war.
There are those who say I split the people.
I did not.
The people split themselves.
They could not split me.
I think now I was happiest when I taught
Mathematics to teachers in their training.
From nineteen hundred and six to nineteen sixteen
I taught the teachers.
Then the trouble started.
In jail, I often sat for hours
Especially at evening
Thinking of those mathematical problems
I loved to solve.
Here was a search for harmony,
The thrill of difficulty,
The possibility of solution.
Released from jail, I set about
Making a nation,
A vicious business,
More fools among my friends than in my enemies,
Devoted to what they hardly understood.
Did I understand? You must understand
I am not a talker, but a listener.
Men like to talk, I like to listen.
I store things up inside.
I remember what many seem to forget.
I remember my grandfather
Telling of his brother's burial in Clare.
The dead man was too tall
To fit an ordinary grave
So they had to cut into a neighbour's plot,
Break the railings round a neighbour's grave

To bury a tall man.
This led to war between the families,
Trouble among the living
Over a patch o' land for the dead.
The trouble's still there. Such things, as you know,
Being a countryman yourself,
Are impossible to settle.
When my grandfather scattered things on the kitchen floor
He used strange words from the Gaelic.
I wonder still about the roots of words.
They don't teach Latin in the schools now.
That's bad, that's very bad.
It is as important to know
Where the words in your mouth come from
As where you come from yourself.
Not to know such origins
Is not to know who you are
Or what you think you're saying.
I had a small red book at school,
'Twas full of roots,
I still remember it.
Roots...and crops. Origins...and ends.
The woman who looks after me now
Tells me to sip my brandy.
Sometimes I forget I have a glass in my hand
And so I do what I'm told.
I have been blind for years.
I live in a world of voices
And of silence.
I think of my own people, the tall men,
Their strange words, the land
Unmoved by all our passions about it,
This land I know from shore to shore,
The Claremen roaring their support
And all the odds and ends
(What was that word he had for them?)
Scattered on my grandfather's kitchen floor.

Oliver Speaks to His Countrymen

I have no rhetoric, no wit, no words.
The Dispensations of God upon me
Require I speak not words, but Things.

I speak of the Being of England,
Of the endeavour and design of its common Enemies
Whether abroad or at home
In London or in Rome.
I will now specificate our Enemies.

Our great Enemy is the Spaniard.
The hatred in the Spaniard is the hatred of God.
Led on by superstition from the See of Rome
The Spaniard will never come to good.
Have no trade with him; with him your only trade
Is duel to the death. Consider
The Spaniard's invasion of Ireland,
His designs of the same kind upon England,
Public designs, private designs, all manner of designs
To accomplish this great and general end.
If you do not know your Enemy, you cannot know your Friend.
Know this: we'll suffer more from peace with Spain
Than from Spain's intense hostility.
When Philip the Second married Queen Mary
And since that time, through Spanish instigation,
Twenty thousand Protestants were murdered in Ireland,
I think it my duty to win by the sword
What is not to be had otherwise.
The sharpest sword is the sharpest word.
This is the spirit of Englishmen.
If so, it is the spirit of men who have higher spirits,
Men who are Englishmen and more,
Believers in God's Gospel –
Clumsily said, but not clumsily meant.
England is Protestant
And will be to the end.
(Know your Enemy: know your Friend.)

Our danger from the Common Enemy abroad,
The Devil apeing the Face of God,
Is headed by the Pope,
Leader of the anti-Christian Interest.
He has an interest in your bowels; he has so.
This is the danger you must know.

At home, there is danger from Priests and Jesuits,
Papists and Cavaliers.
Dark, spectral Jesuits, the Spaniard,
Levellers and discontented persons
Make one black anti-Christian mass
To overwhelm us all. I am an outcast from eloquence,
I have poor words, yet speak my Nation's will.
When my Nation is threatened, I grieve
And do my duty, though men may not believe.
Therefore, I will not cease to say
England cannot be safe
Until Malignants be swept away.
This Pope has a certain zeal for his religion,
A man of contrivance, wisdom, and policy.
He wishes to unite all popish Interests
In the Christian world, against this Nation above any,
Against all the Protestant Interest in the world.
I will not shake the hand of such a man.
Christ and Antichrist had better not
Shake hands; no good will come of it.

I speak plainly. I have no words, no wit.
I love England. I love the very thought of it.

I would lay open the danger
Where in my conscience I know we stand.
If you do not see what is obvious here
We shall sink, our house will fall about our ears.
I tell you plainly what is dangerous.

I see what threatens us.
I know what is.
Sluggish men will not acknowledge this,
Preferring the happiness of lies.
I see what is. I speak what is.
These are things – not words!

Here is a Thing.
An officer was engaged to seize me in my bed
And shoot me dead;
Another, to put gunpowder in my room
And blow me up.
Both these men are gone to their doom
But not I to mine.
I'll wait awhile. There are battles to win.
Herod and Pilate were reconciled
That Christ might die.

Some Fifth-Monarchy men and Commonwealth men
Are reconciled in their dislike of me.
These are unquiet men, a troubled sea
That cannot rest, its waters throw up
Mire and din, such men we find
Leading the bloody massacres in Ireland,
Such troubled men I here pronounce to be
Against the Interest of England.

To be English is to be more than English:
It is to be a Christian man
Who knows Jesus Christ:
To be English is to face the hardest test.

To be English is never to quibble about words
Or matters of no moment.
It is to have a conscience and be free
To enjoy that conscience.
To be English is to believe in Christ
In the remission of sins through His blood
In the grace of God,
To know the debt we owe to God
When we enjoy our liberty.

True tolerance is noble,
True intolerance nobler still.

Hate the inessential.

Study books, if you will.
Study your own hearts, if you are able.

A man is a mind, the mind is the man.
Otherwise, he's a beast.

If I had the tongue of an Angel
If I were inspired as men of God have been
I could live in you till you would live
To save your nation.
You are the true Protestants of this world.
Do not go blind-eyed into ruin.
If a man scruple the plain truth before him
It is vain to meddle with him.
Leave him alone to shipwreck his soul.
Let him eat the heart of his own will.

My countrymen, who live in my heart,
Have peace among yourselves.
I am in union with you, united
In faith and love with Jesus Christ
And his peculiar Interest.
If that is not true, let me curse myself
And pray God may curse me too!
I know too much of God to fool with Him
Or be bold with Him in these things.
I hope I never shall be bold with Him
Who has my trust.
I shall be bold with men
If Christ be pleased to assist.
I have a little faith.
I have a little lived by faith
And so I may be bold.
Therefore, in the fear and name of God,
Accomplish what you know
And have been told.

God told me a psalm last night:
'Lord, Thou hast been favourable to Thy Land
Thou hast brought back the captivity of Jacob
Thou hast forgiven the iniquity of Thy People
Thou hast covered all their sins
Thou hast taken away the fierceness of Thy Wrath
Tell us, o God, of our salvation
And cause Thine anger towards us to cease.
Wilt Thou be angry with us forever?
Wilt Thou draw out Thine anger to all generations?
Wilt Thou not revive us again
That Thy people may rejoice in Thee?
Let Mercy and Truth meet together,
Let Righteousness and Peace kiss each other.'

Earth is Heaven's dream.
This poor English earth
Is an emblem of Heaven
Where God's blessing is supreme
Where Falsity and Greed,
Cruelty, Sin, Fear
And all the Hell-dogs of Gehenna
Lie chained under our feet
In proper postures of defeat.
This is England, gentlemen, England
August and brave and sweet.

Other people see a little of the sun
But we have great lights.

May God invest you with His presence.
He made your hearts and mine.
Let Him live in His own creation.

God bless you all, my countrymen.

Points of View

A neighbour said De Valéra was
As straight as Christ,
As spiritually strong.
The man in the next house said
'Twas a great pity
He wasn't crucified as young.

Calling the Shots

He was half a mile from the road, in the fields,
When they shot him from a moving truck.
He fell like a collapsing scarecrow.
They didn't bother to stop
But took the first turn
Right and pressed on,
Having a village to burn.
The grass accommodated a dead man.
He lay there
Long enough to leave his shape in the grass
Like a resting hare.

I got the loan of a rifle from Danny King
Who loved wild geese.
I knelt by a paling-post and barbed wire
And fired at a seagull in the mud.
He fell like a doll knocked from a mantelpiece.
The incoming tide lifted a wing like paper
Shuffled by the wind.

I never met the man in the fields.
I hear he was clearing scutch,
I wonder if the soldier laughed or shuddered
Or simply forgot. Was he practising
His art? Did anyone congratulate
Him on being so accurate
From such a difficult position?
I won't forget
The seagull's wing lifting in the lazy tide
Like a hand in blessing
Moments after the shot.

The House That Jack Didn't Build

In the beginning was my house, Jack said
And my house was good.
And I was in my house
And outside my house there was nothing.
And the light moved through my house
Until it was my house
So that I was made to see
Myself
Master
Of other people's houses, made from darkness
And my light shone in their darkness
But their darkness could not comprehend it,
And I willed my light to brighten all their houses.
Inspiration being my common condition
I had this divine idea.
I walked in and took them.

There was this little house
Nicely situated on the side of a hill
Within walking distance of the sea.
The moment I saw it I said to myself,
That's mine. That house was built for me.

So I walked in.

The occupant kicked up a stink.
Who do you think
You are, he asked.

I'm Jack, I said. I like houses.
I collect them.
Yours pleases me well.
A crime, you say? Nice word, crime.
You'll admire my light in time.

One can't imagine
How much I improved that house.
To start with, the garden was a mess.
He'd let it run wild.
I tamed it, gave it the sort of symmetry
Which is a perfect expression
Of the civilised mind.
Eden is what I build, not what I find.
It cost me the honest sweat of my brow.
There's not a weed there now.
I changed all the rooms.
This took me quite a while
Visitors comment on their style.
It's simple. I do everything well,
Not exactly, to be fair, in a spirit of love
But with a genuine desire to improve
Others, particularly

One thing worries me, though.
The former occupant won't go
Away.
He has found a small place in the hills,
A cave, or something like that.
Sometimes I hear him
Skulking outside at night
Staring at my little house
Here on the side of the hill
Within walking distance of the sea.
He's a moody brute and might kill
Me if he got the chance.
Why is he not content
To be?

I am taking all necessary precautions
Though I am bored by complaints
And plans for vengeance.
On the other hand
He might just learn to understand
And appreciate my superior position.
Yes, I'm sure he would, if he but studied my face.

Still, I don't really trust cave-dwellers.
They smell.
It's a disgrace.

I like this little place
And intend to keep it.
It's as near to perfect as I can get it.

If you saw it, I'm sure you'd agree.

It contains so much of me.

Statement of the Former Occupant

Up here in the hills
Rain rules most of the time.
Darkness drips like blood
In the cave where I live
With bats and rats and skulking shadows.

I have lost touch with my own language.
Nothing is stranger to me than what is my own.
I am an exile from myself.
Words are stones in my mouth.
The bones of my head are trampled on.

And the stink!
Since I took to living in this cave
I reek like a corpse in a grave.

Head down, shoulders bent,
Eyes stuck to clay and rock,
Words slung like corpses across my back,
I mumble

Jack
Walked in, took over my house,
Drove me to this,
Smiling Jack
Civilising Jack

Mannerly Jack
Language-changing Jack
Smooth and fluent Jack
Collector of homes, lover
Of other men's gardens.

Improver.

One day, I shall improve you, Jack.

When I improve you
I shall improve myself,
Drag myself up from the mire
To share in your glory,
Free myself from my stinking pit
To savour your exquisite order,
Abandon this daft mumbling
To achieve your eloquence,
Quit my pigsty behaviour
To emulate your manners.

I may even learn to love myself again.
A rare thing among men.

Don't be disturbed
If you see me skulking
Near your house that was once my house
And may be my house again.

Don't be upset
At assaults on your sleep
Destruction of property
Barbarous uses of language
Some shedding of blood.

Don't be dismayed.
I'm aware of the progress you've made,
The excellence you create.
It's just that I'm not mad about
Gardens that seem too neat.
Even as a child
I loved my garden
Slightly wild.
Although you've made the rooms
More elegant than I can say

It's not my way.

I am, you might say, driven,
An impassioned simpleton
Someone to look down on
Someone to joke about.
And yet
I do not seem to fear
Prison
Gallows
Rack.

Dear Jack, one day
You'll give me back my house

Though now I mumble
And even among my friends
The bats, the rats, the fickle shadows,
I go despised and broke.

On with the joke.

The Joke

Only a few alert stars
Could see the joke forming
On the lips of God.

It grew and grew
Like a spitbubble
That burst over the world,
A black rain of laughter
On parched hearts.

One man stopped another in the street and said
'Did ya hear this one?
It's a bloody howl.
All about a stupid man.'
They were so twisted with laughter
They couldn't see each other.

It was so funny
They would never forget it
For love or money.

And they told it and told it and told it
Because it was funny so funny so funny.

Paddy Taffy Limey Pole Kerryman Black Jew
And all their women too
Believe in a God
As funny as you.
His prize creation must make Him feel blue.
Yahoo!
Who?

You.
Me too.

And so it came to pass
That when he heard the joke
He was back in a parody of catechism class.

Question: Who made the world?
Answer: A little pig
               With his tail curled.
Question: What is the definition
               Of the ultimate Kerryman?
Answer: A Corkman
               Who fucks pigs.

Dear Audience, to cope with narrative problems
In a shifting context, all we must do
Is change Corkman and Kerryman
To Arab and Jew.
In this world of lies, at least that much is true!

When he made love, he wore two contraceptives
To be sure to be sure.
When he listened to sport on the radio
He burned his ear.
If you wanted to touch his mind
You put your hand on his bum.
And you knew all the time
(To laugh is no crime)
The joke made you a very bright boy
And him – stupid old scum,

A stick of ridicule beating reality's drum,

Be dumb
Be dumb

Be dumb be dumb be dumb

The joke was a sly courtier,
It flattered the King's ear.

The joke knew how to kill.
Flatter and kill, flatter and kill
The black rain sang
As it fell
Into minds, into hearts,
Over land and sea,
Over you and me.

Spill me, spill me, the black rain sang,
Tell me, tell me, tell me again,
I'm a good laugh, good laugh, good laugh.

I will lessen your pain.

The joke is growing and growing
And now there's no knowing
How it all began,

The sneer on the lips of God,
The spit of contempt on the world,
The laugh of the bright, sad man.

The Ship of Flame

The ship of flame defined the Irish sea
Bearing Oliver's corpse home to England
But there were maddened people in that island
Who would not grant him final peace.
So the ship of flame turned back to Ireland
Tried Waterford, Cork, Dublin, Galway
But there were maddened people in that island too
Who refused him burial in their earth.
Then the ship of flame embraced the sea
Went down among the other dead
To find repose among the shells and sand
Among the whispers and the thunders and deceits
Among the weeds and bones and watchful rocks

And there was peace because the sea is blind.

8

Voices

Connection

Self knows that self is not enough.
The deepest well becomes exhausted.
We could wander forever in a wood
And through the trees not see a sign of love.
Turn then where windy March blows golden hair
(A drowning man will grasp the thinnest straw)
And slowly in the ceremonious air
Observe irrational redeeming law

Connect the desert with the sun at noon
Revealing open beaks, descending wings
And bones that hint of spirits that are free.
We open in a moment, love, and then
Linked with the livingness of growing things
Express the shell and comprehend the sea.

Shell

I cannot say I came from nothing
But so it seemed when the sea
Began to shape me. How long

It took is not important.
Light and dark passed through me.
Nothing was constant

But the labouring
Fingers of the sea
At their grind of love and making.

This happened where few
Would wish to penetrate
And none could see

But I received my body there
And hid within me
All the voices of my maker

Singing of his work
As I lurched and tumbled
Through the unfathomed dark.

I bear, I am forever borne.
I am complete yet I must turn
And spin with the deep will, a form

Content to be
The still, perfect image of the sea
Or its demented plaything in a storm.

Sea

I am patient, repetitive, multi-voiced,
Yet few hear me
And fewer still trouble to understand

Why, for example, I caress
And hammer the land.
I do not brag of my depths

Or my currents, I do not
Boast of my moods or my colours
Or my breath in your thought.

In time I surrender my drowned,
My appetite speaks for itself,
I could swallow all you have found

And open for more,
My green tongues licking the shores
Of the world

Like starved beasts reaching for men
Who will not understand
When I rage and roar

When I bellow and threaten
I am obeying a law
Observing a discipline.

This is the rhythm
I live.
This is the reason I move

In hunger and skill
To give you the pick of my creatures.
This is why I am willing to kill,

Chill every created nerve.
You have made me a savage master
Because I know how to serve.

The Island

I

Consider the sea's insatiate lust
And my power of resistance.

The waves' appetite
Gives me reason to exist,

This undermining
This daily assault on my body

Keeps me singing
Like the larks that rise from my heather.

The sea would swallow me whole
But I am a shelter
For music that startles the sky.
In my fields and furrows
Is rhythm to rival the sea.

Is this why we fight?
Does my hidden music
Draw the sea to my throat

To suck my secrets into itself?
Must two kinds of music
Clash and devour
Till the crack of whatever doom lies in store?

I am always about to surrender
When the sea withdraws from my shore

And leaves me to hear my own music again.
Nothing stranger!
I am consoled
By the voices of creatures
Whose wings are made of my pain.

II

This morning my fields sigh with relief
Because they have survived a storm.
When the sea explodes in rage or grief

What can they do but take it as it comes?
My fields are not interested
In suicide or martyrdom

But in green joyful endurance,
In those changes that are mine also.
If I could imagine a happy man

He would be like my fields before
And after storm.
He would live close to the battered shore

But flourish in his own way.
He would accept the sky's changes
Absorb its fury

Be an image of repose in its light.
But I know nothing of men
And must content myself with

Green peace that knows how to survive.
Worse storms, I know, are gathering
But my fields will live.

The Sandwoman

After the tide went out this morning
The islandboy started to make me out of sand.
How clear and purposeful he was, concentrating
On my head, neck, shoulders, breasts, hands,
All my body made from sand of the sea.

I heard the horizon whisper its awe
When the islandboy stood back and looked at me
Who'd been imagined according to his law.

Then, with the tide on the turn, he touched me
As he'd not touched me in the making.
He kissed my face and hands, he loved me then
As the sea returned to witness his ecstacy.
I swallowed his sheer seed, my body breaking
Where the raping waves dispersed me into grains again.

Bread

Someone else cut off my head
In a golden field.
Now I am re-created

By her fingers. This
Moulding is more delicate
Than a first kiss,

More deliberate than her own
Rising up
And lying down,

I am fine
As anything in
This legendary garden

Yet I am nothing till
She runs her fingers through me
And shapes me with her skill.

The form that I shall bear
Grows round and white.
It seems I comfort her

Even as she slits my face
And stabs my chest.
Her feeling for perfection is

Absolute.
So I am glad to go through fire
And come out

Shaped like her dream.
In my way
I am all that can happen to men.
I came to life at her finger-ends.
I will go back into her again.

Lightning

At a decent distance
From the heads of men
I happen

And am gone.
This is how
I light up heaven

And define the dark.
You think I must
Be something of an exhibitionist,

A dramatic braggart of light?
I am a mere moment
Between this and that

Yet so much that moment
I
Illumine the sky

And the small homes of men,
Flash through their fears, spotlight their joys.
My deepest nature is quiet and private.
I cannot escape the noise.

Book

You come to me with such avid eyes
I wonder what you expect to find.
When you turn my pages

It is not me you see, but you.
Is there anywhere in the world
You do not meet yourself?

What the rain writes on the ground is for you alone.
What the wind screams between the houses
Cannot so be heard by any other man.

You see and hear the wind and rain
And never know the pain
That made me.

Something has sentenced you to yourself.
Your only world is where you are,
What your eyes look at,

Open or shut.
You are an unspeakable secret,
A prison that walks about.

When you consider me
You involve me in your secret.
I extend and deepen it,

I enlarge you as I lose myself, word by word.
I am part of a story you invent
Like a rumour you once heard

And decided to make your own.
When you believe you possess me
You are most alone.

House

I am youth slipping like water
From that cracked tap in the yard.
They are many. I am one.
Thinking of me, they will always be children.
Every leaving will be a return
To me who sheltered their dead.
They ran to me out of streets and fields
When I gave them the smell of hot bread.
That oven in my belly
Helped them grow in the sun.
They are many. I am one.
They will live in others,
Stare out of cities, over seas
To find me,
They will hear their noisy hearts
Beat in my silence,
They will not overcome the surprise
Of finding surprise in me,
They will scour a world for evidence
Of what never dies in me.

They happened in me.
They can happen only once.
This drives my children out-of-sense.

Listen! You can hear the dance
Starting on the kitchen floor.
They are learning the steps
Becoming the music
Reaching the skill, the fever,
Doing what I've always wanted.
Dancing through me, dancing their beginning,
They are learning to be haunted.

Crow

When I croak
I half-lift one wing.
Not bad for a tarry black laughed-at thing.
It's as near as I get to harmony.

Who are you
and what do you think you do
when you sing?

The Singing Tree

In Grafton Street you seehear me sing
    leaves sprouting out of my ears
while all around the children gazing
    forget their fears

Two passing Gardaí stand and smile
    at cockahooping me
branches dancing on my shoulders
    in tickledpinky glee

The sun is strolling down Grafton Street
    I promise you it's not long
till light collaborates with me
    in a greenleaf song

And when the rain comes shopping down
    Gardaí children sun
join with the big magnanimous drops
    in the cutprice fun

But even singing trees grow tired
    I gather the day's fruits
and amblebramble evening streets
    to find my sleepy roots

and dream as every tree must dream
    of love and care
Gardai and children wonderstruck
    love-songs in the air

night serving notice on Grafton Street
    a boy alone
prone in the doorway of a Bank
    under a tourist moon

loitering across the sky
    shedding on land and sea
the kind of light that floods the heart
    of your average singing tree

The Tree's Voice

Felled at the forest's edge,
hewn, yanked, chopped, shaped until
I governed this noisy hill,
I am the scene of crime and privilege.

I carried him
who'd caused good sap to flow like blood
through leaf, branch, trunk, eternal bud,
made strong each limb;

watched me grow sturdy, sent
sun and wind and rain enough
to hint at every miracle of love.
I became his punishment.

Wan, as was predicted, the young hero stepped
up to me, stopped at my unwithering root;
I dumbly bore my awful fruit
while all creation wept.

The Cherry Trees

Destroyers ranged last night
Through Stephen's Green in Dublin,
Uprooting marigold, juniper and roses.
Gathering the striped chairs of summer
They raised a sacrificial pile
To blaze beneath the bland, man-conquered moon.

Quick as a bad rumour
The fire ran, stretched,

Touched
Three cherry trees, three queens of summer
And blackened them with hate.

It takes a long time to grow a cherry tree.
I appreciate the anarchy that beats in every branch,
The balance throbbing in unopened blossoms.
Man's hand is needed here
To cut in early spring
A white image of limitation.

Perfect images are rare.
They live
In drudgery and care.

They move through summer dark,
Whispering words to goad them on,
Rush like bulls among the flowers,
Ruining in a moment
What devoted months have moulded.
Madness grows,
Hate is hot beside the midnight fire
Guiding the flame with hands of power
Where
Perfect, vulnerable,
The cherry trees are in flower.

We, in our beds,
Have guided these hateful hands.
We have been standing at this fire,
Trees' bodies blackening before our sight.
This could never happen in daylight
The time for labour and creation.

There is a time for killing too.

Peter saw that treachery was easy
And he wept.

Shall we say that we are innocent
Because we slept?

I see a martyr burning,
A traitor turning his furtive head,
A virgin screaming with desire.
A soldier prepares to spit

Into the leaping cherry-fire
That rises from the human pit
In shapes that lash our dreams
Until in morning light we lie awake
Bewildered, grateful, still.

The cherry trees have always burned in Ireland.

They always will.

Mr Thomas Harte, Park Superintendent,
Saved as much as he could
Working fiercely
With the Dublin Fire Brigade.

'The amount of damage done,' he said,
'Would indicate that it was done
With some purpose in mind.'

He watched the raped earth
Where red and yellow roses used to grow.

'Though what that purpose was
I'll never know.'

Three girls, slim and supple in their beauty,
Nod to each other,
Laugh.

Three dead things, scarred and black,
Blaspheme the light.

There will be pain
Until the violated earth
Is confident again.

The cherry trees define my failure too.
I have known my purpose go astray in words
Stammering like broken blossoms through the air.

Perfect images are rare.
They live
In drudgery and care.

The Speech of Trees

The ceiling is lonely
The walls are lonely
The trees shiver with eloquence
Where have you gone?
There is a sound behind all sound
The sound of souls
Rustling each other like trees
In a clipping wind.
A friend died yesterday
A friend will die today
A child will be abandoned
A girl go to Libya
('There must be people somewhere who say what they think')
Where have you gone?
The speech of trees gives nothing away,
If I could listen truly
I might hear what they have to say

And find some reason
Why your speech is like the speech of trees.
I cannot listen.
Where have you gone?

Latin

You know what it's like to say me
without knowing what you're saying.
A nine-year-old boy

you discovered me
at the foot of the high altar.
I was thriving in your head,

a flute, a bell, a fiddle, a drum:
Ad deum qui laetificat
juventutem meum.

Sure any eejit could say it in English
and swallow the meaning like a pill:
To the God who gives joy to my youth.

Joy. To say without knowing.
Taste without eating.
Love without hurting.

I was the hare in the grass
you startled one Sunday afternoon
in a field near the Shannon.

I ran he ran you ran
the Shannon ran until
the hare vanished and the world was still.

So I ran through your head
when the man who coughed and prayed
drank the wine, ate the bread

talked of footballers famous
in every mouth that opened itself
as yours did, to say *Adoremus.*

And when the thorny wire
ripped your leg from ankle to knee
why did I say

Fiat voluntas tua
sicut in caelo
et in terra?

Was it because my music
was the only meaning
reached you, sick

in caelo et in terra,
ringing through you like a desire
to curse that bloody thorny wire

leaving a scar
rehearsing other scars,
later?

You forgot me for years.
I came back
in bits of dreams,

glimpses of light on a dark road,
strangers offering help
when no help was expected,

stray music in the stillness of night,
from nowhere I came
like sudden small flowers without a name,

with roots somewhere in a boy's head,
bells and angels, mornings bright and blessed:
Et verbum caro factum est.

And when the word was made flesh
the singing trees became a choir
to celebrate hearts born to perish.

Word

If you call me anything
Say I'm a maker of men.
I was in the beginning

I will be there at the end.
I have named everything
You have sought and found

And I will name whatever
You can discover.
I live in the air

Awaiting the call
You know you must make
And are scarcely able to make.

I
Serve
Your most inarticulate cry

From depths you often ignore,
The darkest reason there is
For your brightest endeavour,

What you believe you mean
By love and by pain.
I will serve you again and again

If you use me, sensing my worth,
Master and slave
Making something of earth

A few will recognise as more
Than the lies
Increasing at the door.

Loneliness

I have my friends though they
may see me as their enemy.
I am insatiable energy

roaming forever
from heart to heart.
Some evict me but others

let me stay, set up house,
live at the core of their being.
I don't scream or shout,

remain quiet, calm, unbeatable.
The deeper I am
the harder it is to see me.

I like hawks, the way they hover
and plunge. When I dive
into a troubled lover

my wings beat in his mind and blood,
this may be our first meeting
but now that we're introduced I have him for good

though I may lie low for a while.
I never vanish completely,
I wait in the shadows, taking it easy

knowing my turn will come again.
When I'm not hovering, I live under
everything.

Under skin, under grass, under love,
under breathing, under all the words.
All the words. My poets, diplomats, singing birds,

actors, critics, publishers, teachers, philosophers, clowns,
my children, my future, my agents.
Listen. All the words. Flesh, blood, bones.

How light they are, how faithful,
intent on revealing
yet somehow concealing

me. Masks made of sound. Don't be hard on them.
They work hard, do their best, poor things.
Think of lip, skin, tongue, thigh, belly, breast,

I'm under all these, I never sleep
even when masks of sound are laid aside.
I hover, plunge when I can, creep

when I must, possess in good time
my almost invisible kingdom
between sky and dust.

Dust
works, plays, walks the streets, makes love, spawns its kind.
I work and play in its heart, its mind.

I know you, you saw me once or twice:
Mary Teresa's eyes
The Greek's face

Kavanagh's silence.
This is the kind of truth that sticks
like limpets to the rocks.

Once you see this, you know it.
Once you know it, you learn how to bear
burdens of earth and air.

We know each other, on that we agree.
More than love, I define the strangeness of creatures and things.
Of you, for example. Of me.

Tide

                        I bring
a red rosepetal, a white plastic spoon, a fly, a shell, a bee,
              a bottle, a pebble, a blue plastic bag,
a stick, a feather, a ring of green weed, the sole of a shoe
                   and the body
                 of Mossie Hanley
             who used to trouble his head
             about the Albigensian Heresy
                and the Nicene Creed.

Bullet

She dropped at his feet
in the quarrelling street.
The night turned red.
Love never tore her heart apart
like I did.

Peace

I am
Beyond all things
Even your dream

Of me.
I am farther than
The last syllable of the

Last poem.
It is so still
Where I am

That the infant's breath
Is monstrous
And death itself

Is a swilling pig
In a sty of silence.
Here

I quiet the boisterous stars,
Obliterate
All thought of war

While my influence
Breathes in the dog's throat
And the moulded stones

Of the sea that wait
For the bully's hand
To hurl his hate

Through the night
Of smashed families
You soon forget.

Yet I exist for him, for you
What you wish, I am.
You speak of me

But do not accept me.
Let me be more to you
Than a vague wish,
An excuse to kill.
I will change you if you let me.
I will.

Skin

I cover secrets
that help you to live.
They could kill you yet.

I can't pretend to know
what's going on in there,
at my back. It feels so

alive most of the time
yet sometimes I feel
like the scene of a crime

deserving a life-sentence.
This passes and the secrets
move like a happy dance.

Almost everyone needs a cover.
Who could bear
to go naked forever

though it's surprising how many
dream they would love to?
I'm covered too, every living day.

Night is freedom for me.
Secrets feel easier then,
relaxed, calm. I think of men

and women touching me. Midnight. Dawn.
We get things moving,
give birth to passion.

So much blood waits to be stirred.
Touch me, I'll make you new,
out of my silence I give you my word.

Touch me, I won't last forever
or even for long. Touch me,
your blood is Edensong.

Sing it. No one can sing it
like you. Sing it.
You have the secret,

the deepest secret I cover.
Out of my dividing, uniting silence I give you my word:
lover.

Scar

I make my way
    from the side
        of her left eye
            to the corner
                of her mouth.

Over the years, I've become
a public part of her life.
        They look straight at me
        trying to look as if they're not.
        They wonder
        what caused me to be:
            fist
                plate
              glass
                  bottle
                  knife?

I make no reply
    to wondering eyes.
When she laughs
    I am her midnight cries.

Bomb

Though I nestled in Adam's brain
he'd no time to think of me when
day and night he longed for Eve
and the inane birth of human love.
I wandered through the mind of Cain
and through the hearts of murderous men.
I was the alert, indifferent star
contemplating fields of war.
I was vigilant and relaxed,
the death-arc of a flashing axe,
the candid claymore, the sly sword
killed as they listened to my word:
In the beginning was the Bomb.
In the end will be the same.

The holy images I defiled
became for me a deformed child
unknown, unseen, grotesque, absurd.
In the beginning was his Word:
darkness cannot know the light,
why should darkness want to, since it
palls and shrouds each little mind?
I am what light can't comprehend.
I am the quarrel in the marriage bed
when he longs to choke her dead
and when their children face each other
in hate, I am each murdering brother.
Hatred I love, and still I hate
peacemongers out to pray and prate.
For centuries I strove to be
born but my children ignored me.
Children of hatred love to play
and pitch the world into disarray,
to hear the maimed and wounded scream.
I could have realised their dream
but still they couldn't make me exist
until one morning, hate be praised,
a gifted son made me come true
and down to earth to trouble you,
I'd waited centuries to become
the one and only ultimate bomb,
to turn the seas into seas of blood
to prove the stupidity of the good
to annihilate in one small hour
superb creations of man's power
to show that only fools create
while I'm content to devastate
this earth some potty god has given,
a lunatic substitute for his heaven.
I burn everything for I know well
men work hard to make their hell
to sweat their way from cradle to grave,
graceless, ageless, insatiate slaves.
So I offer myself, my explosive style,
to comfort and beguile you while
you prattle, argue, haggle, chide.
I'm waiting here, your invented god
hoping you find courage at last
to lay yourself and your world waste.
I rest assured you'll do your best.
Who knows? Another world may begin

mythologising grace and sin
and I'll go into the dark once more
till a chosen child will find me there
and his heart will hurt with joy
hearing my heart, Destroy! Destroy!
I rest my case until you find
me ready in your ticking mind.
When I go off, your world goes blind.
Bloodspattered stars can't hear a sound.

Freckle

I live under
the deep light of her eye.
A few have looked at me with wonder

but most gloss over me in the light of day.
Her skin is my privilege.
I'm a tiny hedgebird near a highway's

insanely ordered traffic.
I reflect her in the whole of her health.
I measure her when she's sick.

I thrive at the edge of her daring.
I share the names in her dreams.
I ripple and skip in her singing.

I see her dispensing her light.
I'll witness her ageing,
be with her when she's not

here anymore.
That's how I see it anyway.
Maybe I'm wrong.

Maybe I'll wither like a bit of skin,
drift off into a freckleheaven
purged of my original sin,

transfigured into that state of grace
I spend each moment of my tiny life
loving in her face.

Time

You have given me thought
And have theories about me.
Something too much of that.

You're impressed by my patience and appetite.
Promises I make and fulfil,
The way I let everything rot.

This is your problem – you happen in me.
Whatever you do, wherever you go
I am your land and your sea,

Your image of youth and of age.
You bicker and think in my grip.
That is your privilege.

Hugely enduring and passive
I simply let everything happen
And am therefore the source of destruction

In your suffering eyes.
But consider.
When you feel revulsion or hunger

For me, when you hate what you think
Is my work in your body and mind,
When you freeze at the death

Of men in their prime,
Do not curse or blame
My pitiless hand

Because the pity you expect
Docs not exist in me.
Nor am I savagery itself

Though that's your belief.
I do not intrude
On your grief

Or your joy.
These come from you
But they happen in me,

Pour and turn in my silence.
I give you that portion of myself
You are capable of possessing

And I will take it back
When you are done with it,
Share it with every pebble and rock

In this provided world.
I would like you to sing
Of the small offering

I make of myself.
It may help you to find
Something of your heart and mind,

Something of what lies behind a name.
I do not offer more to anyone
Before I make my claim.

Worm

How did I get away with it for so long?
The thrush bends his head sideways and listens,
grabs me, slides me down his throat,

breaks into song.
Poetic types stand and listen,
wonder plastered all over their gobs.

Jonah in the whale's belly got a better deal than me.
Devil the thought you'll give me
delighting in my killer's ecstasy.

There's no deep singing without deep greed.
Whose ecstasy does your body feed?
Do you take time off to bleed

nourishing the gifted other

as you vanish into his hunger?

Ecstatic bastard, sing me back to earth

where I can wriggle my way
   like a randy lover

      or a smarmy Chief Executive
         planning a takeover.

Money

You've made me your way, your truth and your life,
the only God you adore.
I grant, in return, what your heart most desires:
more.

Rumour

Gully Smart slurried his gob at a dinner-table
and I was born. I enjoyed the most
confidential beginning possible,

a whisper so confidential you'd swear
only two chosen souls would
ever know

what I'm about. What am I
about? I spark from mouth to mouth
with a kind of electricity

growing in power and meaning
collecting poison like pay-cheques.
I never rest, each morning

propagates my gospel and when
good souls gather to drink and eat
I am stylish, articulate venom.

May I tempt you to make a contribution
to my being? All it involves
is a word or two passed enlighteningly on.

Just sit there and be imaginative.
Let on you're writing a poem
or creating a character in a novel

that'll gobble The Prize.
Now you're moving, baby.
This fiction means convincing lies

so what's the girl's name?
Why did he sell his shop
and go to live in Trim?

Why did he dump his friends
if it's true he ever had any?
The world knows he was mad for money

even as a boy.
Now you're moving, baby.
Mouth me on to Priscilla Joy

who'll mouth me on to Clotilda Lynch-Hunt
who'll confide in Sebastian Brownhead
who'll whisper me in bed

to Imelda Black who'll open her thighs
and eyes wide in disbelief
and pass me on to –

pass me on to pass me on to –
you'd think I might be weary with all
the travelling. No. Poison

is always young, gets younger
the more it swallows
brands of itself.

One night, I penetrate his head.
Now he knows.
I ripple his brain, trawl his blood,

I know what goes on in him now.
How may he end me? How?

How do you think? Think. Ponder. Say.
Inject me anew with your spirit.
A few words will do. I'm on my way.

Olé!

Silence

Once I was the heartbeat of the world
But am an outcast now.
Why do you find it so difficult

To live with me? I live behind
The eyes of men,
I am the brother of loneliness

And I have never betrayed my kind.
Myself is non-assertion,
A shadow on the ground,

Someone always in the wings
Or just outside the room
Where the party grows exciting,

Voices rising higher
As the night advances.
I do not ask that you should think of me

But of yourself
And what is in you.
I am in you

And wait for you to recognise me there.
Come towards me, I am all there is
Of mercy and repose

For those who drown
Into my deepest lake of sympathy.
I offer no more than

The secret of the dove's breast
On a branch at dawn,
The white fields of December

Purged of contradiction,
Whatever is ignored and gentle,
Your proper calm,

My old capacity
To listen and to trust.
I will be speechless when I wait for you
For when I speak, I'm lost.

Raindrop

Did I ever think I'd come to this?
Alone on a third-storey window,
the wind extorting

homage from the trees, bowing
in submission to the patient
graces of the evening,

not a bird in sight
and a grumpy, dangerous slant
to the summer light.

Yes, I said summer. Maybe that's why
I'm alone up here
above the belligerent city,

transparent as the glass I squat on.
Any moment now, I could be
running down the visible world

to meet my destiny,
kiss it and say
'My dear, you look *so* dry.'

What will my destiny say?
Has it cheek enough to tell
a solitary raindrop to go away,

merge with the universe,
get lost? I think not. Destinies can be
surprisingly shy,

almost afraid at times,
trembling at the prospect of contact.
Once I get moving, I love to act

my part in the cosmic play.
I frolic with the sun,
become a jewel in the eyes of men,

get tossed like a childbird in a storm
yet manage to land
somewhere, cool, fluid, strangely firm.

That's how I am just now
so why should I complain
of sudden, cold or heavy rain,

this friend of mine,
colleague, brother, sister,
means of transport, end and origin

on a third-storey window high above
rich prose of violence,
rhymed mysteries of love?

Key

Back near the cliffs Gráinne Stack
caught the lobster this morning,
gave it to you with a smile,

you set out, the lobster
in the black-and-white bag.
What's it like to die in boiling water,

you wondered, passing the hole
where three girls drowned
in nineteen-fifty-four

and an old priest breathed prayers
into their bodies, grateful
they were found.

Past the house of Rock McCarthy
who said a lie is no sin
if the truth refuses an invitation to come in

but insists on staying outside
because it feels offended or maybe
a bit uppity. Truth is proud,

Rock says, and moody too.
The salmon are rising fine this year, he adds.
The trout are generous too.

I'm in your pocket all this time;
HD 1A British Made.
At the bottom of the Doon Road

you turn right, down for home,
stop at the brown door,
turn me in the lock, place the bag

on the kitchen floor.
Time for fire.
Time for boiling water.

Who eats must kill, or agree with killing.
For the most part, anyway. I know
the savage darkness in the sweet light of skill.

Whenever I enter the lock, open the door,
you take me for granted. Why not?
That's what I'm for.

Heart

I cannot thrive outside my cage,
those red bars that make all possible.
Pluck me out from this

I am a dead bird in the dust.
A passer-by might lift the body by one wing
and comment on lost flight,

days of freedom in the air.
He would be wrong because
my freedom is my cage

here in this bloodworld
of unresting rivers
flowing to the sea beyond the skin

beyond the loves and conflicts
and the relish of uncertainty.
I have such a life (limited, it is true)

that you should know
I beat for you.
I beat the storms for you

with rhythm
the world would ask you to relinquish
because the world's a dumb

stump lacking blood but not malice.
Listen to my music,
it is yours also,

why do you turn away?
Look into me, hear me.
I am all you have to say.

Poetry

I'm waiting to be born.
Emptiness is a womb
where I await my turn

to dare the daylight,
say things glimpsed
the other side of the threshold

of myself, not just age and death and love
but mad craythurs out of nightmare,
words buried in your heart for fifty years,

innocent water scalded to death
and these eruptive moments of surprise
lighting up grey days

that reward responsibility.
I will amaze you
if you pay attention to me,

I echo your darkness now and forever,
we meet in a street or a room
or a bridge over a slow, brown river

whose nonchalance and buzz
I delight to imitate.
My tide drifts in, my tide slips out

transporting you for the fun of it.
Under the shadow of the bridge
we pass, calm and privileged

parts of each other, mingled. The world is
bigger, deeper than I dreamed it was,
see my dream, I add to it, it passes

through me like pictures in your head,
pictures push me into being,
I celebrate the living and the dead

as I wait in silence, on a page, in a book,
wait for eyes, a voice, a savouring
of words yearning to sing.

I'm happy to know I'm a song
born of emptiness.
Out of it I came, into it I go

like the slow, brown river no one
has poisoned yet.
The threat is always there,

all it takes to kill a river
is one who doesn't care.
Open me, flow in me, let me flow

through you, young blood of wonder.
In this moment of surrender
we're together.

Game

Heaven is kept under lock and key.
Play me and set Heaven free.
May God forgive theology, imagine play
for all eternity

or at least for the rest of today.

Fun is the key to Heaven.
Play me, I'll play you back
on the oldest record in Devon,

Dublin, Belfast, Lower Listowel.
Play me on and off the dole.
Play me when I'm up the pole
and when I score that winning goal.
Hell is a gloomy hole,

has no answer to kids yelping in delight
when the Atlantic cools their arses
with foaming rhythms and smashing verses
and young versions of old catharsis.

The daft old Atlantic enjoys the craic.
At school we learned that Paradise was Lost.
Play me, we might win it back.
There's time enough to count the cost.
Time enough to count the cost.

9

That music may survive

The Gift

It came slowly.
Afraid of insufficient self-content
Or some inherent weakness in itself
Small and hesitant
Like children at the tops of stairs
It came through shops, rooms, temples,
Streets, places that were badly-lit.
It was a gift that took me unawares
And I accepted it.

Blackbird

This shiny forager cocks his head
As if listening for the sound
Of killable phenomena
Underground.

He depends entirely
On the sharp eye and ear,
On the ravening stab
Of a yellow beak

From which just now,
Spontaneous as light, pure as flame,
Impassioning the chill day,
Such music came

I scarce believe his murderous competence
As he stabs to stay alive,
Choking music
That music may survive.

God's Laughter

Someone had mercy on language
changed it into something else I can touch
I can touch
        grow to love, murmured Ace
as he heard the stranger talking of how
laughter comes from God.

Who, hearing words from his own mouth
and from others, can stop himself
laughing or freezing in terror

at sound bubbling up out of infinite
emptiness? Well, fill it with pride
and let vanity strut along for the ride.

When the ride peters out at the edge
of small daring, that other sound
opens.

        This is the sound of God's laughter,
like nothing on earth, it fills
earth from grave to mountain-top,
lingers there a while, then like a great
bird spreading its wings for home or somewhere
like home,
        heads out into silence,
gentle and endless, longing to understand

children, killers of children, killers. Mercy. Silence. Sound.
Mercy. Sound. Word. Sound. Change, there must be
change. There is. Say flesh. Say love. Say dust.
Say laughter. Who will call the fled bird back?
Stand. Kneel. Curse. Pray. Give us this day
our daily laughter. Let it show the way.
Thank God someone has mercy
on the words we find we must say.

Living Ghosts

Richard Broderick celebrates
This winter's first and only fall of snow
With a midnight rendering
of *The Bonny Bunch of Roses O*

And Paddy Dineen is rising
With *On Top of the Old Stone Wall.*
His closed eyes respect the song.
His mind's a festival.

And now *Romona* lights the lips
Of swaying Davy Shea.
In a world of possibilities
This is the only way.

His face a summer morning
When the sun decides to smile
Tom Keane touches enchantment
With *Charming Carrig Isle.*

I've seen men in their innocence
Untroubled by right and wrong.
I close my eyes and see them
Becoming song.

All the songs are living ghosts
And long for a living voice.
O may another fall of snow
Bid Broderick rejoice!

The Singers

They take their places on
The stage. Shuffling into
Symmetry, it seems they
Hardly know what to do
In their coloured disarray.

They begin to be a form;
Ordered in their silence now
They wait. He comes from the right,
A dark manipulator,
Dramatic in the light

That drowns us into one
And shows him in command,
A certain harmony in his head,
Raising a controlling hand,
Expressing what cannot be said.

The singers celebrate
The world that moves
Inexorably among
Its hates and loves.
Praise is at the heart of song.

The clumsy city tolerates
Human words and cries of birds,
Concord radiates his face
As he leads the singers towards
Pinnacles of grace.

Nothing can be separate now
All is unified
Orion and Mars join hands with us
Tyrants time and space are dead
The hour is marvellous.

And then it's over. There's
A silence eloquent as death;
As harmony withdraws
Hundreds seem to catch their breath.
Applause, applause!

Smiling singers bow and break.
He bows upon the stand,
They (good ladies, gentlemen)
Seem the happiest in the land.
Confusion spawns and teems again.

Published at Last!

Ace stood on O'Connell Bridge, dropped
his poems in the Liffey. One by one
they floated down the air, fell
into the scummy water. One by one
by one they went from him as they had
come to him,
                    down the foul air
      into the foul river –

                  all he knew of love
                  killers he'd met in public
                  his education in hate
                  stories sharp as
                  Janey Mary's words
                  dreams nightmares readings
                  wisps of hope and horror
                  bits and pieces of the city
                  that raged and slept in him
                  like hell and heaven and the little
                  he knew of earth

fell-floated
      down the air
            into the Liffey
                  and drifted
                        out to sea
                              slowly
                                    calmly

like happy ghosts.

He never felt stronger in his life.

   The slate was clean.

Could be he'd start again.

He knew he still wanted to know how he felt
      about children, women, men

                  and pass it on,
the fleshmessage of a skeleton.

Silently, he blessed the poisoned tide
and turned to face

a croak of seagulls heckling

his riverdance race.

The Singing Girl Is Easy in Her Skill

The singing girl is easy in her skill.
We are more human than we were before.
We cannot see just now why men should kill

Although it seems we are condemned to spill
The blood responding to the ocean's roar.
The singing girl is easy in her skill.

That light transfiguring the window-sill
Is peace that shyly knocks on every door.
We cannot see just now why men should kill.

This room, this house, this world all seem to fill
With faith in which no human heart is poor.
The singing girl is easy in her skill.

Though days are maimed by many a murderous will
And lovers shudder at what lies in store
We cannot see just now why men should kill.

It's possible we may be happy still,
No living heart can ever ask for more.
We cannot see just now why men should kill.
The singing girl is easy in her skill.

Sing and Be Damned To It

Let the ironies kill if the ironies will.
Five willow trees are making a tall
Effort to say what is in their roots,
Shadows on either side
Of the darkened white line
Whisper their secrets in public,
One place they're sure not to be heard,
Even the bald monument
To one of the most distinguished

Solemnities of the nineteenth century
Is wagging its tongue at the start
Of the rain prattling down for the day.
A seagull, fabulously famished
Under a cloud that will not please
The farmers, addresses a window-ledge
Of the Catholic Communication Centre
And a blackbird that has hopped
Undiminished out of a thousand poems
And mornings, savages the grass
With a blazing, yellow rhetoric all his own.
They have little enough time for the ironies
That gather and move like rat-packs
Through the speaking streets of our cities.
I'm game enough to face them
Should they happen to fall on me
Whether the day be warm or cold, dry or wet.
Let the ironies kill if the ironies will.
Meantime,
Sing and be damned to it.

The Wren-boy

The little eagle-conquering wren has died
for him, tautly poised on the threshold there,
gaunt in his fomorian pride;
white feathers in his hair,
swaddled in gold and green,
his right fist flicks the swarthy stick
and beats the goatskin tambourine.

The majesty of Stephen's Day
is on his face, grown proud as Lucifer
as he begins to play;
lithe bodies stir
to his music, cries
of praise unfold and
fierce pride leaps in his eyes.

As the ancient drumbeat rings
from beaten skin, he steps
into the days of unremembered kings.
Alone, he tops
this day of hectic moments in a flood
of notes, their gay swashbuckling passion
crashing through his blood.

Christmas townlands wait,
Rusheen, Carrig, Lenamore,
road and field, they undulate
to every open door.
Village, byre and frosty ways
show farmer, townie, whining crone
grow generous with praise.

He knows dominion now
and leaves behind
the heavy spade, the ponderous plough
for glory in the mind
and blood; a man whose pride
in stick and drum commemorates
the little eagle-conquering wren
that died.

Sounds

Mice scuttled up and down Mozart's back,
he heard sounds in his head.
He did what the sounds asked him to do,
the seas surrendered their toe-tapping dead.

The Voice-of-Us-All

Then the stones cromwelled my head
– O my dandruffed crucified nut –
And I knew I'd never be protected
From this governing rain. I went out
Into the world for the first time in days
Trying to escape, but the first thing I saw
Was a girl with shivering eyes
Singing on a bridge for fear of the law.

The river, polluted as the town,
Made, nevertheless, an effort to flow
Like a cripple determined to live.
I started dancing to avoid the stones,
The girl sang, the law frowned, the river straggled below
And the voice-of-us-all guttered 'Forgive! Forgive!'

Star

Does not complain
When gaped at,
Bother to reply when

Lied about,
Remains unmoved
When someone with his wits

On fire begins
To worship it as though
In expiation of his sins.

It sees starved hearts from where
It may become
A confirmation of their fear

Or the convenient food
Of busybodies
Ravenous for distant gods.

They turn on it
And curse its silence.
It will not blab or prate

In answer to each troubled whine
But is
Here, now, as it has been,

Will be,

Star in its own sky,
Fire of time,
White eye of eternity.

The Whiteness

No dream that I remember
Can touch it.
Not even my childspicture of Christ's cloak

On Easter morning was white as this.
It surpassed
The white bounce of the waterfall

And the secret of wheat,
It put to shame
The names of girls

And the frosty breath of old men,
Fingers of women who have lost blood
In their sickness

And seem hardly able to contain
Heaven
Bursting through their skin.

It was whiter than the whitest part of my mind
Or a sheet of paper lying on the table
Undefiled by words.

Though I could not look at it
It enveloped me.
I drowned in the whiteness,

Felt it filtering through every gross bone,
Cold and impeccable.
I was in a country where sin was unknown

And error did not exist.
It was simply that because of the whiteness
Ice and rain and mist

Could not be thought of.
In the whiteness there seemed no need
Even of love.

Which, I believe, was why
I closed my eyes to find the darkness,
To try to banish the whiteness.

And I did.
And I found
A scatter of ants on the ground

And though they blundered hither and thither
Like drunken guests at a wedding
They did not maul each other

But did what they had to do at my feet
Before my eyes
From which the whiteness is vanishing still
Though it never dies.

Entering

To be locked outside the image
Is to lose the legends
Resonant in the air
When the bells have stopped ringing.
If water soaks into the stone
And sunlight is permitted to caress
The worm and the root
And the feather lodged in the bird's flesh
Contributes to its flight

It is right
To enter the petal and the flame
Live in the singing throat
Mention a buried name
And learn the justice of the skeleton.

Entering,
I know that God is growth
In this garden of death.
I will always love the strangeness
And never be a stranger
In that thought
As I parry the shrivelling demons
And do my failing best
To rest
Among the flowing, growing forms
That open to my will,
Give access to their mercy
And share their skill.

I can't find you anywhere

It was no crushing terror, it was a quiet style.
Had I been stoned by the encircling soldiers
I might have run mile after crucifying mile
Till I reached the community of farmers
Working their bullish land in the shadow of the hill.
They'd have sheltered me for months, even years.
All the encroaching soldiers did was smile
As if they were allies of mine and yours.
Yours? Yes, you were suddenly there at my side
Your eyes fixed on each horrific smile
Your left hand raised as if to protect your face.
The leader sneered, 'I want you not to be proud,
Go your different ways, be free, that's all.'
Now I can't find you anywhere in this smiling place.

Mud

Then I saw all the bodies becoming mud
Like philosophy or my best attempts to speak and sing
Of the generating works of God
Manifest in men, women and children becoming
Mud:
        and I see this toothless man
Taking a narrow path through a cornfield
Beating a goatskin drum in the morning sun.
Dozens of concerned faces come to see
And offer food to the man who tells them they are mud
Singing:
        'Let our prime boys and beautiful girls know
They are mud in the hands of the makers of pots and plates
And cups at their lips on wine-happy nights
And walls between neighbours to challenge the wind
And the makers themselves are mud when the same winds blow
Like thoughts like old coats wrapped round a freezing mind.'
        Do you blame me, then, if on certain days
I tend to see my friends as articulate lumps of mud?
At such moments, I grow intolerant of lipstick
While fashions in clothes and writing almost cause me
To scream in the streets. How pay proper homage
To the best-dressed Mud of the Year? Yet there have been
Distinguished lumps of mud such as Oliver and Ed
Spenser down in Cork stanzaing his Queene
Despite the afforested natives threatening to drive him mad.
The buried fertility of mud is thrilling:
Disciplined armies are stirring underground,
Sound chroniclers, critics, advocates of the life to come,
Scrupulous creators of new styles of killing
And a youngster, awakening to the people of his mind,
Flexing his fingers to play a goatskin drum.

Prayer to Venus

(after Lucretius)

Mother of my friend's people
    Bringer of pleasure to gods and men
You inspirit the hospitable sea
    The land we think we own

Every living creature owes itself to you
    You are responsible for light
You console the winds dismiss the clouds
    Make the sea smile

You inject love like blood into creatures
    So that their desire
In mountains rivers seas bird-throbbing thickets
    Is to spawn their kind

You stand alone at the helm of nature's ship
    Therefore I find
You are my sole associate as I write
    This poem for my friend

He is a gifted man
    I revere his name
I pray to you now aspiring
    To be the same

As I pray for excellence I pray
    That you may kill war
War is not what I am or will be
    War is not what you are

War is a barbarous business
    Over land and sea
You alone can give to mortals
    Your blessing of peace

I have seen war crawl into your lap
    Stretch itself there
Feast on your face with greedy eyes
    Manoeuvre your hair

Breathe grim mysteries into your lips
    Rest on your holy body
I beg you take war into your arms
    Kiss its life away

Let your transfiguring words flow
        Through its heart and head
Till it knows that as much love is lost
        As there are dead

I pray to you my loved one
        Because wherever I look I find
Broken people in a broken country
        And I wish to write with a peaceful mind

A Soft Amen

The unbelievable dawn is again
Upon me like a chain-letter
Informing me I'm cursed as a man
Unless I copy it out fifty times where
I am right now and send the copies to
Fifty strangers who in turn will each send
Copies to fifty others who in turn...

                        I
Rise instead,
        Greeting light as a friend
Inviting me out to walk through the grass,
First music of earth, Adam's ears, still in tune,
Filling the world like a soft amen.

This music loves my heart and eyes,
It caresses my blood, kisses my skin
When I bend to pick up a mushroom
Shaped like the white roof of nightmare
Caving in on my sleep.
I know how to laugh, I know how to weep
As morning explodes inside me here
And I'm scattered like, well, I hope

Like Mum and Oliver, Spenser, the giant, William
And all the others striding through me,
Prisoners on parole from history,
Striving to come alive as I think I am,
Finding their food in me, chewing hungrily
First at the edges, then at the core

Of my heart, beating its victim-victor blood
Begetting, forgetting through all my dark and light.

I peel the mushroom, moist flesh of earth and air,
I taste ruined cities of man and God
I hear the makers calling (are the makers mad?)
In the light of day and the light of night.

At home
(for Michael Longley)

Who is that young lad
    with the wild white beard
at home in the sun and the snow
    praising the hare
finding the word
    for every twitch of Orion's toe?

The Adventure of Learning

Nakamaro bit his hand and wrote in blood
    of the moon rising
above Mount Mikasa at far-off Kasuga:
    the loneliness of learning.

The talkative Liffey goes stubborn and free;
    rambling, twisting, turning
on its journey to the sea:
    a way of learning.

Across the world a light shines
    binding our lands
together, webs of light linking
    island to island.

Distance. Loneliness. Islands. Seas. Light.
    We go home to each other
through puzzling, winding roads becoming
    mother, father, sister, brother, lover.

We phone, write letters, prowl through books,
    dream of losing, winning
love and fortune. And always, always,
    the adventure is beginning.

There Will Be Dreams

'Oh yes, there will be dreams,' Oliver said
'Be assured, there will always be dreams.
And there will be men, willing makers
And willing destroyers of governments and homes.
I walked the bank of the Cashen this morning
And I stood watching at the edge of the tide
I saw the Ballyduff men turn to their fishing
And every man of them was humble and proud
In his dreaming, touching what he knew to be
True in himself. I saw the boats heading out
And I knew why my life is a long war.
Any man will kill who has known the land's beauty
And though his heart suffer stabs of doubt
This land is a dream to be damned and saved for.'

Like the swallow

A white feather drifts past the window
seeking, like you and me,
some corner of home.

Jesus, Mary and Joseph, protect
the innocence of the poem
before knife-eyes bleed it to death

like the swallow I saw yesterday
broken in pieces
on Clonliffe Road.

Begin

Begin again to the summoning birds
to the sight of light at the window,
begin to the roar of morning traffic
all along Pembroke Road.
Every beginning is a promise
born in light and dying in dark
determination and exaltation of springtime
flowering the way to work.
Begin to the pageant of queuing girls
the arrogant loneliness of swans in the canal
bridges linking the past and future
old friends passing though with us still.
Begin to the loneliness that cannot end
since it perhaps is what makes us begin,
begin to wonder at unknown faces
at crying birds in the sudden rain
at branches stark in the willing sunlight
at seagulls foraging for bread
at couples sharing a sunny secret
alone together while making good.
Though we live in a world that dreams of ending
that always seems about to give in
something that will not acknowledge conclusion
insists that we forever begin.

Index

Index of titles and first lines

(Titles are shown in italics, first lines in roman type.)

BRENDAN KENNELLY

Cromwell

Buffún is wracked by the living nightmare of Irish history. His torments are surreal but no less frightening than the awful truth. When Oliver Cromwell turns up, the hapless buffoon can't cope. This Cromwell is a cocky tyrant who wants to run a football team, or start a taxi business. Enter the Belly, the IRA, an Irish giant, and Billy of the Boyne: 'William of Orange is polishing pianos / In convents and other delicate territories,/ His nose purple from sipping turpentine.'

Kennelly's *Cromwell* scandalised readers in Ireland when it first appeared 20 years ago. New readers will be just as shocked and shaken by this extraordinary, extravagantly Irish act of revenge.

'This is an astonishing book…an intense poetic outcry. It is energy and honesty that make this book of horrors humanly tolerable' – SEÁN LUCY, *The Tablet*

'Brendan Kennelly has got guts. And a large portion of those are served up here. This book is not for the squeamish' – MARK PATRICK HEDERMAN, *Irish Literary Supplement*

'One of the most extraordinary books I have ever come across in my life' – GAY BYRNE, *The Late Late Show (RTE)*

'*Cromwell* is explosive, expansive, prolific, explicit' – EDNA LONGLEY

'Kennelly has invented a Cromwell for the modern conscience, a figure to taunt the comfortable soul of a progressive Dubliner' – PETER PORTER, *Observer*

BRENDAN KENNELLY
The Little Book of Judas

The Book of Judas, Brendan Kennelly's 400-page epic poem in 12 parts, became the number one bestselling book in Ireland. *The Little Book of Judas* is a distillation of that literary monster, purged to its traitorous essence. But Judas never goes away. He continued to worm his way into Kennelly's imagination long after the original book was "finished", and *The Little Book of Judas* includes some damning new revelations from the eternal scapegoat and outcast.

Not merely lost but irredeemable, Kennelly's bitterly articulate Judas speaks, dreams and murmurs – of past and present, history and myth, good and evil, of men, women and children, and of course money – until we realise that the unspeakable perpetrator of the apparently unthinkable, in penetrating the icy reaches of his own world, becomes a sly, many-voiced critic of ours.

'This is our most ambitious work of literature since Beckett's prose trilogy…It is a labyrinthine confessional, clamorous with sin, guilt and malice, with no hint of absolution. The gesture of betrayal re-shapes itself in a thousand promiscuous writhings – sexual, political, social economic; the hells of Dante and Hieronymus Bosch rendered in steel-glass corridor, pedestrian arcade, academic cloister, with devils and damned in cashmere, denim, corduroy, polyester… It is the work of moral terrorism, a modern sensibility struggling with medieval demons. You would have to fare far to encounter in literature or life such naked fear – and its attendant self-loathing – so bravely confronted. *The Book of Judas* is magisterial, a work of supreme technical maturity' – AUGUSTINE MARTIN, *Irish Independent*

'*The Book of Judas* is an epic achievement and as over the top as the subject deserves. This is poetry as base as heavy metal, as high as the Holy Spirit flies, comic and tragic, from litany to rant, roaring at times, soaring at other times. Like David in the Psalms, like Robert Johnson in the blues, the poet scratches out Screwtape letters to a God who may or may not have abandoned him, and of course to anyone else who is listening' – BONO

BRENDAN KENNELLY

Poetry My Arse

Brendan Kennelly followed his shocking epic poem *Cromwell* with the even more notorious *Book of Judas*. This new piece of mischief, *Poetry My Arse*, out-*Judas*es *Cromwell*, sinking its teeth into the pants of poetry itself.

When anyone snaps 'Poetry My Arse!' they may not be dismissing poetry, but they are certainly pouring scorn on the intellectual élitism often associated with poetry, or on the posturing arrogance of some poets, or on the ways in which poetry is talked about or "taught". *Poetry My Arse* is written in that spirit of scorn, trading self-glory for self-abuse.

In *Poetry My Arse*, Brendan Kennelly plays devil's advocate, exploring the 'poetryworlds' of one Ace de Horner, who is slowly going blind. As the poem digs into Ace's vanity, visions, fantasies, failures, dedication and absurdity, the reader becomes party to his painful efforts to relate to poetry, to his jocular distortions of language and to his pained perspective on the world.

Poetry My Arse is also an anatomy of mockery – and a poem about Kennelly's Dublin, a city of parody and caricature, an attractive, scruffy centre of scandal and gossip where slagging, piss-taking and ridicule keep boredom and the terrors of self-knowledge at bay.

'A dazzling, Swiftian elegiac satire on the intellectual élitism often associated with poets and poetry' – ANTHONY CLARE, *Sunday Times* Books of the Year

'*Poetry My Arse* is not so much a book for the coffee-table as one for the butcher's block. Essentially about desire and responsibility, it also takes in Dublin, Ireland, love, betrayal, destruction, begrudgery, solitude and loneliness, and the Beckettian tug-of-war between speech and silence, truth and lies' – PAT BORAN, *Sunday Tribune*

BRENDAN KENNELLY
Glimpses

In a frantic world, the momentary glimpse can spark a sudden flash of insight. This resonating glimpse – caught on the move – ripples through the mind, illuminating past and present, fast-forwarding in a split second to reveal future possibilities. But in an instant it is gone, lost in the bustle of everyday life.

Keats wrote of the blindness that accompanies the sense of purpose. In *Glimpses*, Brendan Kennelly opens his eyes – and ours – to the world and times we rush through without looking. With their quickfire wit and timeless wisdom, his glimpse-poems are short, quizzical word-creatures in the tradition of riddles, epigrams and proverbs. Sublime or profane, joyous or crazily raucous, Kennelly's vivid *glimpses* have a life of their own, leaping beyond the words used to summon them up on the page. When lightning flashes, the graveyard dances.

'Brendan Kennelly is famous as the author of roomy, controversial bestsellers like *The Book of Judas*. *Glimpses* is a large collection of tiny poems, powered by an epic momentum. It is based around a simple *aperçu*: that the intensity of modern life denies us much time for meditation, but compensates with the glimpse, a momentary communion of the corner of the eye...The language is fiercely inventive and unquotably bawdy...Kennelly gives us both brevity and largesse' – W.N. HERBERT, *Scotland on Sunday*

'Every page you come upon something so arresting in its bawdiness or bile or wisdom or in its sheer lyrical openness to the little mysteries of life that you pause for a few seconds in recognition of something truly felt and perfectly expressed before flicking onwards to another page. Read in this way, *Glimpses* is a book crammed with glittering little jewels' – JOHN BOLAND, *Irish Independent*

Glimpses was chosen by Bill Cullen on BBC Radio 4's *Desert Island Discs* as the one book he would want to be marooned with (along with the Bible and complete works of Shakespeare).

BRENDAN KENNELLY

Martial Art

This mischievous poet is alive and kicking. He is a satirist trying to define generosity, happiness and love, with scurrilous candour and piercing clarity, in brief punchy poems. But no matter how savage his attacks, he is always playful and compassionate. He is a sharp, visionary writer who knows the world about him and is in touch with the world within himself, at once bewildered, attentive and bitingly articulate. *Martial Art* is a book that packs a punch.

'If he'd been a boxer, he'd have developed a new kind of knockout punch, smiling at his victim as he walked back to his corner. His themes are many and varied. He writes of money, food, wine, furniture, style, power, sex, corruption, love, hatred, streets, darkness, families, poverty, snobbery, poets, poetry, polished deceit, aesthetic back-stabbers, High Art, low artists, metropolitan egotism and arrogance, politics, escape to the countryside, property, law, education, greed, manipulative men and women, cliques, loners, talkers and chatterboxes of every shade and motive, patrons, misery, the happy life, clothes, enemies, gossip, friends, flattery and the old constant problem of personal survival and hope of self-renewal. That's Rome two thousand years ago. That's Dublin today… Is one translating Martial? Or is Martial, smiling and mischievous as ever, translating the translator?' – BRENDAN KENNELLY on the Latin poet Martial

'His translations breathe new life into Martial' – PAUL DAVIS, *Guardian*

For a complete catalogue of Bloodaxe titles, including Brendan Kennelly's plays and essays, please write to:

Bloodaxe Books Ltd, Highgreen, Tarset, Northumberland NE48 1RP

www.bloodaxebooks.com